COUNSELING
in the
UNITED STATES

HARROP A. FREEMAN
Professor of Law
CORNELL UNIVERSITY

Prepared from a Survey, 1962-65, financed by
THE WALTER E. MEYER RESEARCH INSTITUTE OF LAW, INC.

1 9 6 7
OCEANA PUBLICATIONS, INC.
Dobbs Ferry, N. Y.

Library of Congress Catalog Card Number 67-24526

Manufactured in the United States of America

PRINTED
IN
U.S.A. THE ALPERT PRESS INC., BROOKLYN, N. Y.

TABLE OF CONTENTS

Preface

This volume reports a three year study of counseling in the United States (particularly that of lawyers, doctors and clergymen), the pattern or lack of pattern in counselor training, and the deficiencies and successes of counseling as seen by actual and prospective clients. The author is a law teacher, trained in psychology and sociology, for thirty years engaged in religious and marriage-premarriage counseling, adviser to Quaker and liberal students on a college campus, a member of the American Association of Marriage Counselors. The research was sponsored by the Walter E. Meyer Research Institute of Law, Inc., and was conducted from 1961-65 in selected communities from the east to the west coast through questionnaires and interviews. It is believed that this is the first complete study of counseling in the three ancient professions and of their clients. In completing this study we used over twenty-five interviewers, coders, analysts. Their names are not here listed but they already know our deep indebtedness to them and our appreciation for their devotion through laborious and discouraging tasks. I have been aided and sustained throughout these years of study by my wife, Ruth St. John Freeman, who has served as research assistant during most of the period. The meticulous and exhausting detail, the almost limitless checking of thousands of bibliographical citations and scoring of data would have been impossible without her steady hand. To further thank her would be like commending oneself—so close has been our collaboration.

I decided to use a very informal committee to guide the study— members who would be consulted individually and make recommendations as to methods of research, hypotheses to check, form and content of questionnaires to use, method of coding, priorities to be given to materials emerging. The following have served in one capacity or another as such a committee (it will be seen that the committee includes practicing and teaching medics and psychiatrists, psychologists, clergy, sociologists and lawyers):

Committee

John Bennett.....................................Union Theological Seminary
Louis Brown............................University of Southern California
John Cook........................New York City (psychiatric practice)

Jerome Frank..Johns Hopkins University
Erich Fromm..University of Mexico
Seward Hiltner............................Princeton Theological Seminary
Robert Jones..Columbia University
Saxton Pope............................University of California, Berkeley
David Riesman...Harvard University
Howard Sacks..Northwestern University
Nevitt Sanford..Stanford University
John Summerskill...Cornell University

The committee (and many others who cannot be listed) have proved of immense help—in encouragement, in hard-headed realism when my plans might have been too flighty, in discussion of alternatives, research productivity, hypotheses, and priorities.

My special appreciation goes to Professors Ralph E. Brown, Maurice Rosenberg and David Cavers of the Walter E. Meyer Research Institute; Arthur Young, Director of Chicago Legal Aid; The Education Testing Service of Princeton and Dr. Harry De Wire of the Ministry Studies Board; Dr. L. Z. Friedman of the Department of Psychiatry, University of Chicago; Dr. Robert Hutchins of the Center for Study of Democratic Institutions; Dr. Arthur J. Brodbeck, Dr. Frank Freeman, Dr. Lewis Greenberg, Dr. Lorne Kendall, Dr. Kenneth Reichstein, Dr. Robert Redmount; Katherine Davis, M.A., Bertram Sippola, M.A., Frances Poynter, M. S. W. These friends made material from other unpublished studies available, opened agencies for my research, helped devise the coding procedures or most creatively projected their minds to pose the questions we tried to answer.

As pointed out in Chapter 1 and following, this report is explorative and tentative. We have collected much data which cannot yet be included in a report like this. We hope and encourage others to use our data or other data and to more completely study the counselor, the counselee, the counseling process and the counseling outcome.

Ithaca, New York
December, 1965

Introduction

Although "counseling" as a popular or almost vernacular word may be of recent prominence, it surely relates to an art and profession as old as man's experience (Ch. 2). The Old Testament warns against the danger of rejecting counsel (Proverbs 1:20-26, Jeremiah 23:18, 22), recommends good counsel (Proverbs 12:15, 13:10, 20:18, 27:9) and wisely suggests the safety in multiple counsel (Proverbs 11:14, 15:22, 24:6). The picture of the wise old family lawyer, clergyman, or doctor is as prevalent as that of the modern psychiatrist, marriage counselor or psychologist. Nor is the use of "case material"—the reference to actual counseling practices and cases—of recent vintage. Nathan referred to a case to advise David in his affair with Bathsheba (II Samuel 12) and Jesus employed case incidents (good Samaritan, the compassionate shepherd, the prodigal son, the woman taken in adultery, etc.) with telling effect.

Most of us are aware of the volume of books and articles being written on counseling (in Freeman and Freeman, *Counseling: A Bibliography with Annotations,* New Brunswick, Scarecrow Press, 1964, are listed about 9,000 items since 1950). But an examination of these reveals that few are concerned with exploring the fundamentals of counseling and virtually none study the counselor and counselee in actual operation.

This book is an expanded report of research conducted between 1961 and 1965 under grant from the Walter E.

Meyer Research Institute of Law, Inc., whose purpose in part was "a better understanding of human relations" and "developing new methods of inquiry or advancing the use in law of the techniques and knowledge of the other social science disciplines." The Meyer Foundation and its Board of Directors have been the center for the movement to add this dimension to the field of law.

If the underlying Alpha purpose of this research were to be stated it would be: find where and how to improve the teaching of counseling—and incidentally achieve methods of interrelating counseling materials and experience among the professions, particularly law, medicine and the clergy. Although sometimes diverted by the sheer size of the field and the fascinating leads developing, your researcher has tried to keep to the central purpose. It was always intended to conduct a pilot or exploratory rather than a definitive study. It was recognized that none of the professions had been adequately studied—law least adequately; and that the function of "counseling" was the portion of the profession nearly forgotten. It was felt that the three ancient professions (law, medicine, religion) should be studied together—and this proved an extremely wise choice.

From the beginning, these four areas were marked out (see the two outlines of research pp. 52-53):

Survey of Professional Schools
Survey of Actual Practicing Professionals
Study of Clients
Collation of Books, Articles, other material.

It was hoped that recommendations could be made to the professional schools, that "materials for casebooks" would emerge, that "eventually bibliographies . . . and interdisciplinary materials" would result. Already a casebook (*Legal Interviewing and Counseling: Cases with Comments*, St. Paul, West Publishing Co., 1964) and a bibliography (*Counseling: A Bibliography with Annotations*, New Brunswick, Scarecrow Press, 1964) have been published.

The actual research on which this book is based was

completed under the following plan (a more complete outline of the research constitutes Ch. 4):

I. We questionnaired as to their counseling training and the absence of or desirability of training, all Law Schools, Medical Schools and Theological Schools (See pp. 61-61a for questionnaire form), obtained a fairly high percentage of replies and increased our depth coverage by interviews. We examined any other available studies of professional schools.

II. We surveyed, by questionnaire (see form, Appendix) and/or interview, about 1/10 of the lawyers, doctors (including psychiatrists) and clergymen in Los Angeles, San Francisco, Chicago, Queens and selected upstate New York and Illinois communities. We received between 11 and 25% replies.

III. It early became evident that the most difficult (not previously undertaken) and most rewarding study would be of clients. Almost without exception we found it impossible to get to individual clients of practicing counselors. Through good fortune we were able to questionnaire (See form, Appendix) and/or interview as two control groups about 3,000 "neutral" or public-cross-section subjects as well as 1,000 members of "Parents without Partners" (divorced, separated or widowed persons). This latter group was different from the general "control" sample in having a specific type (marital) problem, but were similar to the general group and acted as a second control group since we could not know whether any had been to counseling. We also questionnaired 2,500 persons who had been to psychological—psychoanalytic —psychiatric clinics, about 3,000 clients who had been to a legal aid clinic, and about 1,000 persons who went to religious counselors. In each of the client surveys, except the control groups, we arranged to see or obtain a report of the counselor's handling and evaluation of the case for comparison with the client's recorded view.

Our supervising committee strongly advised taking advantage of special groups and separate projects willing to fit into the research rather than to follow a preconceived and wholly self-contained pattern. The above outline shows how singularly fortunate we have been in getting to materials never previously tapped while at the same time putting these together into, a meaningful pattern. The warning was early given by sociologists and psychologists that it would be hard to get a 10% response, that any sample chosen might be considered not typical, that a "tight" sociological study was almost impossible, and that the use of special groups, as above, would still further endanger the statistics of our study. But they all encouraged the research and that it be made as broad as possible, precisely to pioneer in the field and open the professions to empirical examination. It was early concluded that there was an educational job to be done in these professions and that the very process of receiving a letter, a questionnaire or a call for an interview was of major value, educationally. I am increasingly convinced this was true.

When this research was first conceived we envisioned some kind of a definitive sociological report on counseling in the United States. As the project moved forward this seemed increasingly undesirable for these reasons:

1. The mass of material grew beyond the ability of one person to assess and report it as supporting or disproving a limited number of pre-stated hypotheses.

2. The number of potential hypotheses to be checked expanded toward infinity.

3. The demand of the professional schools was that we attempt to advise them by private discussions and articles what we learned from the school surveys, and also from the study of practicing professionals and clients, even though we had no definitive conclusions about counseling and its teaching.

4. As the scope of the project became known, and particularly as people heard of our bibliography, we were besieged with requests that we publish a first bibliography on counseling—annotated. For there existed no such bibliog-

raphy. Not only did lawyers, doctors and clergymen (and their professional schools) emphasize the need, but psychologists, social workers, guidance advisers, marriage and student counselors added their voices. We too came to conclude that excellent material exists in each discipline, known often to only a few within that profession and rarely known outside.

5. An equally persistent demand was for a casebook of legal counseling. Psychiatry, psychotherapy and religion had produced several casebooks. Law had produced not one. And when courses on legal counseling, legal aid or clinical practice were attempted in law schools at Northwestern, Temple, Yale, Harvard, Michigan, Minnesota, California and elsewhere there were no ready cases. Social workers and all the professionals, who saw legal aspects in their cases, wanted to see the legal mind at work and to have available a collection of cases with legal connotations.

6. Those persons who had been most cooperative in producing material and were presumably most interested in new frontiers of counseling, impressed us with their need for informal reports and data on their own problems. Consequently much time has been given at this initial stage to sharing portions of the data where it would be of most help, even though the material was not ready for inclusion in this or any other report.

7. Much of the data was inconclusive from a strictly sociological standard. On the other hand, the material was extremely suggestive and challenging. The mere fact that we rejected certain hypotheses as unproved by statistics did not seem as important as the insights or visions developed in the process.

This volume is based upon our research and the guidance it gave, but it does not present merely a statistical support for a few fixed conclusions. Where the research suggests observations which could not be studied sufficiently to make them definitive, they are nevertheless advanced where sufficiently confirmed and where needed to round out

the picture. In portions of our study we used, where confirmed by our research, insights into the dimensions of
counseling and interpersonal dynamics on which others had
written. We have not seen it as desirable to footnote these
item-by-item. Instead, we have added at the end of each
chapter a limited bibliography and designated the master
"key" to our *Counseling: A Bibliography with Annotations*,
which will lead to additional material. We have not included
material unconfirmed or unrelated to our research.

Our study attempts to report the state of training and
practice in counseling, the apparently accepted definition of
counseling and its distinction from other disciplines, the expectations and reactions of clients, and guides to better
counseling practice and training. It is explorative and in a
sense tentative. We hope that others, either using the data
which we have or from other data, may further the inquiry
along these lines to the end that a more complete and accurate picture of counseling can result.

The book offers, in chapters 2 and 3 conclusions as
to the nature of counseling and professionalism and the
accepted elements of good counseling and interviewing. It
may seem strange that these should precede chapters 4-7
which detail the research and results of the research. But
it was felt that chapters 2 and 3 represent general observations from the total research to confirm the better published
material in the field and that this sense of the nature of our
subject was needed as preliminary to understanding the
problems to be researched, the format for the research and
the items on which conclusions were sought. Chapters 4-
7 discuss the actual research results. In chapters 5 (professional training) and 6 (the practicing professional) we
have restricted ourselves to percentage statistics in the body
of the manuscript, without reproducing all of the table from
the IBM programming, as a means of uninterrupted discussion. Only in chapter 7 (clients) have we extensively set
forth the statistical tables so that the reader can check our
methodology and conclusions against the raw data. We did

consider that an exploratory and readable presentation was generally more important than the most detail proof, but we presented this one chapter in the more orthodox report form. Finally, chapters 8 and 9 are to round out the picture of substantive materials and community resources which the better counselors desired to use.

Chapter 2

Counseling: The Old Professions and The New Callings

Increasingly modern man's language has embodied the word "counseling". Our study showed that the concept which first came to most people was "marriage counselor", and that everyone from friends to psychiatrists were utilized as counselors. Yet our statistics did not bear out the seeming corollary that marriage was the major problem taken to counselors or that psychiatrists were favored or usually employed as counselors.

We chose to study the three ancient professions—lawyers, clergymen, doctors—because these were the first recognized counselors, because we believed they showed qualities and similarities which marked the nature of counseling as a profession, because with them were developed the legal regulations and protections (*e.g.* confidentiality of communications) which others sought to apply to the newer counseling processes, because we believed that they would show a unity of attitude and aim but diversity of action and work characteristic of all counseling callings, because these professions had not been adequately studied and because they permitted us to understand the counseling process both from the counselor and counselee point of view.

Priests from the beginning were counselors to the rulers and the earliest legal systems (Egyptian, Mesopotamian,

Chinese) had legal counselors as available advisors. Medicine included the counseling process. The Hippocratic Oath of 600 B.C. and its earlier Egyptian counterpart of 2000 B.C. refer to "nor will I counsel", and Maimonides' *Guide to the Perplexed* is a counseling handbook. From the time of the Roman proconsuls on, the counseling or giving of opinions and assistance in the law was a recognized profession. Lawyers were early described as "counsellors" in England and most American states admit qualified candidates as "attorneys and counselors-at-law," the job of the lawyer being viewed as counseling the Court as well as his client. Another historical note joins these three professions. The title "doctor", in Latin meaning "teacher", was first conferred in the Faculty of Law at Bologna and in the Faculty of Divinity in Paris in the 12th century and next conferred in medicine in the 14th century—this marked these men as learned and experienced beyond the bachelors and masters, placed on them a teaching obligation and set them aside as the helping professions.

Marriage counseling, as one of the recent counseling callings may be compared with this history. Marriage counseling appeared as a separate discipline after World War I in Germany and Austria. The first center for "Information and Advice on Sex" was established at the Berlin Institute for Sexual Science in 1919 and in 1922 Vienna founded a "Center for Sexual Advice." The first marriage counseling centers in the United States were those of Paul Popenoe in Los Angeles in 1930, Abraham and Hannah Stone at Labor Temple in New York in 1932 and the Philadelphia Marriage Council, 1932. The first state to license Marriage Counselors (California) did so in 1963. The American Association of Marriage Counselors now nationally enrolls and prescribes the qualifications of marriage counselors, but has so acted for only five years.

The largest number of persons who advertise themselves as "counselors" are psychologically or otherwise trained school guidance counselors. One surprising result of our study was this: while most of our client respondents had received school "guidance-counseling", virtually none of them recognized this or listed it as counseling. There seemed to be a feeling that this was merely "test interpretation", at most a part of the education process; that the counselee shared no confidences with the counselor; that the process was largely imposed by the counselor rather than sought by the counselee; that it did not aim to put the whole life in balance, and thus lacked the elements of true counseling. There was also an underlying feeling that the guidance personnel were not highly competent or respected.

One of the real cutting edges of the present report may be precisely at this point: that these new callings want to monopolize the term "counseling" for themselves (and claim it as a profession), whereas the clients and the old professions will not so view them. We purposely submitted the Report to a testing-psychologist vocational-counselor and this was his reply—"It is *not* a report on 'professional counseling in the United States,' it is a partial study of counseling as done by representatives of three selected professions— law, medicine, clergy. In fact, it really is a study of *non-professional* counseling, since by design it excludes such professional trained counselors as school counselors, counseling psychologists, social workers, vocational counselors, etc. And the whole counseling in educational settings is arbitrarily eliminated although 1600 of the 8000 items in the Freeman and Freeman Bibliography are classified in these areas."

In our survey we listed a variety of broad but partial definitions of counseling: "verbal or non-verbal advice, guidance or direction to a person submitting or constituting a problem," "the giving of advice or guidance or helping a client to develop his own pattern of orientation, based on information communicated or obtained through diagnosis or research," "any aid by one viewed as a counselor in the solution of a problem which a counselee has." All these phrasings were tentative, to cause the respondents to react.

Every questionnaire or interview asked, "How would you define counseling?" And each questionnaire contained from 5 to 20 multiple-choice questions to cross check the respondent's concept of counseling.

What appears from the study is a fairly clear recognition of all counseling as showing well-defined common elements and differentiated from other activities with which it is sometimes confused. Both counselors and counselees looked upon counseling as a helping profession, practiced by one who through superior education and experience was able to understand and approach problems in a more objective and successful way, who held himself out to the public as willing to listen and intervene for a fee (or in the clergy's case, as part of his paid job), who had special tools to supplement mere advice when necessary (lawyer utilizing legal power, doctor with medication, pastor with absolution and grace). It seemed axiomatic to most that there was not just a doer and a receiver, but that counseling was a two-way street and few counselees could be helped who did not want and actively try to help themselves. An often used expression was the triangularity of the relationship of counselee, counselor and problem. There was also an emphasis on relation to "wholeness"—that the counseling was not a limited function addressed to one problem or facet, but an attempt to reinstate homeostasis or balance to the total person through presented problems.

Equally clear was the need felt to distinguish counseling from advising, confessionals, guidance, interviewing, the performing arts (preaching, court pleading, surgery and the like), psychoanalysis, depth analysis, psychiatry or psychotherapy, teaching and testing. Thus, such distinctions as these were common between interviewing and counseling: (1) interviewing as information getting, counseling as advice and interpretation giving; (2) interviewing as procedure, counseling as substance; (3) interviewing as the preliminary step, counseling as the final stage; (4) interviewing as a tool, counseling as a process (yet both described as interpersonal relationships flowing in two directions and problem oriented). Again, counseling was defined as operating at the conscious level with a counselee assumed more or less normal, one who was still in the main stream of society although some problem threatened to force him outside of the community (divorce, prison, mental breakdown, or neuroses). By comparison, psychiatry was seen as properly working with the abnormal, non-rationally motivated, at the unconscious and psychoses level (there were many who felt that psychiatrists in fact operated 80% of the time with normal people because they would pay the fees and that in this area psychiatrists had no greater, perhaps not as much, ability to act as successful counselors as those who trained for problem handling at the normal, conscious level).

The present study and certain others, notably those at Merrill-Palmer Institute in Detroit, have shown a hesitancy of the recognized professions to accept counseling as a separate profession or the newer callings as professions at all, even while willingly using their services in consultation or referral. One of the key aspects of this attitude relates to confidentiality and its protection. As already pointed out, our client respondents did not see "guidance" as counseling, in part because the counselee was not the initiator of the relationship and shared few confidences. The same would largely be true of the accountant, the finance and investment counselor (and the Courts have consistently refused to view these as more than "agents", without professional protection). The social worker may be primarily serving an agency rather than the counselee and relying on social facts (job, environment, health) rather than on shared confidences. But, says the marriage counselor, the client does seek me and share confidences with me (the most personal of confidences), and I do give him my primary loyalty. True. But, for what purpose and in what way related to the original legal protection given to doctor, lawyer and clergyman? Lawyers generally say that it was not merely the sharing of confidences which produced the legal protection. All these elements were operative: a person was forced by a societal standard outside himself, a potential punishment (charged with heresy, crime or banishment for disease), was told to seek skilled aid, to defend himself. The professional thereupon committed himself solely to the client's interest. The client shared unrestricted confidences in order that the skilled counselor might sort out the pertinent. Society was willing to license, recognize and regulate a limited number of callings for this purpose.* Each profession provided for self regulation and an apprentice training which preserved the ethic of the profession. It may be seen that nearly all of the new callings lack one or more of these elements, though some (marriage counseling, for example) are fast gaining these. Society hesitates to open the gates to every person who

---

* This is not the time to completely review the legal protection of confidentiality. Only the lawyer originally had it completely. Under the English common law and that of about 20 American states, though the Hippocratic Oath requires "Whatever . . . I see or hear in the life of men which ought not to be spoken abroad, I will not divulge", the physician may be required by a court to testify and this is deemed to free him from his oath. The clergy are generally protected only as to matters "in the course of discipline enjoined by the church to which he belongs". This covers few churches, little more than the confessional, and perhaps not such matters as marriage counseling. Nurses associated with physicians, secretaries and accountants associated with lawyers, secretaries and religious assistants to clergy are not generally protected. New York and Illinois have recently extended the privilege to registered psychologists and done so in language as broad as the protection of lawyers (this author helping draft the provision for psychologists). This is an issue most pertinent to the growth of counseling. The other side of the coin is also important—what is the client's right to privacy (for, as is suggested later, some use of clients' cases, some taping of sessions, some demonstration for trainees is essential to counseling training). The right of privacy is guaranteed in at least 25 states; the medical profession has avoided the problem by requiring clinic or ward patients, and more recently semi-private patients, to consent to use of their case for teaching purposes; legal aid follows a similar theory. But what of guidance tests and scores available to school and employer, social worker reports available to agency and community and like "semi" confidential material?

holds himself out to counsel. If a criminal can close the lips of every friend, every accountant, every social aid agency by spilling out his confession to them, what has become of the ancient confidentiality dimension. In studying counseling we were made aware by counselors, training schools and counselees, how much we needed to keep in mind the original elements yet recognize new knowledge, new movements and new demands. The data for definitive answers on these important issues as to recognizing new professions and extended protections is not yet available. Our research again and again revealed the problems.

Bibliography Chapter 2

See Freeman, Counseling — A Bilbliography with Annotations
Code K-I, 3, C-I, A, 9

American Psychological Association—Counseling Psychology as a Specialty. (1956) Am. Psychol. 11:282-285.

Aptekar, Herbert H.—Casework, Counseling and Psychotherapy: Their Likeness and Difference. (1950) Jew. Soc. Serv. Q. 27:163-174.

Barber, Bernard—Some Problems in the Sociology of the Professions. (1963) Daedalus 92:669-688.

Beardsley, B.—Images of the Professions. (E. Lansing, Michigan State Univ., 1958).

Berg, I. A., Harold B. Pepinsky, Seth Arsenian, Joseph C. Heston— Age, Income, and Professional Characteristics of the Members of the APA's Division of Counseling and Guidance. (1952) Am. Psychol. 7:125-127.

Blanton, Smiley—The Contribution of the Religio-psychiatric Approach to Family Life. (1965) Past. Coun. 3:3-6.

Blaustein, A. P.—The American Lawyer: A Summary of the Survey of the Legal Profession (Univ. of Chi. Pr., 1954).

Bordin, Edward S.—Psychological Counseling. (New York, Appleton, 1955).

Bucher, Rue, Anslem Strauss—Professions in Process. (Jan. 1961) Am. J. Soc. 46:325.

Cannon, W. J.—A Study of the Use of Psychological Concepts, Approaches and Methods by Pastoral Counselors (D.A. XX, 748, 1960).

Cantoni, Louis and Lucile Cantoni—Lay and Professional Counseling. (1965) Rehabilit. Lit. 26:169-171.

Carlin, Jerome—Lawyers on Their Own (Rutgers Univ., 1962).

Carr-Saunders, Alexander M.—Metropolitan Conditions and Traditional Relationships. In R. M. Fisher, ed.—The Metropolis in Modern Life. (New York, Doubleday, 1955) 401 pp.

Cavanaugh, J. J.—The Lawyer in Society (Phil. Lib., N. Y., 1963).

Cogan, Morris L.—The Problem of Defining a Profession. (Jan. 1955) Ann. Am. Acad. Pol. Sci. 297:105-11.

Cook, Stewart W.—The Psychologist of the Future: Scientist, Professional or Both. (1958) Am. Psychol. 13, No. 11:635-644.

Davis, F. James, et al.—Society and The Law: New Meanings for an Old Profession. (New York, Free Press, 1962) 488 pp.

DeWitt, B.—Privileged Communications Between Physician and Patient (New York, Thomas, 1958) 548 pp.

Donovan, John D.—The Catholic Priest: A Study in the Sociology of the Professions. (Dr. Dissert., Harvard, 1951).

Eaton, Joseph W.—Whence and Whither Social Work? A Sociological Analysis. (Jan. 1956) Soc. Work 1:11-26.

Eissler, K. R.—Medical Orthodoxy and the Future of Psychoanalysis. (New York, International Universities, 1965) 592 pp.

Ellis, Albert—Legal Status of the Marriage Counselor: A Psychologist's View: (1951) Marr. Fam. Liv. 13:116-120.

Erikson, Erik H.—Psychoanalysis and Ongoing History, (1965) Am. J. Psychiat. 122:241.

Family Service Association of America—The Lawyer and the Social Worker (New York, Family Service Association of America, 1959) 33 pp.

Fletcher, F. M., Jr.—Occupations in Counseling. (April-May 1949) Ed. Res. Bull. 28:93-100, 127-37.

Foster, Robert F.—Marriage Counseling in a Psychiatric Setting. (1950) Marr. Fam. Liv. 12:41-43.

Frank, Lawrence and Rollo May, eds.—Psychotherapy and Counseling. Nov. 7, 1955 Annals of New York Academy of Sciences 63 Art 3:319-432. (New York, Academy of Sciences, Section of Psychology held Dec. 3 and 4, 1954).

Freund, Paul A.—The Legal Profession. (1963) Daedalus 92:689-700.

Friedman, Maurice—Existential Psychotherapy and the Image of Man. (1964) J. Hum. Psychol. 4:104-117.

Froehlich, P. C.—Is Counseling Becoming a Profession: (Feb. 1950) Sch. Life 32:75.

Gardiner, James A.—A Re-evaluation of the Attorney-Client Privilege (1963) Vill. L. Rev. 3:279.

Gawke, John O.—The Role of a Counseling Service in an Urban University (Dr. Diss., Columbia Univ. 1957).

Goode, William J.—Community Within a Community: The Professions. (April 1957) Am. Soc. Rev. 22, No. 2:194-200.

Greenwood, Ernest—Attributes of a Profession. (July 1957) Soc. Work 2:45-55.

Harper, R. A.—The Professional Status and Relationships of Counseling Psychologists. (1961) J. Counsel. Psychol. 8:278-279.

Harper, R. A.—Should Marriage Counseling Become a Full-Fledged Specialty? (1953) Marr. Fam. Liv. 15:338-339.

Harris, Emerson W.—The Rural Minister and Counseling. (Oct. 1962) Past. Psych. 13:31-37.

Hiltner, Seward—Tension and Mutual Support Among the Helping Professions. (Dec. 1957) Soc. Serv. Rev. 31:377-389.

Hughes, Everett C.—Professions. (1963) Daedalus 92:655-668.

Johnson, Paul E.—The Pastor as Counselor. (1955) Ann. N. Y. Acad. Sci. 63-423-26.

Kerckhoff, Richard K.—Interest Group Reactions to the Profession of Marriage Counseling. (1955) Soc. and Soc. 39, No. 3:179-183.

Kerckhoff, Richard K.—The Profession of Marriage Counseling as Viewed by Members of Four Allied Professions: A Study in the Sociology of Occupations. (1953) Marr. Fam. Liv. 15:340-344.

Kitson, H. D.—Is Counseling a Profession? (Oct. 1949) Occupations 28:41-42.

Kremen, Benjamin G.—Counselor Certification in the United States. (1951) Occupations 29:584-586.

Lawyers Earnings and Prestige Shrinking Because They Fail to Counsel Their Clients Personal Problems? Cur. Med. 7:45 (May 1960).

Loeb, Eleanor—Some Concepts for Interdisciplinary Practice. (Oct. 1960) Soc. Work 4:83-90.

Mace, David R.—What Is a Marriage Counselor? (1954) Marr. Fam. Liv. 16:135-138.

Miner, Roy W., ed.—Psychotherapy and Counseling. (1955) Ann. N. Y. Acad. Sci. 63:319-432.

Moser, L. E.—Counseling: A Modern Emphasis in Religion (New York, Prentice Hall, 1962).

Mudd, Emily H.—The Practice of Marriage Counseling. (New York, Association, 1951) 366 pp., Rev. (1952) Marr. Fam. 14:178-179.

Nelson, Harold A. and Edward C. McDonagh.—Statuses and Images of Profession. (Oct. 1961) Soc. Res. 46, No. 1:3-16.

Nemeschy, Robert B.—The Status of Privileged Communication in the Field of Counseling. (Dr. Diss., Indiana Univ., 1956) (D.A. XVII, 1938, 1957).

Parsons, Talcott—The Professions and Social Structure. In his Essays in Sociological Theory, Pure and Applied. (Glencoe Free Press, 1949) 379 pp.

Parsons, Talcott—A Sociologist Views the Legal Profession (U. of Chi. L.S. Conf. Sec. #11, Dec. 1952).

Peterson, R. and F. Featherstone—Occupations of Counseling Psychologists. (1962) J. Counsel. Psychol. 9:221-223.

Polansky, Norman A., et al.—Social Workers in Society: Results of a Sampling Study. (April 1953) Soc. Work J. 34:74-80.

Pollak, Otto—Image of the Social Worker in the Community and the Profession. (April 1961) Soc. Work 6, No. 2:106-111.

Ratigan, William—Conflicts within Counseling and Guidance in Broad Historical Perspective and in Contemporary Professional Focus. (Doctoral Dissertation, Michigan State Univ., 1963) (D.A. XXIV, 2384, 1963).

Redmount, R. S.—Pantoscopic View of Law and Psychology, J. Leg. Ed. 10:436 (1958); Attorney Personalities and some Psychological Aspects of Legal Consultation, U. Pa. L. Rev. 109:972 (1961) and other articles.

Reese, Seward P.—Confidential Communications to the Clergy. (1963) Ohio St. L. J. 24, No. 1:55.

Rettig, S., et al.—The Status of the Professional as Perceived by Himself, by Other Professionals, and by Lay Persons. (1958) Mid-West Sociologist 20:84-89.

Riesman, David—Law and Sociology, Stan. L. Rev. 9:643 (1957); Observations on Law and Psychology, U. Chi. L. Rev. 19:30-44 (1951); Toward an Anthropoligical Science of Law and the Legal Profession, Am. J. Soc. 57:121 (1951).

Rueschemeyer, Dietrich—Doctors and Lawyers: A Comment on the Theory of the Professions. (1964) Can. R. Soc. Anthro. 1:17-30.

Sedler, Robert A.—The Realities of Attorney-Client Confidences, (1963) Ohio St. L. J. 24, No. 1:1-55.

Soloman, Robert B.—Counseling Concepts in Selected Social Agencies (Doctoral Dissertation, Stanford Univ., 1957) (D.A. XVII, 2675, 1957).

Soni, B. C.—Sociological Analysis of Legal Profession, J. Soc. Sci. 1:63-70 (1958).

Stokes, Walter R.—Legal Status of the Marriage Counselor. (1951) Marr. Fam. Liv. 13:113-115.

Strauss, Anselm, et al.—Psychiatric Ideologies & Institutions. (New York, Free Press, 1964) 418 pp.

Wade, Andrew—Are Ministers Qualified for Marriage Counseling? (1951) Soc. and Soc. Res. 35:106.

Walker, C. and P. London—Psychotherapists: The New Clergy (April, 1961) Christian Cent. 78:515.

Watson, Andrew S.—Some Psychological Aspects of Teaching Professional Responsibility, J. Leg. Ed. 16:1 (1963).

White, R. Clyde—Prestige of Social Work and the Social Worker. (Jan. 1955) Soc. Work 36, No. 1:21-23.

Whitehouse, Frederick A. and Miriam G. Collier—Teamwork: Philosophy and Principles, Social Work Practice in Medical Care and

Rehabilitation Settings, Monograph II. (Washington, D.C., American Association of Medical Social Workers, 1955). 29 pp.

Zinberg, Norman E.—Psychiatry: A Professional Dilemma. (1963) Daedalus 92:808-823.

Chapter 3

Counseling and Interviewing: Elements

Introduction

As we suggested in the previous chapter, counseling is a separate function to be distinguished from advising, interviewing, the confessional, psychoanalysis and like activity. Here we shall briefly treat the interrelation of counseling and interviewing and describe some of the elements of each. Our conclusions are based on the observations of the many counselors and counselees we interviewed supplemented by the best writing in the field; they are an amalgam of ideas emphasized by the most knowledgeable, probably none of whom would assemble the material in just this way—this latter is our contribution.

Interviewing-counseling is an interpersonal relationship, the *yang* or active-initiating and the *yin or* passive-receiving: complementary parts which together make wholeness or the complete Chinese circle. Any counselor can *give* advice, but until the client *takes* counsel and it becomes part of him and his actions it is worthless.

The single most important observation from our survey was the cardinal need to emphasize the two elements—the counsel*or* and the counsel*ee*. Never before had counseling been so studied from the client view. The client saw as unsuccessful and unacceptable the counselor who went his

21

merry way unrelated to the client, acting as though counseling were only his (the counselor's) affair, and successful counseling was seen as that in which the counselor correctly appraised the counselee, his abilities, his needs, his problems, that made counseling a mutual relation with primary emphasis on the counselee.

The counselor's business is to help clients find appropriate action to resolve problems which they have not, cannot or will not solve for themselves and which they choose to bring to him. To do so, he must get all the facts. He must find what solution the client desires. He will apply his knowledge to outline the alternative potential solutions, and he will give advice. He will attempt to gain the client's cooperation in accepting and utilizing some or all of the counsel. Even then counseling will not have completed its function, for the counseling experience and his evaluation or reaction thereto will be stored by the counselee and become another tool for him to use in later coping with life.

The client faces a problem which he finds stressful or hazardous. Our study showed with the greatest clarity that he defines it in a certain way in which he is willing to face it, and thereby defines the counselor he is willing to see. He brings expectations to the counseling session. The counselor has a role both as he defines it and as the counselee defines it. The broad role concept, against which both operate is this: The counselor is in that service group which meets clients somewhere between normal social life and social discard. We might picture people as in three zones: Zone I-Normal Societal Life; Zone II-Within Society but in trouble; Zone III-Lost to Society, disabled. The average man operates in Zone I—(the home, school, church, job, recreation, growth and development). He solves his problems without help or help of the simplest kind (a loan). Occasionally he is pushed by some stressful situation such as illness, bereavement, marital, business or criminal problems into Zone II —(normally functioning but unable to cope with this serious problem). This is the critical preventive zone. Here clergy, physicians, attorneys, social workers, marriage and other counselors work to solve the current problem and keep the individual operating in and productive for society. They seek to keep him out of Zone III—the area of mental and physical disability, criminality, societal and family breakdown. It is extremely hard for even deep therapy to return a man from the third to the first group. The professionals' responses seemed to sense this picture of counseling in which they were engaged. They felt they operated in the real area of potential salvage (within the second circle) and that this was more important to persons and society than therapy or treatment for those who had lost contact with society.

The Client

When a client enters a counselor's office he presents himself and his problem and he takes the measure of the counselor.

For some reason this man or woman who now enters the office has taken steps to become a client. Why? Why seek counsel? Why this profession? Why this counselor? Why now? Why for this problem and not others? Driven by what forces? With what expectations? How ready? How certain? How able or likely to interrelate with and benefit? All these and many more questions enter an office with the client. And the wise counselor must gauge each of these factors as he progresses with interview and counsel.

From our national survey we can here make certain overall and specific observations on some of these questions (for detail see Chapters 6 and 7). The client, in order to become a client, has decided he can make more progress with a helper than alone. The problem seems important enough to do something about it *now*. The client is willing to face the problem and try an interrelation with *this* counselor. He seeks a counselor who he thinks is competent or able to help and benevolent or willing to help. He is not sure the counselor will aid; only that here is potential help. He expects the interviewer to do something.

The client is an individual—an individual with a desire to communicate something formulated as a problem. A speaking mouth in need of a listening ear. He is motivated (appropriately or not). He has his own personality, prejudices, anxieties, repressions, defenses, fears and hostilities, and his own degree of communication ability.

Each of the above items and many more go to the very core of interviewing and counseling—both positively and negatively. Consider anxiety. This is far from being just a negative item, as so long thought by psychiatry. Extensive studies have shown (and our counselors sensed) that without a degree of anxiety few will seek counseling or aid, and further that the degree of anxiety (a reasonable anxiety, rather than too little or a paralyzingly great amount) is necessary to successful counseling. The existence of the right amount of anxiety is one of the primary factors determining interviewing or counseling "readiness".

Some of the specific related conclusions from our study include: clients of lawyers are mainly men (compared to clients of clergy and doctor-psychiatrists who predominantly are women); the client seeks out the counselor appropriate to the way in which the client is willing to formulate his problem; client readiness is as important to success as counselor competence; the client generally seeks "affective" or "feeling" topics and relationships rather than "cognitive" ones; the client wants "action" and when possible "collaboration". The client brings to the interview a wide variety of expectations, aims and goals. He may seek information, support, love, friendship, skills, problem solution, decision making, a way out of unpleasantness, movement toward a goal, change in inner feelings, etc. His satisfaction will depend on the degree to which his original or later created expectations are met.

The Counselor

The counselor must be recognized both as an individual and as a professional. He has a religion or value orientation, a personality, a family, personal problems, pressures, anxieties, blind spots and clarity of perception, communication abilities and defects. He is a complex person, and every bit of him sits in interview or counsel, whether he will or not.

As each counselor is a singular individual, so each counseling profession has its uniqueness, its "role". A lawyer may represent a legal specialist, a higher class or respectability, the law or authority, logic or reasonableness, broad coverage of typical problems. The clergyman may be viewed as the shepherd or pastor, conscience, morality, right and wrong, grace, absolution, mediator to God. The physician (and psychiatrist) may seem to operate in the field of sickness, to heal, to treat the whole body. The social worker, psychologist, marriage counselor is by his calling placed in a different role.

In chapter 2 we outlined some of the common role functions of counselors. Dr. F. E. Fiedler of the University of Illinois has described the kind of person who makes a good counselor, negotiator, mediator or therapist. These people are found to be at peace with themselves, effective in functioning, reality oriented. They perceive situations accurately and other persons positively and they adapt behavior accordingly. Our counseling survey came to substantially the same conclusions and supports another theory of Dr. Fiedler. In studying negotiation he concluded that two types of leadership were required at different stages— the first, the ability to bring persons together (empathetic, emoting, liking, pleasant, relaxed) and the second almost the opposite, the power to push others up toward a constructive solution (one who utilizes stress, is dissatisfied, looks for new solutions, throws his mind around). In negotiating, a team representing both types is often used and each plays his role. The counselor as a single individual must somehow embody both and be able to appropriately shift from one to the other.

If not openly formulated nevertheless semiconsciously the client makes a composite picture of all these roles and expects the counselor to take the interview lead and somehow bring out the essential facts necessary to understand the client and his problem, examine these with his trained eye and be able to communicate a solution or approach to the problem which the client could not have found on his own. The client expects the counselor to treat his problems and him as distinct, individual and living.

The Interviewing Process

This author has written elsewhere (Legal Interviewing and Counseling, p. 8) that the interviewing process may be said to involve seven interrelated and somewhat overlapping stages, over all of which hovers the all-pervading problem of communication.

Stages of the Interviewing Process.

Recognition of Participants, Roles, Expectations, Purposes, Goals. Formulating Strategy of the Interview.	Precede interview proper
Establishing Optimum Interrelation. Obtaining Maximum Information. Structuring, Correcting, Further Exploration.	Interview core
Analyzing, Summarizing, Formulating. Opinion, Conclusion, Counseling, Therapy.	Utilizing interview results

We have already said much about the *participants and their roles, expectations and goals.* The *matter of strategy* presents limitless possibilities. It was the item many counselors desired to talk about and on which countless books have been written—even on the minutia of where the light should be placed, pictures hung or shelves of books appear. But the good counselor wanted to go below these superficialities. He wished to consider items like these: Where can I get the information? Who is available; who willing; who able to give it? To what degree should I get it from records, documents, elsewhere? Is this interviewee to supply me the information, or give entree to others who will? Will the atmosphere be hostile, friendly, intermediate? Ambivalent or polarized? Should there be single or multiple contacts? Should I be "sponsored" by anyone? Who would be the best interviewer (taking into account age, sex, ethnicity, personality, etc.)? How can the role of the interviewer best be presented—as lawyer, friend, marriage counselor, community leader, what? Will I be a member of the in-group or the out-group? A subordinate, peer or superordinate? What is the best time? Place? Other setting? What should be the sequence of contacts? How to avoid leakage, crossover, or contamination of information? How structure the interview? How much existing information shall the interviewer share with the interviewee? How to reformulate strategy in the course of an interview? These are all general problems that our interviewers said they constantly face.

Each of these may seem simple in itself, but a few illustrations furnished by our survey, will show the complexity and importance of taking each into planning consideration. Take sponsorship. If one seeks to obtain highly confidential information from a closed community (let us say the Italian community) there may be two or three power figures controlling that community. An interviewer attempting to interview without one of these vouching for him may run up against a stone wall. At another time the sponsorship of such an individual may be the "kiss of death". Sponsorship assumes a relation of the sponsor to the purpose of the interview; it will color the interview; it will shape the informant's concept of what he is doing. No sponsorship may be better than even good sponsorship on occasion, and certainly better than bad sponsorship.

Or consider the in-group and out-group choice. Each role has its advantages and disadvantages, mainly related to the type of information sought. The outsider has the advantage in matters relating to violation of the in-group code, for he does not represent ego-threat or in-group judgment. He also is at an advantage whenever a person is looking outside the group for assistance, as where a woman may not want her religious community to know of plans for divorce. He is at an advantage where secrets may be shared that would cause loss of face, or condemnation within the group, or where new meaning is sought from outside. He will be at a disadvantage in those cases involving information which the community wants no one else to share. The in-group interviewer has the advantage of using the same jargon. He is assumed to be sympathetic to the group mores and to stand with the in-group against public norms. He is not treated as a visitor, empathy is easier. Strategy will require the ability of the counselor to emphasize or de-emphasize a given role and, as pointed out on the next page, the development of skills and techniques to maximize the flow of information of communication.

For the *third element, establishing maximum interrelation,* each counselor must find his own methods. Our respondents had much to say about this. The interviewer-counselor should be friendly and informal, but professional. He must show he is a sympathetic, interested and attentive listener. Tolerant and non-judgmental. Neutral as to the subject matter, concerned as to the person. He must empathize and create rapport, being neither emotionally under or over-involved. It is desirable to share identification— feeling "with" rather than "for" the client. At the same time the interviewer must put the client at ease and committed to the interview. He must reduce embarrassment, irritation, suspicion, fear, intimidation. The counselor must as objectively as possible, assess what is inhibiting and what facilitating relationship. Errors and barriers may come from the interviewer, the interviewed or the situation: from prejudices, emotional residue from other experiences, preconceptions, ego attack, transference, displacement, bad communication or observation.

The study revealed that almost every professional counselor accepted the above description of interviewing and
developed an almost sixth sense for achieving interrelation
and an understanding of roles and goals. But he had an
almost complete inability to describe just how he acted,
why he related better to some, the strategy he fol-
lowed. "Intuition" was his usual answer. But intuition is
probably nothing but unconscious experience. Therefore, in
trying to set forth skills necessary for the fourth factor—
gaining information and achieving maximum communication,
we shall try to do this in the form of advice distilled from
the study confirmed by various writings on interviewing:

The skills and the techniques for gaining and handling
information will basically be: getting understanding of the
information needed, motivating the giving of information,
assuring that information is given accurately, hearing and
observing fairly, remembering, recording, analyzing and
evaluating. Each interviewer will need techniques to aid in
developing and supporting his skills. Studies increasingly
show that no specific technique (*e.g.* non-directive compared
to directive) is universally superior to another, but that pre-
tested techniques are easier to learn than skills and give the
interviewer a sense of structure or safety from which to
operate. Thus the interviewer may use the technique of
silence to indicate he is unhurried and secure, or to create a
thoughtful mood, or to allow the client free thought without
interruption, or as an invitation. In using verbal techniques
such as questions, he can develop rules as to vocabulary:
common words, questing words, non-loaded words. Or he
can tactically use different forms of questions: general,
specific, even those that suggest the answer. Each has its
use and each will produce a type of answer. One technique
will be used to handle the hostile witness, another to interview a resistant person, still another to meet a seductive
client, one who is frightened, one clearly neurotic. Different
sequence patterns can be used. One may hold the client to
chronological sequence to be sure continuity is achieved and

items are not missed. Or an "outline sequence" may be
utilized, the important topics first, filled in by subtopics. Or
does one choose the "funnel sequence" working from the
broad and open mouth to the focused fine point? Many interviewers follow a check list of information on a given problem; but, use this with care lest it preclude information that
may be uniquely more important for this client. Even sum-
marizing, hypothesizing, tentative or partial advice may be
a technique to induce the client to proceed further as he sees
that all is working out satisfactorily thus far. The acceptance or rejection of a tentative diagnosis may be as
revealing as a ten year chronology.

Since interviewing is interrelation with the purpose of
communication, we will report in some detail what our respondents thought constitutes good and bad communication.

Consider the client. The interviewer is trying to get
his story as he sees it, in his own words. Words are slippery
tools. The client must try to select the words that exactly
convey all his meaning (he will not); words have to bridge
the gap to the interviewer with the same connotations (they
will not). Real effort should be made to encourage choice
of words and symbols that will communicate the intended
meaning. Beware of one word replies to questions; refuse
to accept replies like "depends", "don't know". Try to get
all the information—clear, relevant, complete. Try to ex-
haust the client's information. Watch out for irrelevant,
vague, general, ambiguous expressions. Clarify what is
unclear before moving on. Spoken language can be unconsciously as well as consciously motivated. When a client
uses "she" in place of "he", "glad" instead of "bad",
these Freudian slips may reveal words really fitting the
client's thought which is being covered by acceptable expressions.

The client is communicating to the interviewer verbally
and non-verbally. He nods, smiles, grimaces, stammers,
blushes, sweats, shakes, shows a tic, lights a cigarette,
crosses his legs, loosens his collar, etc. This "body language"

often carries more content than spoken language. His pauses, hesitations, silences, averted eyes are also communicative. "Listening" thus must become a receptive ear and an observant eye. The interviewer must learn not to read too much into a motion. A man may take off or put on his glasses purposefully—because he needs them to read. That is appropriate behavior. But if he puts them on and off from nervous habit, as a defensive mannerism, then you are witnessing unconscious body communication.

An interviewing counselor is also communicating to the client and sets the pattern for the client to follow. Good communication mechanics are to speak to the client, speak slowly, speak clearly. The interviewer's words and gestures, his body language should show him as self possessed, calm, qualified, attentive, expectant. They should put the client at ease, put the interviewer in control and encourage communication. He must be prepared to structure the interview; the client will expect this.

Now the counselor must settle back to listen. Listening is hard. We are used to reading and reading rapidly. We like to talk rather than listen. We are able to listen three or four times as fast as a person talks. We can hear many sounds at one time. The outer ear and the inner ear can hear simultaneously. Therefore, we tend to be "hearing" and also "thinking" something beyond what the client is saying—we call up related information, our own emotions and other problems, what we think is the likely solution; we anticipate. In short, we cease to really listen. A good rule is for the interviewer to constantly try to identify four aspects in every communication: the manifest or stated content, the associated emotional aspects, the client's reaction to the interviewer and the interviewer's response to the client and his affairs.

What active part may the professional take to improve communication? One client appears tongue-tied, slow or hesitant in speech. Another may have diarrhea of the mouth. One must be speeded up, another slowed down. The client may be given an outline through questioning. He may be encouraged to overcome his difficulty by saying, "You appear to be having some trouble telling me about this."

Wherever the client is adequately verbalizing, the job is to keep the train of thought going with the least interruption and the greatest encouragement. Indication that one is attentive and following the conversation is needed— nodding, "uh-huhs", tentative 'yes . . . yes", "so that's how it was", "I see", etc., can help. At some points the counselor must not allow a topic to be slighted, must shape direction, must probe, possibly must cross examine. But he must be sure he is a catalyst, not creating a new compound.

There are "inhibitors" and "facilitators" of communication. Some have to do with the client's willingness to communicate and others with his ability to do so. If we speak of inhibitors, the first type is represented by: competing time or energy demands, unpleasant associations, concepts of propriety or etiquette, ego-defenses; clients use evasion, omission, denial, distortion, fabrication, shame, confession, impersonalization, minimization or maximization, dramatization or many other patterns to take the pressure off the ego. The second type may be illustrated by the difficulty of witnesses in remembering and presenting facts: forgetfulness, chronological inaccuracy, habit and other unconscious behavior, inferential errors both inductive and deductive are always present; no two persons observing the same happening give the same report; no report is wholly accurate or complete; memory is fickle and recall a thief; emotions and conclusions pose as facts; a person may assert as true what he knows is not and fail to communicate that which he knows is. We must in interviewing somehow lead communication through these errors of perception, memory, emotional coloration and recall.

To counterbalance these inhibitors there are recognized facilitators: ego strengthening by recognition and attention; expectation fulfillment; catharsis; appeal to accepted values;

communicated sympathetic understanding; non-commital communication encouragers (uh-huh, yes-yes, etc.); reassurance; revelation or development of meaning; challenge.

We might summarize the concepts developed as to interviewing by a few do's and don't's:

Good interviewing is to recognize that the process is interpersonal; is obtaining maximum information flow; is an art, the skillful appearance of smooth, spontaneous and relaxed interchange and interrelation, developed however from thorough study and training in the nature of the process. Good interviewing is listening and observing; is to start where the client is; is effective communication; proper questioning; selection and going beneath the surface. Good interviewing is sharing confidences and always confidential; it is empathy, being oneself and at the same time maintaining a professional relationship. Good interviewing is framing a purpose and a goal, determining the client's need, collecting, verifying, synthesizing information; it is framing hypotheses and making correct diagnosis. Good interviewing is the recognition of the prejudices, anxieties, moral cubbyholes, ambivalences of the interviewer and interviewee, and of the objective and subjective aspects of every situation.

The Counseling Process—Definition with Illustrations.

Although in Chapter 2 we listed some of the elements which our surveyed sample thought important to describe counseling, we did not attempt to define the counseling function both as a *content,* or what the counselor seeks to accomplish, and as a *method,* or how the counselor carries out this purposeful interrelation. In this chapter we shall deal largely with the *how.* A counselor's training in his specialty and his general wisdom gained from experience, and from psychological or other materials will determine the *what.* Selecting from the piecemeal definitions of respondents, and giving weight to the more important and more frequently referred-to elements, this author's preferred definition of the art of good counseling is:

> "An interpersonal relationship characterized by acceptance and understanding, whereby a counselor viewed as competent seeks to help a counselee, by intervention in a stressful situation, to develop insight, work through problems, make decisions and effectuate solutions, so as to move effectively and creatively in appropriate directions, in his total life and societal milieu."

As in all arts, practice makes perfect. This was underscored by our national survey which showed that personality and exeperience were more important than book learning, and that those who did little counseling were least competent, most resistant or fearful, while at the same time overly sure of themselves.

Let us explore further the eight elements of our definition. *Interpersonal relationship* ranked highest in our replies and is the cardinal quality emphasized by counseling writers. The center of all counseling is the living, feeling human being in whom the problem is centered. Chapter 9 on Socio-Psycho Dynamics is devoted to interpersonal relations. It is axiomatic that the counselor is going to have to deal with male or female clients, the old or young, the hostile or frightened, the dependent or unmotivated, the neurotic or psychotic, the seductive or distant, etc. And the counselor is going to have to deal with himself—his prejudices, problems, blind spots, irrationalities. The survey showed that counselor and counselee did in fact choose each other and that most counselors were marked by a particular type of client.

One side of interpersonality not sufficiently discussed is how one deals with superordinates, peers and subordinates, and who are considered to be in each class. We can illustrate this by the case of lawyers. A subordinate usually expects

the lawyer to be directive, advice-giving, power wielding—
and the lawyer usually is. In theory lawyers should inter-
personally relate easily with upper classes (they being of
this stratum) and achieve the give and take of good counseling. We found however a tendency to abrogate this function
precisely with this group and to become merely technicians
to accomplish decisions the upper class client had already
made.

Acceptance and understanding are another hallmark of
counseling. King Solomon prayed not for wisdom, but for
an "understanding heart". Clients are both facts and feelings. An understanding heart reaches into the other's feeling world and accepts it. Acceptance is real concern effectively expressed. It is neither approval nor disapproval;
it is the golden mean. The counselor must share enough of
the counselee's feelings to have a good investment but not
enough to become tied up and anxious as the client is—else
he will be as ineffective as the client has been. The counselor
can erect a barrier which the client will not cross by as
simple a thing as giving a prejudiced opinion or non-dis-
criminating praise.

Competence is assumed in a professional. Doesn't his
diploma prove it? But competency is more than passing a
test. Competence involves being aware of one's limitations,
and keeping up with new applicable knowledge. Our survey
showed how few really *kept* themselves competent.

Intervention occurs when a new force is brought into an
existing situation. A moment before, the problem rested
only with the client; when the counselor is brought in it is
no longer the same problem; his intervention is a new factor.
Two heads are in fact better than one. And intervention
is not to be lightly undertaken. Here is the place where one
must ask, "Am I the best person available under the circumstances?" And neither false pride nor false modesty should
dictate the answer. Our survey emphasized both that the
client has selected this counselor and may never again get
up the motivation to go to another, and also that interven-

tion makes certain promises, creates certain expectations. One cannot non-perform or withdraw without hurting someone.

Managing Stress. Stress is the pull or strain on human functions caused by life situations, by any sudden alteration in the field of forces affecting a person so that his view of himself or others must change. It is caused by such incidents as birth of a sibling or death of a loved one, inheriting or losing money, school entrance or change or failure or graduation, job getting or loss or promotion, being sued or charged with fraud, marital or business problems.

Stress may be good or bad. Pull on a rubber band gives power to propel a missile. Unmanageable stress blocks normal functioning, but manageable stress is power and activates. In fact, our study again proves that without the right amount of anxiety few will recognize that they have a problem or seek counsel. The counseler should expect stress. He should recognize that the stress may be related to him, to the problem or unrelated to either. Stress is emotional, a matter of feeling and not reasoning. Therefore, the way to handle it is to empathize, encourage expressions of feeling, be non-committal, "stay loose." Do no try to manage stress by logic. One will get nowhere by saying to a distraught person, "now calm yourself." Stress is a fine fulcrum on which to work. The counselor's role is to use it to manage and mediate the crisis, to lift the anxiety that is barring creative action, and to bring the client to use available forces to bear on the solution of his problem. Helping a person to manage one day-to-day stressful situation tends to create in him the ability to handle other stressful situations realistically.

Insight and working through places the emphasis where it belongs—on the client seeing his way and working out of the problem; it is "helping people help themselves." Freud characterized thinking as "action in rehearsal." If the counselor can get the client to face and rehearse appropriate reactions to situations, the client will act similarly in real life.

This may depend on understanding and using "transference" —the psychological process by which the client associates with the counselor some residues from the past (*e.g.* fear of father or authority) and, in the trust and security of the relationship, learns to face these and their relation to his problem realistically. The counselor must himself be secure enough not to fear transference, nor to react to it as reality. This insight and working through is to be compared to advice of the type which tells the other person what to do. Giving direct advice may at times be dangerous. It places the burden of being right on the counselor. It may dispose of, rather than solve, problems. It tempts him to play god, and the client to seek miracles. Similarly the matter of referral can constitute abrogation of function or rejection of the client; it can attack the client; it can be sheer carelessness. And refusal to refer can be selfish, even crass. But properly used, referral may be the best working through possible and direct advice may often be necessary.

Movement in appropriate directions shifts the emphasis of our definition to testing by results. No person who is growing and maturing stands still. There will always be forces in the individual, his society or other individuals which should be utilized. And there will be resistances which restrict the forces. Movement depends upon utilizing both. As a sailor, I cannot think of a better analogy than that of a sailboat. A sailboat moves forward by the force of the wind on the sail meeting the resistance on the hull and keel to form the power of a wedge. We then say, "she runs free," a very small rudder with almost fingertip control balancing force and resistance. Good counseling is furnishing that rudder.

"In the *total life* and social milieu" points to the fact that medicine, psychiatry, sociology, personality theory, counseling are all today wholeistic. A problem does not exist in isolation. You cannot avoid affecting the whole life even by trying to treat only the problem.

Counseling is Applying Socio-Psycho Dynamics. In an important sense this whole chapter could be entitled: Applying Socio-Psycho Dynamics. Men tend to seek magic protection. We call our new medicines "miracle drugs." The counselor must not be a medicine man. Counseling requires hard work. A lawsuit, a "document," a divorce or muttering "abacadabra" is not enough.

All behavior, bizarre or ordinary, has its cause. Some is obvious to everyone, some only to the client, and still other is hidden even from him. As the Bible records: "for that which I do, I would not; and that which I would, I do not; and that which I hate, I do." All situations are composed of objective and subjective facts. Objective facts can be observed by all; subjective facts are emotional and personal. The objective can be tested as true or false; the subjective can never be so tested—we can only ask whether they are operative. All persons are ambivalent in making choices as they go through life. Each choice is associated with conflicting interests and pulls, desires and emotions. What one chooses is almost never 100% what he wants and some attachment remains to every discarded choice. People do tend to escape responsibility. Internally this may take the many forms of ego defense and regression; or externally they can blame society, slums, injustice, poverty, discrimination, overcrowded schools.

The counselor must cope with these and many more applications of Socio-Psycho Dynamics. He must understand motivation, take account of ambivalence, refuse to be judgmental, recognize ego defenses and escape mechanisms—and he must work hard and help the client to work hard through his problems to a relatively satisfactory solution.

In Chapter 9 we review the most up to date concepts of Socio-Psycho Dynamics revealed by our most sophisticated respondents as used in counseling. To that chapter turn for enlargement of the present theme.

Finally, to what degree did our surveyed counselors embody good interviewing-counseling? A very high percentage, perhaps 80-90% as can be seen from Chapter VI, would define interviewing-counseling elements accurately. A somewhat smaller percentage (perhaps 60%) would consistently practice accordingly. A percentage as low as 30% would probably be considered by psychologists-psychiatrists as following psychological routine. The counseling widely varied from counselor to counselor and profession to profession; it was strongly eclectic. But we concluded that at least 60% of the counselors had somehow (often without formal training therein) grasped the essentials of good professional interviewing-counseling and adapted them to the distinct problems and powers with which they dealt. For further analysis, see Chapter 9.

Bibliography Chapter 3

See Freeman, Counseling—A Bibliography with Annotations
Code F, G (particularly 1, 3, 4), H, I
See also Bibliographies Chapters VI, VII.

Alfred Adler Institute, N. Y. C.—Manual for Adlerian Family Counseling.

Anderson, Floyd M. and Leon G. Smith—Conjoint Interviews with Marriage Partners. (1963) Marr. Fam. Liv. 25:184-188.

Aptekar, Herbert H.—Dynamics of Casework and Counseling. (Boston, Houghton Mifflin, 1955) 262 pp.

Arbuckle, Dugald S.—Counseling: Philosophy, Theory and Practice. (Boston, Allyn, 1965) 415 pp.

Bamber, Laurene—Point the Way: Nine Steps in Counseling; a Handbook for Counselors. (St. Louis, Mo., American Red Cross, 1951) 39 pp.

Barbara, Dominick A.—The Art of Listening (New York: Thomas, 1958).

Barbara, Dominick A.—Psychological and Psychiatric Aspects of Speech and Hearing. (New York, Thomas, 1960) 756 pp.

Becker, Howard S. and Blanche Geer—Participant Observations and Interviewing: A Comparison. (1957). Human Org. 16, No. 3:28-32.

Benney, Mark, David Riesman and Shirley Starr—Age and Sex in the Interview. (1956) Am. J. Soc. 42:143.

Berezin, Annabel G.—The Development and Use of a System of Diagnostic Categories in Counseling. (Doctoral Dissertation, Univ. of Missouri, 1957) (D.A. XVII, 3087, 1957).

Berdie, R. F.—Psychological Processes in the Interview. (1943) J. Soc. Psych. 18:3-31.

Berdie, Ralph F., ed.—Roles and Relationships in Counseling. (Minneapolis, Univ. of Minn. Press, 1953) 37 pp.

Biestek, Felix P.—The Non-Judgmental Attitude. (June 1953) Soc. Casework 34:235-239.

Bingham, Walter Van Dyke, Bruce V. Moore and J. W. Gustad—How to Interview. 4th ed. (New York, Harper, 1959).

Blenkner, Margaret—Predictive Factors in the Initial Interview in Family Casework. (1954) Soc. Serv. Rev. 28, No. 1:65-73.

Blenkner, Margaret, J. Hunt and Leonard S. Kogan—A Study of Interrelated Factors in the Initial Interview with New Clients. (1951) Soc. Casework 32:23-30.

Boomer, D. S.—Speech Disturbance and Body Movements in Interviews. (1963) J. Ner. Ment. Dis. 136:263-266.

Bordin, Edward S.—Counseling Methods: Therapy. (1950) Ann. Rev. Psychol. 1:267-276.

Brammer, Lawrence and Everett L. Shostrom—Therapeutic Psychology: Fundamentals of Counseling and Psychotherapy. (Englewood Cliffs, Prentice-Hall, 1960) 447 pp.

Brams, Jerome Martin—The Relationship Between Personal Characteristics of Counseling Trainees and Effective Communication in Counseling. (Doctoral Dissertation, Univ. of Missouri, 1957) (D.A. XVII, 1510, 1957).

Brayfield, Arthur H.—Readings in Modern Methods of Counseling. (New York, Appleton, 1950).

Brookes, Crittenden E.—Personality Theories Underlying Two Views of Counseling. (Doctoral Dissertation, Stanford Univ., 1956) (D.A. XVII, 91, 1957).

Bruch, Hilde—Some Comments on Talking and Listening in Psychotherapy. (1961) Psychiatry 24:269-272.

Bucher, Rue, Charles Fritz and E. L. Quarantelli—Tape Recorded Interviews in Social Research. (1956) Am. Soc. Rev. 21:359-364.

Buchheimer, Arnold and Sara C. Balogh—The Counseling Relationship (Chicago, Science Research Associates, 1961).

Burton, Arthur—Case Studies in Counseling and Psychotherapy. (Englewood Cliffs, Prentice-Hall, 1959) 431 pp.

Callis, Robert—A Casebook of Counseling. (New York: Appleton, 1955).

Callis, R., P. C. Rolmantier and E. C. Roeber—Five Years of Research on Counseling. (1957) J. Counsel. Psych. 4:119-123.

Campbell, Robert E.—Influence of the Counselor's Personality and Background on His Counseling Style. (Doctoral Dissertation, Ohio State Univ.) (D.A. XXVII, 3739, 1962).

Cannon, William J.—A Study of the Use of Psychological Concepts; Approaches and Methods by Pastoral Counselors. (Doctoral Dissertation, American University, 1959) (D.A. XX, 748, 1960).

Cantoni, Louis Joseph—Counseling Your Friends. (New York: William Frederick, 1961).

Carnes, Earl F. and Francis P. Robinson—The Role of Client Talk in the Counseling Interview. (1948) Ed. Psych. Meas. 8:635-644.

Cartwright, Rosalind D. and Barbara Lerner—Empathy, Need to Change and Improvement with Psychotherapy. (1963) J. Consult. Psychol. No. 2, 27:138-144.

Cecil, R. L. and R. F. Loeb (A foreword of) D. W. Atchley—Patient-physician Communication. A Textbook of Medicine. 10th ed. (Philadelphia, Saunders, 1959)

Chance, Erika—Mutual Expectations of Patients and Therapists in Individual Treatment. (1957) Hum. Rel. 10:167-178.

Coburn , Herbert H.—An Experimental Comparison of Relationship-centered and Problem-centered Counseling. (Doctoral Dissertation, Wayne Univ., 1954) (D.A. XIV, 2123, 1954).

Cole, Charles W.—Effects of Verbal Stimuli in a Counseling Analogue. (1965) J. Counsel. Psychol. 12:408.

Coleman, Jules V.—The Initial Phase of Psychotherapy. (1949) Bull. Menn. Clinic 13:189-197.

Coleman, William—The Counseling Process. (1957) Rev. Ed. Res. 27:202-209.

Correll, Paul Thomas—Factors Influencing Communication in Counseling. (Doctoral Dissertation, Univ. of Missouri, 1955) (D.A. XVI 497, 1956).

Cottle, William C. and N. M. Downie—Procedures and Preparation for Counseling. (New York: Prentice-Hall, 1960).

Cottle, William C.—Some Common Elements in Counseling. (1953) Personnel Guid. J. 32:4-8.

Dahlberg, Edwin T.—The Pastor as an Amateur Counselor. (Feb 1960) Past. Psych. 11:31-36.

Danskin, David G.—Roles Played by Counselors in Their Interviews. (1955) J. Counsel. Psych. 2:22-27.

Davis, Stanley E.—An Investigation of Client Character Shown in Interview Behavior. (Doctoral Dissertation, Ohio State Univ., 1953) (D.A. XVIII, 1855, 1958).

Dean, John P. and William F. Whyte—How Do You Know If the Informant Is Telling the Truth? (1958) Hum. Org. 17, No. 2:34-38.

Deutsch, Felix and William Murphy—The Clinical Interview. (New York: International Univ. Press, 1961).

Deutsch, Felix—Correlations of Verbal and Non-Verbal Communication in Interviews Elicited by the Associate Anamnesis. (1959) Psychosom. Med. 21:123-30.

Dicks, Russell L.—Creative Listening as a Method in Marital Counseling. (1950) Marr. Fam. Liv. 12, No. 3:91-94.

Dittman, Allen T. and Lyman C. Wynne—Linguistic Techniques and the Analysis of Emotionality in Interviews. (1961) J. Abnorm. Soc. Psychol. 63:201-204.

Doane, Calvin J.—A Study of Empathic Ability and Related Variables

Among Trained and Practicing Counselors. (Doctoral Dissertation, Indiana Univ., 1955). (D.A. XV, 2096, 1955).

Dodd, Aleck D.—Counseling Step-By-Step. Part I (Nov. 1955) Past. Psych. 6:27-34. Part II (Dec. 1955) Past. Psych. 6:40-52.

Doniger, Simon—Pastoral Counseling Centers. (1963) Past. Psych. 13:5-8.

Drasgow, James—A Graphic Description of Counseling Relationships. (1960) J. Counsel. Psych. 7:51-55.

Dreikers, Rudolf—The Psychological Interview in Medicine. (1952-1953) Am. J. Indiv. Psych. 10:99-122.

Ebaugh, Franklin G.—Evaluation of Interviewing Techniques and Principles of Psychotherapy for the General Practitioner. (1948) J. Omaha Clin. Soc. 9:29-35.

Elkin, Meyer—Short-Contact Counseling in a Conciliation Court. (1962) Soc. Casework 43:184-190.

Erickson, Clifford E.—The Counseling Interview. (New York, Prentice-Hall, 1950) 174 pp.

Farres, Miriam—Hostility in Short Term Counseling. (1958) Personnel Guid. J. 36:627-628.

Fenichel, O.—Concerning Unconscious Communication—in Collected Papers. (London: Routledge, 1954).

Fenlason, A. F.—Essentials in Interviewing: For the Interviewer Offering Professional Services. (New York, Harper, 1952).

Fey, William F.—Acceptance of Self and Others, and Its Relation to Therapy-Readiness. (1954) J. Clin. Psychol. 10:269-271.

Fiedler, F. and J. McGrath—The Nature of Teamwork, Discovery, Feb. 1962; Dynamics of the Negotiation Situation (Unpublished, 1963).

Finesinger, J.—Psychiatric Interviewing. Some Principles and Procedures in Insight Therapy. (1948) Am. J. Psychiat. 105:187.

Fisher, Herbert—Interviewer Bias in the Recording Operation. (1950) Int. J. Op. Att. Res. 4, No. 3.

Fitz-Hugh, Ann K.—The Conceptual Structure in Spontaneous Client Laughter During Counseling Interviews. (Doctoral Dissertation, Univ. of Michigan, 1956-57).

Fortas, Abe—The Legal Interview. (Feb. 1952) Psychiatry 15:91.

Foster, Robert G.—How a Marriage Counselor Handles a Case. (1954) Marr. Fam. Liv. 12:41-43.

Frank, Jerome D.—Patient's Expectancies and Relearning as Factors Determining Improvement in Psychotherapy. (1959) Am. J. Psychiat. 115:961-68.

Frank, Lawrence and Rollo May, eds.—Psychotherapy and Counseling.

(1955) Annals of New York Academy of Sciences, 63 Art. 3:319-432.

Frankl, Viktor E.—Man's Search for Meaning: An Introduction to Logotherapy. (New York, Washington Square Press, 1963).

Frizzo, Gabriella—Correspondence as a Casework Tool. (1950) Smith Coll. St. Soc. Work 20:149-172.

Froehlich, Clifford P.—The Completeness and Accuracy of Counseling Interview Reports. (1958) J. Gen. Psychol. 58:81-96.

Garrett, Annette—Interviewing: Its Principles and Methods. (New York, Family Service Association of America, 1960).

Gehrke, Shirley and James Moxom—Diagnostic Classifications and Treatment Techniques in Marriage Counseling. (1962) Family Process 1:253-264.

Geist, Joanne and Norman M. Gerber—Joint Interviewing: A Treatment Technique With Marital Partners. (1960) Soc. Casework 41:76-83.

Gelbman, Frank and F. R. Wake—An Experimental Study of the Initial Interview. (1949) Psychiat. Q. Supp. 23:248-253.

Gilbert, William M.—Counseling: Therapy and Diagnosis. (1952) Ann. Rev. Psychol. 3:351-380.

Gill, Merton M., et al.—The Initial Interview in Psychiatric Practice. (New York, International Universities Press, 1954).

Goldman, Leo—Counseling: Content and Process. (1954) Personnel Guid. J. 33:82-85.

Goldstein, A. P.—Patient Expectancies, Symptom Reduction and Aspects of the Initial Psychotherapeutic Interview. (1961) J. Clin. Psychol. 17:129.

Goldstein, A. P.—Therapist-Patient Expectancies in Psychotherapy. (New York, Macmillan, 1962).

Gomberg, Robert and Frances T. Levinson, eds.—Diagnosis and Process in Family Counseling: Evolving Concepts Through Practice. (New York, Family Service Association of America, 1951) 243 pp.

Gordon, Raymod—Interviewing: Theory, Strategy, Techniques and Tactics. (New York, Basic Books, 1964).

Grater, Harry A.—Client Preferences for Affective or Cognitive Counselor Characteristics and First Interview Behavior. (1964) J. Counsel. Psychol. 11:248-250.

Guerney, Bernard G.—Client Dependency, Guardedness, Openness, and Resistance in a Reflective and in a Leading Psychotherapy. (Doctoral Dissertation, Penn. State Univ., 1956) D.A. XVI, 1492, 1956.

Gullerud, Ernest and Virginia L. Harlan—Four-way Joint Interviewing in Marital Counseling. (1962) Soc. Casework 43:532-537.

Guze, Samuel—An Analysis of Some Features of the Interview with the Interaction Chronograph. (1959) J. Abnorm. Soc. Psychol. 58-269-271.

Hall, Bernard and Winifred Wheeler—The Patient and His Relatives: Initial Joint Interview. (Jan. 1957) Soc. Work 2:75-80.

Harms, Ernest and Paul Schreiber—Handbook of Counseling Techniques. (New York, Pergamon, 1963) 506 pp.

Harris, Natalie and Gordon Connelly—Symposium on Interviewing Problems. (1948) Inter. J. Op. Att. Res. 69.

Heilbrun, Alfred B., Jr. and D. J. Sullivan—The Prediction of Counseling Readiness. (1962) Personnel Guid. J. 41:112-117.

Heller, Melvin, Esther Polen and Samuel Polsky—An Introduction to Legal Interviewing. (Nat. Leg. Aid and Def. Assn., 1960).

Herbert, W. L. and F. V. Jarvis—The Art of Marriage Counseling, A Modern Approach. (New York, Emerson, 1960) 125 pp.

Hiltner, Seward—Pastoral Psychology and Pastoral Counseling. (1952) Past. Psych. 3:21-28. Also in S. Doniger, ed.—Religion and Human Behavior. (New York, Association, 1954) pp. 179-195.

Hiltner, Seward—Timing in Counseling. (1950) Past. Psych. 1, No. 7:20-24.

Hoffman, Simon—Diagnosis and Evaluation in Counseling. (1959) Personnel Guid. J. 38:229-231.

Holzman, Mathilda S.—The Significance of the Value Systems of Patient and Therapist for the Outcome of Psychotherapy. (Doctoral Dissertation, Univ. of Washington, 1961) D.A. 4073, 1962.

Howe, Reuel L.—Overcoming the Barriers to Communication. (1963) Past. Psych. 14:26-32.

Hugerth, Christine S.—Some Factors Affecting Interviewers' Judgments. (Doctoral Dissertation, Yale Univ., 1957-58).

Hummel, Raymond C.—Interviewee Responsiveness as a Function of Interviewer Method. (Doctoral Dissertation, Columbia Univ., 1958) (D.A. XIX, 1846 1959).

Jaffe, Joseph—An Objective Study of Communication in Psychiatric Interviews. (1957) J. Hillside Hosp. 6:207-215.

Jewell, Walter O.—Differential Judgments of Manifest Anxiety, Defensiveness and Effectiveness, and Effective Problem Solving in Counseling. (Doctoral Dissertation, Univ. of Minnesota, 1958) (D.A. XIX, 3010, 1959).

Johnson, Ray W.—Number of Interviews, Diagnosis and Success of Counseling. (1965) J. Counsel. Psychol. 12:248.

Jurjevich, Ratibor—The Effects of Ego-inflating and Ego-deflating Responses of the Psychotherapist. (Doctoral Dissertation, Univ. of Denver, 1958-59).

Kadushin, Charles—Individual Decisions to Undertake Psychotherapy. (1958) Admin. Sci. Q. 3, No. 3:379-411.

Kadushin, Charles—Social Distance Between Client and Professional. (March 1962) Am. J. Soc. 517-531.

Kahn, Robert L. and Charles F. Cannell—The Dynamics of Interviewing. (New York, Wiley, 1957) 368 pp.

Kanfer, F. H. and J. F. McBrearty—Minimal Social Reinforcement and Interview Content. (1962) J. Clin. Psychol. 18:210-215.

Kanfer, F. H.—Verbal Rate, Eyeblink and Content in the Structured Psychiatric Interviews. (1960) J. Abnorm. Soc. Psychol. 61:341-347.

Kirk, B. A.—Interval Between First and Second Interview. (April, 1958) Personnel Guid. J. 36:529-33.

Korman, Maurice—An Investigation of Semantic Difference Among, and the Inferential Process of, Psychiatrists, Psychologists and Psychiatric Social Workers. (Doctoral Dissertation, Univ. of Minnesota, 1957) (D.A. XVIII, 1491, 1958).

Kounin, J. and N. Polansky—Experimental Studies of Client's Reactions to Initial Interviews. (1956) Hum. Rel. 9:265-293.

Krasner, L.-—Studies of the Conditioning of Verbal Behavior. (1958) Psychol. Bull. 55:148-170.

Kunkel, Fritz and Ruth Gardner—What Do You Advise? A Guide to the Art of Counseling. (New York: Washburn, 1946).

Lawton, George—Neurotic Interaction Between Counselor and Counselee. (1958) J. Counsel. Psych. 5:28-33.

Layton, Wilbur L.—Constructs and Communication in Counseling: A Limited Theory. (1961) J. Counsel. Psychol. 8:3-8.

Lesser, William M.—The Relationship Between Counseling Progress and Emphatic Understanding. (Doctoral Dissertation, Michigan State Univ., 1958). D.A. XIX, 3367, 1959.

Leventhal, Allan M.—Prediction of Number of Counseling Interviews. (1964) Psychol. Rep. 15:106.

Lewin, K. K.—Nonverbal Cues and Transference. (1965) Arch. Gen. Psychiat. 12:391-394.

Lief, H. I.—Silence as Intervention in Psychotherapy. (1962) Am. J. Psychoanal. 22:80-83.

Line, W.—Scientific Aspects of Counseling. (June 1950) Nat. Assn. Deans Women J. 13:147-151. Same (April 1951) Col. Univ. 26:330-335.

McCauley, William A.—An Analysis of Aspects of Counselor and Client Behavior in the Counseling Interview. (Doctoral Dissertation, Syracuse Univ. 1956) D.A. XVI, 2386, 1956.

McGowan, John F.—Client Anticipations and Expectancies as Related to Initial Interview Performance and Perceptions. (Doctoral Dissertation, Univ. of Missouri, 1954) D.A. XV, 228, 1955.

Maier, Norman—The Appraisal Interview. (New York, Wiley, 1958).

Marsden, Gerald—Content-analysis Studies of Therapeutic Interviews. (1965) Psychol. Bull. 63:298-321.

Matarazzo, J. D., H. F. Hess and G. Saslow—Frequency and Duration Characteristics of Speech and Silence Behavior During Interviews. (1962) J. Clin. Psychol. 18:416-426.

Matarazzo, J. D., et al.—Interview Content and Interviewer Speech Duration. (1963) J. Clin. Psychol. 19:463-472.

Matarazzo, J. D., et al.—Interviewer Mm-Hmm and Interviewee Speech Duration. (1964) Psychotherapy:T.R.P. 1:109.

May, Rollo—The Art of Counseling. (Nashville, Abingdon, 1957).

Mellinger, Glen D.—Interpersonal Trust as a Factor in Communication. (1956) J. Abnorm. Soc. Psychol. 52:304-309.

Mendelsohn, Robert A.—The Effects of Cognitive Dissonance and Interview Preference Upon Counseling-type Interviews. D.A. XXIV, 2987, 1964.

Miner, Roy W., ed.—Psychotherapy and Counseling. (1955) Ann. Acad. Sci. 63:319-432.

Mitchell, Howard E., et al.—Anticipated Development of Case from Content of First Interview Record (1953) Marr. Fam. Liv. 15:226-231.

Most, Elizabeth—Measuring Change in Marital Satisfaction. (1964) Soc. Work 9:64-70.

Mudd, Emily—The Practice of Counseling. (New York, Association, 1951).

Murphy, Carol R.—The Ministry of Counseling. (Wallingford, Pa., Pendle Hill, 1952) Reprint (Dec. 1957) Past. Psych. 8:15-32.

Narramore, Clyde M.—The Psychology of Counseling. (Grand Rapids, Zondervan, 1960).

Oates, Wayne E.—Counseling and Communication. (1955) Rel. Ed. 50:103-105.

Oppenheimer, Oscar—Some Counseling Theory: Objectivity and Subjectivity. (1954) J. Counsel. Psychol. 1:184-187.

Parukh, Soli K.—General Semantics—An Approach to Communication with Reference to Counseling. (1959) Ind. J. Soc. W. —No. 4, 19:253-271.

Patterson, C. H.—Control, Conditioning and Counseling. (1963) Personnel. Guid. J. 41:680-686.

Payne, S. L.—The Art of Asking Questions. (Princeton, Princeton Univ. Press, 1951).

Pepinsky, Harold B.—Counseling: Theory and Practice. (New York, Ronald, 1954).

Perez, Joseph F.—Counseling: Theory and Practice. (Reading, Mass., Addison, 1965) 186 pp.

Phillips, J. S., et al.—Relationships Between Descriptive Content and Interaction Behavior in Interviews. (1961) J. Consult. Psychol. 25: 260-266.

Pittenger, Robert—The First 5 Minutes: A Sample of Microscopic Interview Analysis. (Ithaca: Martineau, 1960).

Pohlman, Edward W.—A Study Involving Client Preferences for Counselor Behaviors in Counseling. (Doctoral Dissertation, Ohio State Univ.) D.A. XXI, 3167, 1961.

Polansky, N. and J. Kounin—Clients' Reactions to Initial Interviews: A Field Study. (1956) Human Rel. 9:237-264.

Polansky, N.—The Concept of Verbal Accessibility. (1965) Smith Coll. St. Soc. Wk. 36:2.

Poole, Aileen—Counselor Judgment and Counseling Evaluation. (1957) J. Counsel. Psychol. 4:37-40.

Pope, Benjamin and Aaron W. Seligman—The Effect of Therapist Verbal Activity Level and Specificity on Patient Productivity and Speech Disturbance in the Initial Interview. (1962) J. Consult. Psychol. 26:489.

Powdermaker, Florence—The Techniques of the Initial Interview and Methods of Teaching Them. (1948) Psychiatry 104: 642-646.

Quaytman, Wilfred—Motivation for Psychotherapy: A Comparative Investigation of Motivational Factors in Female Neurotic Outpatients Who Prematurely Terminate and Those Who Remain in Psychotherapy. (Doctoral Dissertation, New York Univ., 1961). D.A. XXII, 4412, 1962.

Rabiner, Edwin L., et al.—Conjoint Family Therapy in the Inpatient Setting. (1962) Am. J. Psychother. 16:618-631.

Redmount, Robert S.—The Analysis of Interview Content in Formulative Legal Counseling. (Unpublished mimeo, 1960).

Redmount, Robert S.—Perception and Strategy in Divorce Counseling. (Sept. 1960) Conn. B. J. 34:249.

Reik, Theodor—Listening With the Third Ear; the Inner Experience of a Psychoanalyst. (New York, Farrar, Straus, 1948).

Richardson, Stephan A.—The Use of Leading Questions in Non-scheduled Interviews. (1960) Hum. Org. 19:86-89.

Ripple, Lillian—Motivation, Capacity and Opportunity as Related to the Use of Casework Service: Theoretical Base and Plan of Study. (1955) Soc. Ser. Rev. 29, No. 2:172-193.

Roberts, Ralph R., Jr., and Guy A. Rengaglia—The Influence of Tape Recording on Counseling. (1965) J. Counsel. Psychol. 12:10-16.

Robinson, Frances P.—The Dynamics of Communication in Counseling. (1955) J. Counsel. Psych. 2:163-169.

Rogers, Carl R. and R. J. Becher—A Basic Orientation for Counseling. (1950) Past. Psych. 1:16-34.

Ross, J. H.—The Initial Interview. (1957) Psychoanalysis 5:46-57.

Routh, Thomas—Counseling and Common Sense. (1964) Personnel J. 43:558-560.

Routh, Thomas—Feelings Are Facts. (1957) Hum. Rel. 6:78-83.

Rubinstein, Ben—An Approach to Humanism in a Medical Setting. (1966) Am. J. Orthopsychol. 36:153.

Rudikoff, Esselyn C. and Barbara A. Kirk—Goals of Counseling: Mobilizing the Counselee. (1961) J. Counsel. Psychol. 8:243-249.

Ryan, T. Antoinette—Influence of Different Cueing Procedures on Counseling Effectiveness. (1965) Proc. of 73rd Ann. Convention of the Am. Psychol. Assoc. 351-352.

Samler, J.—Change in Values: A Goal in Counseling. (1960) J. Counsel. Psychol. 7:32-39.

Sarason, Seymour B.—The Clinical Interview. (New York, Harper, 1954).

Saul, Leon J.—On the Value of One or Two Interviews. (1951) Psychoanal. Q. 20:613-615.

Sinha, S. N.—Perspectives in Interviewing. (1958) J. Voc. Ed. Guid. 5, No. 2:81-87.

Spivak, Mark—Factors Influencing the Formation of a Patient-Percept by Psychiatrists Following the Initial Interview. (Doctoral Dissertation, Univ. of Mich, 1962) D.A. XXIII 341, 1963).

Stevenson, Ian—Psychotherapy—How to Guide Interviews. (1953) G.P. 7:69.

Strauss, A. and Leonard Schatzman—Cross-class Interviewing: An Analysis of Interaction and Communicative Styles. (1955) Hum. Org. 14, No. 2:28-31.

Strupp, H. H.—The Performance of Psychiatrists and Psychologists in a Therapeutic Interview. (1958) J. Clin. Psych. 14:219-226.

Sullivan, Harry S.—The Psychiatric Interview. (New York: Norton, 1954).

Tarachow, Sidney—Initial Interview Conference. (1962) J. Hillside Hosp. 11:127-153.

Terwilliger, Gaines and Fred Fiedler—An Investigation of Determinants Inducing Individuals to Seek Personal Counseling. (1958) J. Consult. Psychol. 22:288.

Thorne, Frederick C.—Principles of Personality Counseling: An Eclectic Viewpoint. (Brandon, Vt., Journal Clinical Psychology, 1950) 491 pp.

Tolbert, Elias L.—Introduction to Counseling. (New York: McGraw-Hill, 1959).

Toman, W.—Pause Analysis as a Short Interviewing Technique. (Feb. 1953) J. Consult. Psychol. 17:1-7.

Triandis, H. C.—Cognitive Similarity and Communication. (1960) Human Relations 13:175-183.

Trout, David M.—Why Define Counseling in Medical Terms? (1954) Personnel Guid. J. 32:518-523.

Truax, Charles and Robert R. Garkhuff—Experimental Manipulation of Therapeutic Conditions. (1965) J. Consult. Psychol. 29:119-124.

Tyler, Leona E.—Initial Interview. (April 1956) Personnel Guid. J. 34:466-473.

Tyler, Leona E.—Theoretical Principles Underlying the Counseling Process. (1958) J. Counsel. Psych. 5:3-10.

Wiest, Bernard J.—The Relationship of Interpersonal Responses to Ratings and Content of the Interview. (Doctoral Dissertation, Columbia Univ. 1960) D.A. XXI, 2008, 1961.

Wiggins, James—Some Consideration in Interviewing. (March 1959) Fed. Prob. 23:36.

Williamson, Edmund G.—Meaning of Communication in Counseling. (Sept. 1959) Personnel Guid. J. 38:6-14.

Wise, Carrol A.—Pastoral Counseling, Its Theory and Practice. (New York, Harper, 1951) 231 pp.

Wrenn, C. Gilbert—Counseling: A Way of Living. (1960) Counseling 18:1-4.

Wrenn, C. Gilbert—Counseling Methods. (1954) Ann. Rev. Psychol. 5:337-356.

Zerfoss, Karl—Readings in Counseling. (New York, Association, 1952) 639 pp.

Chapter 4

The Research Survey —
Method and Analysis

Some Preliminary Choices and Forms

If in the Genesis of this study we inadequately grasped the effect of problems of methodology and procedure, this was not true by the time of Exodus, and completely cured before Revelations. A budget dimension first posed the question of how much information could be obtained at how little cost. We knew from preliminary readings that interviews cost approximately 10 to 60 times what a questionnaire does per reply and that writers strongly differed as to whether sufficient additional information resulted from interviews to justify the added cost. Members of our Committee opined that questionnaires would prove adequate. We discussed the matter thoroughly with the Bureau of Applied Social Research in New York, which had done the most in studying lawyers, doctors and clergymen, and they reported a comparative cost of about $10 interview to $1 questionnaire per reply. We thereupon set up a small controlled experiment ourselves, using both questionnaires and interviews.

After several experimental runs it was determined that interviews produced little more data than questionnaires, were about 10 times as expensive per reply, tended to reflect the reaction of the interviewer, were difficult to arrange with lawyers and therefore should be used primarily for analysis in depth rather than original collection of responses. These conclusions were fortified by many studies showing how interviewers color results, through selecting respondents, wording of questions, errors of observation and recording, reaction to and of respondents, personal opinions and attitudes, social distance of parties, and many other factors. Although we knew that the effect of these could be lessened by careful selection of inerviewers we were also aware that we were not permanently enough in the survey business and were covering too wide a sample to adequately rule out error. At one point we tried telephone interviews as a result of some interesting experiments with these. We found the telephone interview to work reasonably well with doctors, less well with lawyers and poorest with clergy. Clergy seemed to have time and desire for face-to-face contact. Lawyers were suspicious.

Almost immediately we issued the first Outline of Research as follows:

Outline of Research on Counseling
(by Physicians, Lawyers, Clergymen)

1. A pilot project to see:
    a) What is being done to teach counseling.
    b) What common elements exist in counseling.
    c) What makes a good counselor.
    d) How do clients choose a counselor.
    e) What is the counselor's concept of himself.
    f) What is the client's concept and reaction.
    g) What methods are usable for studying counseling.
2. Planned stages of the project (to be completed so far as time, personnel and money permit):
    A-1) Questionnaire to all professional schools to determine counseling teaching and plans.
    A-2) Follow-up interviews with professional schools.
    B-1) Selection of test group (2 cities of upstate New York)—Lawyers, Doctors, Clergymen. By interviews, test questions and their analysis of counseling.

B-2) Attempt to arrange for a few in this group to tape regular counseling sessions with clients.

C-1) By interview, test a cross-section group of citizens on whether they have ever been for counseling; how they chose the counselor; what was their reaction and satisfaction.

D-1) By questionnaire attempt to survey a large group of Lawyers, Doctors and Clergymen on training for counseling, methods, purpose, success, etc.

D-2) For this purpose we are proposing every 10th or 20th listed professional in the three groups in Los Angeles, San Francisco, Chicago, part of New York and 2 upstate rural communities.

D-3) Second and perhaps third questionnaires may be sent to all, or to those who respond.

D-4) Follow-up interviews will be conducted with samples from the questionnaire response.

E-1) An attempt will be made to survey the available books, mimeograph material, tapes, etc., on counseling or used in counseling—not only in the three professions but in related fields.

F-1) Conferences and interviews will be held with those in the professions and related fields who are most interested in counseling, have written, etc.

G-1) A few practitioners in each profession will be asked to tape record counseling sessions (obliterating identification).

G-2) It is hoped that interviewers can appear as clients to some practitioners and record what actually happens in a counseling session.

Obviously, we shall, in most areas, be surveying rather than working in depth. We believe this best suited to check the validity of various methods of research.

Not quite a year later we amplified this in a second release, reading:

Research on Counseling by Physicians, Lawyers, Clergymen

The Walter E. Meyer Research Institute is supporting Prof. Harrop A. Freeman of Cornell University Law School in a pilot study of counseling by physicians, lawyers and clergymen.

The *purpose* is to determine whether and how counseling can be studied, whether there are interdisciplinary similarities among the three ancient professions, whether and how the training for counseling (either in or out of college) can be improved. Intentionally, "counseling" has been very broadly defined as being verbal or non-verbal advice, guidance or direction to a person submitting or constituting a problem. All types of clergymen and lawyers are studied, but only general practice, psychiatry, internal medicine and like groups among physicians are examined.

The original outline of research is attached to this statement. As will be seen from what follows, little change has been required in the actual operation of the project except that Professor Freeman doubted the ethics of steps B-2, G-1, G-2, and these have merely been explored rather than utilized. In order to get the most out of the money expended, in realization of the great scope and limited time for the project, and in fulfillment of the purpose to run a pilot rather than a definitive study, Dr. Freeman has worked in subsidiary projects whenever possible and omitted areas of research wherever studies already done or being done by others promised material to help tell the complete survey story.

The Study easily breaks down into *four areas* or levels of research. These areas and the plans under each may thus be outlined:

(1) *Survey of Professional Schools*: By questionnaire to all law, medical and theological schools, and by interviews with the more important in each group, an attempt is being made to study the teaching of counseling. The schools are questioned as to choice of students, place of counseling in the curriculum, teachers and their training, satisfaction with or

plans for change of curriculum, interest of students, availability of teaching or study materials on counseling.

(2) *Study of Actual Practicing Lawyers, Physicians and Clergymen.* In Los Angeles, San Francisco, Chicago, Up-state New York, and part of New York City, a questionnaire survey is to be made of every 10th lawyer, doctor and minister, with an attempt to interview about 1 in 100 in each category. In order that we may have a broader test or comparative group in each profession, at least a New York State-wide questionnaire survey is proposed of doctors, lawyers and ministers. The pattern of the questionnaires and interviews is devised to find out how the professionals actually operate in counseling, their training and ability, their concept of counseling, their relationship to other professions, their referral practices, their need for further training and like details.

(3) *Follow-up Study of Those Who Have Been Through Counseling.* An attempt is being made to complete *five* substudies by questionnaire and/or interview: a) Survey of about 2500 typical persons (as a check group) who may or may not have had counseling. b) Survey of about 3000 persons who have had medical (psychiatric) counseling. c) Survey of a sample (number not yet fixed) of persons who have had religious counseling. d) Survey of persons (number not yet determined) who have had legal counseling. e) Survey of about 1500 persons who have had one type of counseling (marriage) whether by lawyers, doctors, ministers or others. In b), c), and d) we expect to place the counselor's report of the counseling alongside the client's report. In all instances we shall be determining: type of problem counseled, how counselor selected, what he did, success of counseling, when problems are not taken to counselors, degree of client satisfaction.

(4) *Study of Books, Articles and Audio-visual Material Related to Counseling and the Function and Teaching of Counseling in Three Professions.* It is hoped this may give

rise, eventually, to bibliographies, to materials for casebooks, to interdisciplinary materials.

It is Professor Freeman's intention to carry this project as near to completion as possible, as money and time will permit. Later, greater coverage, completion of the study, or more definitive results may be sought.

Next, we attempted to devise three *types* of questionnaires, to be varied slightly within each of the categories. One was for the professional schools (form is at pp. 61-62); one was for practicing professionals (typical form is in Appendix); a third was for clients. So that the reader may see the variations which were necessary from discipline to discipline and in dealing with less or better educated persons we place in the Appendix samples of *all* the forms used with clients: a) the general client (unknown whether he had been to a counselor), b) psychological-psychiatric clinic clients, c) legal aid clinic clients, d) Parents without Partners, e) Clergy counselees. Of course the questions, however worded, had to be kept sufficiently parallel to allow for parallel coding. The variations in questions from one type of professional counselor to another are discussed below.

Our committee recommended a 2-3 page questionnaire for professional schools and professional practitioners (on the assumption they were enough interested to do this much work), and a one page form for clients. All were to provide open-ended questions as the means for getting the most accurate picture and evaluation from those who would answer; all were to embody "traps" and opportunities for inconsistent statements and revelation of defensive and like attitudes. It was recognized that ambiguities would exist in the questionnaires. One of the most hotly debated issues was whether any definition of counseling should be provided: if "yes," then you prejudiced the case in favor of this as *the* definition; if "no," then the responding definitions might be so varied as to render comparison of data impossible, and some might throw away the questionnaire as non-suggestive or uninteresting. We finally agreed on a broad, suggestive definition and set this forth in an accompanying letter as "tentative." It was also decided, rather than formulate a preconceived number of hypotheses and develop questionnaires to answer these, that we should merely list so much of the kind of information likely to be useful in understanding counseling as we could get into the prescribed length questionnaire and then let our hypotheses develop as we collated the furnished material.

[Although, I may, on occasion, be quite critical of the questionnaire forms we used, I am generally satisfied with the information which they yielded and with the coding possible.]

It can be seen that we departed from accepted survey rules. If one is going to compare data from questionnaires it is generally assumed that the form of questions must remain exactly the same. But the practice of lawyers, doctors and clergymen is both similar and different. For example, it was important that we get the lawyer's and doctor's self-image of their worth (the fees they charge) and of their social service (free work); such an inquiry would be meaningless to a minister. The lawyer, the doctor and the clergyman engage in trials, operations and sermons (quite different but all involving "performing")—how phrase the questions to elicit whether they viewed these as counseling or related to counseling. Lawyers did not have within their profession a "specialty" group to whom counseling could be referred, whereas many churches have counseling clergy attached, and doctors may view psychiatrists as their specialist counselors—how determine the different effect of this dimension. Also, to develop a picture of the way in which each profession saw each other profession with regard to counseling, questions had to be phrased in different ways.

The points at which we found it necessary to vary the questions related to the type of work in which the different professions saw their counseling, and their reaction to clients and other professions. Lawyers needed case categories: real estate, business, criminal, and like terms; the medic needed physiological and psychosomatic labels; and the clergy spiritual and moral pigeon holes. *But,* we also had to carry all these professions into like questions, into marital, criminal, psychological, personal, moral categories and thus compare their similarities and differences. This was done through general and specific work, client, satisfaction and success questions. Further discussion of the inquiry items and what we sought to find out is set forth later in the paragraphs on coding.

The Survey Sample

A second decision loomed large in our early planning. What should our sample cover? We were located on the Atlantic Seaboard; the greatest concentration of lawyers, doctors and clergymen was in the large cities. Yet we knew that lawyers in metropolitan districts were not typical of rural and up-state practitioners—and this particularly in the type of clients and the extent of counseling. We suspected the same as to clergymen and doctors (the largest concentration of psychiatrists is in New York City around Fifth and Park Avenues). We rather imagined that different professions served the primary role of counselor in differing communities. It was highly desirable that we should not be provincial, that we should not select those most or least sympathetic to our project. What mid-western state and city might be studiable and reasonably typical? California attracted us because it had an integrated legal bar (admission to bar equalled membership in the bar association), an extremely active Continuation of the Bar training program for practicing lawyers that had shown some interest in counseling training, a large profession of psychiatrists and general doctors with psychological orientation, a fine state-wide education, a most liberal tradition in all three professions. The author's contacts were good in all these areas.

We chose Los Angeles-San Francisco, Chicago-upstate Illinois and Queens-upstate New York as sample areas for practitioners in the three professions because these would parallel where we were surveying clients, represented different patterns of integrated and non-integrated professions, might show the most and least liberal counseling attitudes and practices, covered the northern part of the country, represented rural to metropolitan practices, paralleled the location of most professional schools, were organizable within our financial and time limits, and were most reachable in terms of available personnel and lists. The choice proved good though it may have added somewhat to the cost of the survey.

The survey sample therefore turned out to look like this:

(1) *Survey of Professional Schools*: Out of 132 law schools of the American Association of Law Schools, 99 replied to our questionnaire and about one-half of these were interviewed. Out of 122 theological schools 70 replied and 20 of these were interviewed. Of the 70 medical colleges only 20 replied or were willing to be interviewed (considerable lack of cooperation here; in fact, the American Medical Schools Association refused to authorize our study). Had it not been for a survey by the Chicago Medical School on Psychotherapy Instruction in Medical Education, the questionnaire replies of which we were permitted to use, it would have been hard to make comparison of the three professions. As it was, we got a fair picture of about 40 medical colleges.

(2) *Study of Actual Practicing Lawyers, Physicians and Clergymen*:

Lawyers: In Los Angeles, San Francisco, Chicago, Queens and selected upstate New York-Illinois communities there are approximately 33,000 lawyers. We random mail-surveyed something over 10% of these (4,000) and received usable replies or interviews without replies from 850 or about 21%. Of these about one-seventh were interviewed.

Physicians: We tried to cover basically the same areas but were unable to assure complete parallels. We used a list of one-half of New York State general practitioners and one-tenth of the internists, general practitioners and psychiatrists in Los Angeles, San Francisco, Queens and the two upstate areas. The sample involved 3,500 out of about 30,000 physicians. We had usable replies and interviews from 450. About 75 were interviewed.

Clergymen: The list was composed of one-tenth of the clergy in Los Angeles, San Francisco, Chicago, Queens, up-state New York and non-metropolitan Illinois. The sample involved 3,600 out of about 24,000 clergymen. We received replies from about 520 and 80 were interviewed. Between interview and questionnaire we covered about one-tenth of the doctors and clergymen and had replies from about 15% of the one-tenth.

(3) *Those who Have Been Through Counseling*: Very early it became apparent that this might be the most important part of the program. Unusual success was had in setting up research.

a) As a major control group a survey was made of about 3,000 graduate students and general public (concerning whom we did not know whether they had been to counselors). We received about 750 returns and interviewed 10%. We also used the survey in paragraph (d) as a minor control.

b) Through very good fortune we obtained the co-operation of psychological-psychiatric clinics to survey 2,500 persons who had been through the clinics. We utilized 450 replies, about equally divided between those willing and unwilling to be interviewed. We were allowed by the clinics to photostat the doctor's report on each client (with name and identification obliterated) and compare it to the client's original report and his questionnaire response; and also to interview and questionnaire the counselors.

c) We worked out a study of those who received legal counseling at Chicago Legal Aid (United Charities). We surveyed (by questionnaire) about 3,000 clients in four categories: single visit legal advice cases, current pending cases, cases as closed, closed matrimonial cases on which social workers had aided. The lawyers wrote a report on about 1 in each 10 cases to compare to the client's reply. Because of the lower income group and resistance to survey, 380 replies were usable.

d) We questionnaired 1,000 divorced persons through "Parents-without-Partners" in metropolitan-urban areas, as a separate part of a general questionnaire. Here counseling may never have been had or may have been pre-marital, marital, at the time of divorce or subsequent; and by lawyer, clergyman, physician, other. Replies to our part of this questionnaire were about 20%. We used this sample as a second control group (not known whether had counsel) but different from the general group in (a) above in having a specific type of problem—marital.

e) The survey of persons who had been to religious counselors was least successful; we did not believe this so important because the published literature in this field is greatest. We surveyed 1000 and had responses from about 150. Here again we got parallel reports from the counseling clergyman.

This then, was the data with which we had to work.

At an early stage in the program and from time-to-time thereafter we compiled some thirteen series of questions or issues which seemed likely to come up. It was along the lines of these thirteen series that we asked a group of consultants to "throw their minds around" in drafting questionnaires, reading over some of the interviews and questionnaire replies, and in devising coding. The 13 series of questions were these (the total bank of questions in each appears in the Appendix):

"A" Series — General or Global Approach to material and counseling.

"B" Series — Selection and Training of professions.

"C" Series — Composition of the Profession and the Professional's Practice.

"D" Series — How clients are obtained? How disposed of?

"E" Series — Self Image of the Counselor.

"F" Series — Image or Attitude to Own Profession— Mythology or Professional Image.

"G" Series — Image of Other Professions—Relation to
     Other Professions.
"H" Series — Attitude to Counseling and to Clients;
     Relationship to Clients.
"I" Series — Methodology in Research and Coding.
"J" Series — Practice of Counseling.
"K" Series — Definition or Delimitation of Counseling.
"L" Series — Success or Evaluation of Counseling.
"O" Series — Client Concepts and Expectation.

The "I" Series on Methodology is most pertinent to
this chapter and raised in greater detail all the questions
mentioned as to sample, localities, questionnaires and interviews, pretesting, professional endorsement, cost, using other
organizations or projects. (See the total list of questions in
the Appendix).

Coding

Our greatest difficulty came when we tried to arrange
with Data Processing Coders for coding and analysis of data.
They immediately demanded the "few" hypotheses we wanted checked. When told we had no pre-conceived conclusions
which we sought to verify and that we believed there were
"thousands" of leads we wished to explore, they threw up
their hands. By now we had "thrown our minds around"
on questions suggested by reading through a fair sample of
the questionnaire replies and the interviews. These were
collected in categories which we have referred to above as
Series "A" - "O". The more replies we read, the greater
became the number of our speculations. The whole gamut
of problems, from the global view of the interviewee and
of counseling to detailed questions of training, practice, client relations and satisfaction, were presented.

We therefore tried to discover what catalogue of material
from the questionnaires was most likely to permit either
frequency checks or cross tabulation to answer the greatest
number of these questions or hypotheses in series "A" to
"O".

We decided to use IBM cards with 80 punch lines (horizontal) and 12 punch boxes to each line (vertical). This was the dimension of the machine we had most available. If we could not compress replies to one card then we had to use 2 cards and a third cross-over card. Thus for the professional questionnaires we had to use two cards per subject and then punch another amalgam card of the data most usable in cross-tabulation.

Next, we devised a coding chart for each of the professions and for each group of clients. We worked out a code that was usable for all three professions, (some questions had to have slightly different sub-punches for different questionnaires). The questionnaire and code for Lawyers is at the end of this Chapter (p. 55a). That for Clergymen and Physicians was almost identical. The information we sought and the choices we made are at once apparent. We were satisfied to distinguish metropolitan, urban and rural counselors, in 5 year age groups, by sex, as single, married, divorced or widowed, as Catholic, Protestant, Jewish or of no religion. When we came to the question as to what percentage of work was counseling in what type of case, we met our first major discrepancy of the professions. What we were trying to find out was in what type of cases did the counselor see a counseling situation. For lawyers legal pegs were needed on which to hang thought. General, matrimonial, tax, corporate, real estate, criminal were the types of labels with which he was familiar. In medicine, similar categories were: physiological ailments, psychosomatic. But we also wanted to carry across for all the professions: personal, family and marital relationships, business problems, criminal matters, philosophical, moral and spiritual problems. For the clergy "violation of rules, antisocial" replaced criminal, "psychological" replaced psychosomatic and other categories remained the same. In order to give comparison (*e.g.* lawyers on spiritual, moral, philosophic, marital, family, personal problems), a supplemental question was included. These differentiations were inserted in the questionnaires and used as coding categories, as a result of studying the free responses of early test questionnaires and interviews in each group. We decided it was enough to rate frequency of each type problem as little, medium and much.

We wanted to catalogue clients by sex, age, general occupational and educational group (dimensions constant for all professions), to find out the percentage of each served, the counselor success and interest in each group. Particularly, we desired the *counselor's* view of his success here. Did the client solve his problem, improve, remain unchanged, retrogress? Would he do as well without help? How much did the counseling contribute? It was of interest to see how sessions were scheduled, the time given, the frequency, the duration, the amount charged, the proportion done free.

The counselor's self description was next sought. What was his training: professional, in psychology, sociology, counseling, other? Had he been psychoanalyzed? What were his hobbies, clubs, outside interests? His family situation. His motivation; his reasons for doing counseling, and what he believed contributed to his ability. We wanted to know how he got material usable in counseling: by intuition, observing, listening, empathy, psychology, tests, introspection, cross examining and questioning, taking background histories, discussing cases with others, referral to specialists, experience with like cases, other methods. Our codes tried to record all this, even from the open ended questions. It can be seen that we were looking for extensive material, material to be played against itself to suggest hypotheses rather than to prove conclusions. Many of the questionnaires had the whole back side of the page or two or three extra pages covered with writing.

Against this perspective of material we gave the counselor multiple choice statements about counseling, professionalism, other professions, needed training, rating ability, ethics, client relationships. We laid traps for him. We duplicated some earlier questions for cross-check of answers in different context. The coding of these multiple choice responses (questions 16ff) proved most productive.

Then we produced *a code for clients.* It will be recalled that we were dealing with those known to have gone to a counselor, those who went to a specific type of counselor, those with a specific problem, those of varied sophistication, economic or education level, those who may never have gone to a counselor, and even those who themselves may have acted as counselors. We even wanted to see how the counselee might look upon himself as a counselor under some circumstances. We wanted comparisons. The Code as used generally for clients, with some slight modification from group to group, appears in the Appendix following client questionnaire forms.

In *our process of coding we used an intermediary step* not normal to coding. In between the questionnaire and the normal "number-box" form whereon the coder writes the punch number (1-12) in a box number according to the card lines (in our study 1 to 80), the coder made a yellow sheet using the actual abbreviations for all questions (*e.g.* SM-subject matrimonial, SC-subject corporation) and gave his over-all reaction to the questionnaire. By reviewing these sheets, the present author could at a glance get the global picture of a given respondent without reliance on punch cards and statistics. This helped, both in checking the coder and in my own speed of assimilating material. It kept the analysis from becoming too statistical. It called attention to valuable quotes, to insights of a novel type, to material no code could encompass. This procedure is heartily recommended to researchers.

Next, our key-punch operator transferred all box numbers to key punch cards. From these in all instances we first ran a frequency sort which showed the number and percentage giving each answer. From this would come a table as follows (*e.g.* for general client card sorts):

Sex

75% male
24% female

Religion

      51% Protestant
      7% Jewish
      14% Catholic
      14% no religion
      13% other or no answer

Hometown

      17% metropolitan
      64% urban
      14% rural

Have you failed to go to a counselor when you had a problem?

      44% yes
      41% no
      15% no answer

Why didn't you go?

      25% "solved (should solve) own problem"
      17% "thought unnecessary"
      6% "no one to trust"
      6% "cost"
      27% no answer

To whom did you turn?

      10% doctor
      6% psychiatrist
      8% lawyer
      12% teacher - boss
      17% clergy
      14% other professional counselors
      6% friends
      7% others

Generally the mere card sorts answered many of our questions.

Next, we would cross tabulate, *e.g.*, residence with each of the other pieces of data on which residence might have a bearing. For example, we found residence significantly related to at least 18 different answers of clients. Where we had a parallel record of the counselor this was also cross tabulated. It must not be understood that we have even yet completed all possible cross tabulations—rather only those deemed most potentially productive.

We retained all questionnaires, all preliminary summaries, all punched cards, all cross tabulation sheets for further use, and we welcome others to make use of them, and to carry forward any further cross tabulation, analysis or hypothesis checking.

NOTE: Neither this chapter nor later chapters (except 8) have been presented in the usual "research protocol" form of a report on tight sociological research. To do this would require detailed analysis of the sample population and its choice, the repliers and non-repliers, the usable and non-usable replies, the questions answered and avoided, the degree of cooperation, the exact form and condition of interview, the statistical data, the reliability and validity of the data, the confirmed and unconfirmed hypotheses. We should have had to present not merely percentages but unit breakdowns, item by item. Instead, we have used a form of presentation intended to convey to the reader the problems of research in a new and difficult area, the exploratory nature of the research, the desirability in such exploration not to be tied down to all the rigors of chi square, the value of advancing both fully confirmed and partially supported observations. As we have previously said, our whole methodology was focused on opening explorative studies of the professions and counseling generally. We can now report that we were satisfied with the study for this purpose.

We have found it more appropriate and less confusing to present such statistical material as may be desired in following chapters, usually as percentages in the body of the manuscript and to omit the underlying statistical tables. In chapter 8 (clients), however, we have reproduced a substantial group of tables so that the reader can check our conclusions. Similar tables were used as a preliminary stage on our other chapters.

This questionnaire is a part of a study Professor Harrop A. Freeman, Cornell University Law School, is making as to counseling by clergymen, lawyers and medics. These three are being studied together because they are recognized professions, are protected in confidential communications, have similarity of advanced training, and may show common attributes of counseling. The word "counseling" is employed very broadly; it is not limited to marital or spiritual or personal advice (see Part II). It is hoped that we shall be able to find ways of improving counseling training in our colleges. I recognize this will take some time, but I hope you are this much interested in improving our profession.

The form of this questionnaire is being used by all three professions. We can see similarities and differences only if you answer all questions even though you may think they apply primarily to professions other than your own. *There are 4 parts.* The *Most Important* part is the third, where you discuss concrete cases and give one or more illustrative cases of your own:

Part 1:   Identifies you, and catalogues statistical details.

Part 2:   Defines counseling and gives your attitudes toward counseling.

Part 3:   Gives some concrete case and your reaction thereto.

Part 4:   Gives your reaction to other professions and problems you may encounter.

QUESTIONNAIRE
Part 1:

Your City.......................... Your Age.......................... Sex..........................

Marital Status.. Religion..........................

1)   Do you consider yourself: A general $\begin{cases} \text{doctor} \\ \text{clergyman} \end{cases}$

.....................A $\begin{cases} \text{doctor} \\ \text{clergyman} \end{cases}$ specializing in................................

....

2)   What percentage of your work do you consider to be counseling clients........................%

3)   What percentage of your counseling is with (these may not add to 100%): Men: married............% unmarried............% businessmen..............% laboring men..............% other..............% age over 50..........% 25-50 years..........% 15-25 years..........% Women: married................% unmarried................% business women..................% housewives..................% other..................% age over 50..........% 25-50 years..........% 15-25 years..........%

4) With what age group, sex and occupation:
   a) **Do you prefer to work**...
   b) **Are you most successful**..
   c) **Least successful**...

5) What percentage of your counseling involves the following:
   Business or financial................% Criminal matters................%
   Relationships: personal........% family........% marital........%
   Philosophical..............% moral..............% spiritual..............%
   Other (specify what)..
   ....
   ....

6) a) What is your average fee per hour or visit?........................
   b) What percentage of your counseling would be free or at
      reduced rates..%

7) How do you schedule time for clients:
   a) Is the client given an estimate of the time likely
      involved? ....
   b) Do you fix a specific period for each interview?................
      What ....
   c) Do you try to keep time spent at a minimum?....................

8) Do you attempt to ascertain the unconscious as well as conscious processes at work: a) In the client............................
   b) In yourself..
   c) By what means?..
   ....
   ....

9) Do you have special training in counseling?............................
   What ....

10) Have you undergone psychoanalysis?......................................
    How long in duration?..

11) What percentage of your clients do you think:
    a) Solve their problems........................%, b) **achieve some**
    improvement ....%
    c) Become worse............%, d) Remain unchanged............%
    e) Would they do as well on their own? yes............ no............

12) Please write on the back of this page or on a separate sheet
    any other details which will help to understand the person
    you are: hobbies, clubs, outside interests, children. We want
I to know the type of person who goes into counseling and the
M experience out of which he operates. Why do you believe you
P went into counseling? *What feature of your life do you believe
    contributes the most to your counseling?*

Part 2.

This part deals with defining counseling and your attitude toward counseling.

20) If you were presented the following statements as to counseling, with which would you agree, disagree, have no opinion:

	Agree	Dis- agree	No Opinion
a) "Counseling occurs when a professionally competent person acts in an advisory capacity to a less knowledgeable person."	....	....	....
b) "Based on information communicated or obtained, the counselor is helping the client to develop his own pattern or orientation."	....	....	....
c) "Counseling is the giving of advice or guidance."	....	....	....
d) "A lawyer trying a case, a clergyman preaching, a doctor operating would not be 'counseling' but rather 'performing'."	....	....	....
e) "Flexibility, tact, intuition, understanding are valuable to a counselor."	....	....	....
f) "A counselor is more than a legal, medical or religious technician; he is an advisor on human problems."	....	....	....

	Yes	No
21) Should a counselor have professional training in counseling?	......	....

a) Why? ....
....
....

22) Should a counselor have undergone psychoanalysis? ....
a) Why? ....
....
....

23) Is the religion of a counselor or client important? ....
a) Why? ....
....
....

24) Does the function of a counselor include:
a) Giving advice specifically requested ....

    b)   Giving unsolicited advice   ....

    c)   Probing beyond the client's stated problem   ....

25) Should the counselor's attitude be:
Professional detachment...,
friendly sympathy........................ active interest........................

26) Should the counselor be:
    a)   Emotionally uninvolved..
Emotionally involved..
    b)   Does emotional involvement destroy objectivity.................
    c)   Do you become emotionally involved in clients' problems
without wishing to..

27)   a)   Do clients expect more than objective interest and
advice ....
    b)   Should the counselor meet the client's expectation..............

28)   a)   Should one counsel a person who is a friend or social
acquaintance ....
    b)   Should a professional man be in a different position
from a friend ....

29) Should counseling be fitted to the client.................................
Give example ....
....
....

29)   a)   How do you believe a client selects a counselor.................
Does the client assume the counselor's superiority in a
field ....

29)   b)   What part do you believe "intuition" plays in:
Eliciting facts   little........ some........ much........
evaluating problems   ....
counseling clients   ....

29)   c)   Would you please write on the back of this page your
own frank views on counseling and the improvement of counseling in our professions. How ought our colleges to improve
counseling training?

Part 3.

This part deals with specific cases:

Assume the following cases came to your office, labelled cases (A)
and (B). How would you handle them? Would you take the case?
What next steps toward counseling would you take? Write your answers
on the back of this page.

Case A: A woman, about 35, of foreign extraction but native born,
says she has a husband and two children, a girl 3 and a 4 year old
son. She is obsessed with the idea that she no longer loves her husband
and sometimes feel a compulsion to grab a kitchen knife and run it

through him or the children. This came on suddenly about 5½ years
after marriage. She is deeply religious and she and her mother have
strong faith in fortune tellers, one of whom she visited just before
marrying. She has now separated from her husband without telling him
of her obsessions but only that she cannot stand him any longer. She
has returned to live with her mother. She misses her husband, and
particularly her children, but does not dare trust herself with them.
There is considerable property (a house, stocks, bank account of perhaps $200,000). She believes the huband will want to do anything
fair, but he keeps insisting there is no reason for a divorce or separation.
You know the family and have always considered them well-mated
and happily married.

*   *   *

Case B: Mr. C., a man of 48 manages XYZ Company and owns a
one-third interest. The other two-thirds is owned equally by Miss D
and her brother Mr. E who had brought C in as manager and sold him
the one-third interest. Miss D is 65, dynamic and overbearing. She
educated E (age 40) and gave him his interest. Mr. C has been having
gastric upsets, sleepless nights and quarrels with Miss D. There is an
agreement by which C can leave and sell at "book value" to the others.
But he claims Miss D has fixed it so book value does not reflect actual
value. Mr. C wants "out" but he does not know what to do with his
life then. He feels he has failed in his loyalty to E, of whom he is
very fond. He has a great deal of bitterness toward D.

*   *   *

Case C: Would you please write up, on the back of this page, a typical
case of your counseling, setting forth any observations as to method,
sought for result, relationship or success which you may think appropriate?

Part 4.

This part deals with interrelationship of the professions and
problems common to the practice of more than one profession:

Check after each statement the space which most nearly represents
your view.

		Agree	Dis-agree	No Opinion
30)	Cases often involve emotional disturbances. My training and experience are such that I feel competent to handle these.	....	....	....
	a) Emotionally disturbed clients need more help than I can give.	....	....	....
	b) The only emotional problems I get interested in are the ones			

I think I can help. ....

c) Most emotionally disturbed clients get over the problem, in time. ....

31) My training and experience are such that I feel competent to take on most moral or ethical problems. Cases often present these. ....

a) All problems submitted to counselors involve moral, ethical or religious issues. ....

b) On moral, ethical or religious issues the client should see his spiritual adviser. ....

32) Matters which involve the law are too technical for counseling by anyone but a lawyer. ....

a) A lawyer does not really counsel, he only champions his client. ....

b) A lawyer should be brought in to legally accomplish the desired result only after it is determined what is in the client's emotional and spiritual interest. ....

33) A counselor should *listen* to the client —doing nothing more active than assuring him of his interest. ....

a) A counselor should *discuss* the problem with the client and help him see the various causes and effects of his actions. ....

b) A counselor should *reassure* the client. ....

34) A counselor should aid the client in selecting those more competent than himself in the particular problem. ....

35) There is no reason why the general lawyer, doctor or clergyman should not practice some psychiatry or psychology. ....

a) All three professions do

counsel in fields primarily those of
another of the three professions.   ....
b) Each profession should so
counsel in other fields.   ....
c) Problems submitted to a coun-
selor are so intertwined as to
render such counseling necessary.   ....

36) Would you please write a paragraph on the back of this page as
to how you believe our professions
interrelate and how we migth best
make use of each other.

37) How would you rank the following occupations?

	In contributions to society	In Prestige
Teachers	....	....
Clergymen	....	....
Lawyers	....	....
Businessmen	....	....
Doctors	....	....

a) What proportion of doctors, lawyers, clergymen are
doing less than a competent counseling job? Doctors................
.... Lawyers................................ Clergymen....................

38) a) Would you be willing to be interviewed as to counseling?..................................... b) Would you tape an interview
with a client's consent? ....

CODING PROFESSIONAL COUNSELORS (Lawyers, Doctors, Clergy)
(on 2 IBM cards)
CARD 1
(Horizontal card punch left margin; vertical squares numbers in body;
question numbers appear #......).

		1			2		3		4
1	*Residence*	M (metropolitan)			U (urban)		R (rural)		....
		1	2	3	4	5	6	7	8	9	10
2	*Age*	....-25	26-30	31-35	36-40	41-45	46-50	51-55	56-60	61	....
			1			2		3		
3	*Sex*	M (male)			F (female)		....		
		1		2		3		4		5
4	*Marital*	S (single)	M (married)		D (divorced)		W (widowed)		....
		1		2		3	4		5	6
5	*Religion*	P (Protestant)	C (Catholic)		J (Jewish)	N (none)	O (other)		....
		1		2		3	4		5	
6	*Question* #1	G (general)	SM (matrimonial)		ST (tax)	SC (corp)	SL (real estate)		
			6		7		8		
		SCR (criminal)			0 (others)		....		

		1	2	3	4	5	6	7	8	9
7	*Question* #2	0	1-10	11-20	21-30	31-40	41-50	51-60	61-70	**71-80**

			10	11
			80-....	....

			1	2	3	4	5
8	#3a	MM (married men)	0 (none)	L (little)	M (medium)	Mu (much)	....

			1	2	3	4	5
9	#3b	SM (single men)	0	L	M	Mu	
10	#3c	BM (business men)	"	"	"	"	"
11	#3d	LM (Laborer men)	"	"	"	"	"
12	#3e	Other	"	"	"	"	"

			1	2	3	4	5
13	#3f	Age 50	0 (none)	L (little)	M (medium)	Mu (much)	....
14	#3g	25-50	"	"	"	"	"
15	#3h	15-25	"	"	"	"	"
16	#3i	MM (married men)	"	"	"	"	"
17	#3j	SW (single women)	"	"	"	"	"
18	#3k	BW (business women)	"	"	"	"	"
19	#3l	HW (housewife)	"	"	"	"	"
20	#3m	Other	"	"	"	"	"
21	#3n	Age 50	"	"	"	"	"
22	#3o	25-50	"	"	"	"	"
23	#3p	15-25	"	"	"	"	"

		1	2	3	4	5	6	7	8	9
24	#4a	SM	BM	LM and O	50-....	15-49	SW	BW	HW and O	50-....

		10	11	12
		15-49	0 (other)	....

25	#4b	1-12 *same as above*
26	#4c	1-12 *same as above*

			1	2	3	4
27	#5	BU (business)	L (little)	M (medium)	Mu (much)	....
28		CR (criminal)	"	"	"	"
29		PE (personal)	"	"	"	"
30		FA (family)	"	"	"	"
31		MAR (marital)	"	"	"	"
32		PH (philosophical)	"	"	"	"
33		MOR (moral)	"	"	"	"
34		SP (spiritual)	"	"	"	"

			1	2	3	4
35		O (other)	L (little)	M (medium)	Mu (much)	....

		1	2	3	4	5	6	7	8
36	#6a	1-4	5-8	9-12	15	20	25	30-....	....

		1	2	3	4	5	6
37	#6b	0-10%	11-30	31-50	51-70	71-90	....

		1	2	3	4
38	#7a	Y	N	?	....

		1	2	3	4	5	6	7	8	9	10
39	#7b	Y	N	?	....	¼ hr.	½ hr.	1 hr.	1-2 hrs.	as needed	....

		1	2	3	4		6	7	8	9
40	#7c	Y	N	?	....					

| 41 | #8a (client) | Y | N | ? | .... | #8b (self) | Y | N | ? | .... |

42   #8c (means)   1 I (intuition)   2 OB (observe, listen, empathy)   3 PS (psychology)

      4 TE (tests)   5 IN (introspection)   6 CR (cross examine, question)

      7 H (taking personal history, background)   8 DI (discussing case with others)

      9 REF (referral for analysis)   10 EX (experience, other cases)   11 O (other)

      12 ....

| 43 | #9a | 1 Y | 2 N | 3 ? | 4 .... |

44   #9b   1 PR (prof. school)   2 PS (psychology)   3 SOC (sociology)   4 AN (psych. 5 analyzed)   5 CO (counseling trained)   6 O (other)   7 ....

| 45 | #10a | 1 Y | 2 N | 3 ? | 4 .... |

46   #10b   1 S (short)   2 M (medium)   3 L (long, full)   4 O (other)   5 ....

47   #11a   1 S (solve self)   2 ....20%   3 21-30   4 31-40   5 41-50   6 51-60   7 61-70   8 70-....   9 ....

48	#11b	ASI (achieved some improvement)		1-8 *same as above*
49	#11c	W (worse)		1-8 *same as above*
50	#11d	UC (remain unchanged)		1-8 *same as above*

| 51 | #11e | DAW (do as well) | 1 Y | 2 N | 3 ? | 4 .... |

52   #12   *Sports and Hobbies*   1 VA (very active—baseball, mountain climbing, etc.)

      2 A (active—golf, sailing, etc.)   3 INA (inactive—photography, etc.)

      4 SE (sedentary—reading, stamp collecting, etc.)   5 O (other)   6 ....

53   *Family*   1 L (large—over 4 children)   2 M (medium—2-3 children)

      3 S (small—less)   4 Y (young children)   5 HS (high school or college)

      6 G (grown)   7 GC (has grandchildren)   8 ....

54

Organizations   PRI (many active professional org's) [1]   PR II (some [2]
prof. org's)   CL I (active social clubs) [3]   CL II (some social clubs) [4]
CH I (active in church) [5]   CH II (some church activity) [6]   SE I (active [7]
service or charity)   SE II (some service or charity) [8]   CA I (active [9]
community affairs)   CA II (some community affairs) [10]   O (other) [11]
[12]
....

55

Travel—Intellectual   WIT (widely travel) [1]   TR (travel some) [2]
LI (literature) [4]   M (music) [5]   FA (foreign affairs, peace) [6]   A (art, [7]
painting)   SO (social sciences) [8]   PS (psychology specifically) [9]
REL (religion) [10]   [11] ....

56

Problems Overcome or learned to live with   PH (physical) [1]   PS (psy- [2]
chological)   MA (marital) [3]   PE (personal) [4]   FI (financial) [5]
FA (family) [6]   [7] ....

57

Items Contributing to Counseling   P (public office, politics) [1]
EX (experience, general) [2]   EXP (experience, professional) [3]
TE (technical training or reading) [4]   M (marriage, general) [5]
MP (marriage to trained or insightful spouse) [6]   REL (religion) [7]
EVS (evaluate self) [8]   PS (psychoanalysis, psychiatry) [9]   DI (personal [10]
or family difficulties)   EM (empathy, interest in others, patience, etc.) [11]
[12]
RE (knowledge of where to refer)

58

Why Enter Counseling   CL (client expectation) [1]   PR (part of [2]
professional job)   FA (family, relatives or friend in this profes- [3]
sional counseling)   IA (counseling of others inadequate) [4]   AL [5]
(altruism, obligation to community)   ST (status, prestige) [6]
AP (aptitude) [7]   O (other) [8]   [9] ....

CODING LAWYERS
CARD 2

		1	2	3	4
1	#20a	A (agree)	Dis (disagree)	NO	....
2	#20b	"	"	"	"
3	#20c	"	"	"	"
4	#20d	"	"	"	"
5	#20e	"	"	"	"
6	#20f	"	"	"	"

		1	2	3	4
7	#21a	Y	N	?	....

8   #21b   1 HE (helpful)   2 OB (get objectivity and insight)   3 NN (not necessary,

4
can handle clients without this)   UN (unadjusted. If counselor needs

5
psychoanalysis ought not to counsel. Could hinder)   PS (should use

6
psychology and psychiatry and need training)   EX (experience enough

7
more important)   SP (more specialized knowledge the better)

8   9
PR (existing professional training enough)   NO (no opinion)

10   11
O (other)   ....

		1	2	3	4
9	#22a	Y	N	?	....

10   #22b   Use same categories and code numbers as for #21b (1-11)

		1	2	3	4
11	#23	Y	N	?	....

12   #23b   1 ND (no difference, not important)   2 RI (only important if religion involved)

3   4
BI (helps determine biases, client-counselor)   CO (conflict in some areas-

5
divorce-between religion and law)   PH (understanding philosophy of life)

6   7
EA (easier communication if same)   CA (Catholic more concerned)

8   9   10
MO (motives important)   O (other)   ....

		1	2	3	4	5	6	7
13	#24	YYY	YNY	YNN	NNN	NYY	NYN	NNY

8   9   10   11
YYN   ....(a)   ....(b)   ....(c)

		1	2	3	4	5
14	#25	PR	FRS	ACI	(1) plus (2) plus (3)	(1) plus (2)

		6	7	8
		(1) plus (3)	(2) plus (3)	....

		1	2	3
15	#26a	UN	IN	....

		4	5	6	7	8	9
16	#26b-c	Y	N	....	Y	N	....

17   Combine categories from box #15 and 16 to make up following categories

	1	2	3	4
	(1) plus (4)	(1) plus (5)	(1) plus (7)	(1) plus (8)
	5	**6**	**7**	**8**
	(2) plus (4)	(2) plus (5)	(2) plus (7)	(2) plus (8)
	9	**10**	**11**	**12**
	(4) plus (7)	(4) plus (8)	(5) plus (7)	(5) plus (8)

		1	2	3	4	5	6	7	8
18	#27a	Y	N	?	....	(b)	Y	N	?	....

		1	2	3	4
19	#28a	Y	N	?	....

		1	2	3	4
20	#28b	Y	N	?	....

		1	2	3	4	5	6	7	8	9
21	#28a & 28b combined	YN	YY	NY	NN	-Y	-N	N-	Y-	....

		1	2	3	4
22	#29	Y	N	?	....

		1	2	3
23	#29a	NA (nature of problem)	R (reputation)	RE (referral)
		4	**5**	**6**	**7**
		F (friend)	REL (religion)	CL (clubs, etc.)	FI (cost)
		8	**9**	**10**	**11**
		EM (empathy)	SH (shops around)	O (other)	....

		1	2	3	4
24	#29a	(second part). Y	N	?	....

			1	2	3	4
25	#29b	EF (elicit facts)	L	S	M	....
26		EP (evaluate problems)	L	S	M	....
27		CC (counsel clients)	L	S	M	....

		1	2	3	4	5	6	7
				....	....			....
28	(combinations)	+++	+—+	+——	———	—++	—+—	——+

	8	9
	++—	....

omit #29c   and 3 cases in Part 3

		1	2	3	4	5
29	#30	A (agree)	D (disagree)	No (opinion)	....	changed or crossed out answer
30	#30a	"	"	"	"	"
31	#30b	"	"	"	"	"
32	#30c	"	"	"	"	"
33	#31	"	"	"	"	"
34	#31a	"	"	"	"	"
35	#31b	"	"	"	"	"
36	#32	"	"	"	"	"
37	#32a	"	"	"	"	"

		1	2	3	4	5
38	#32b	A (agree)	D (disagree)	No (opinion)	....	changed or crossed out answer
39	#33	"	"	"	"	"
40	#33a	"	"	"	"	"
41	#33b	"	"	"	"	"
42	#34	"	"	"	"	"
43	#35	"	"	"	"	"
44	#35a	"	"	"	"	"
45	#35b	"	"	"	"	"

		1	2	3	4	5
46	#35c	A	D	NO	....	changed or crossed out

omit #36 and 37 — score separately.

		1	2	3	4
47	#38a	Y	N	?	....

		1	2	3	4
48	#38b	Y	N	?	....

Bibliography Chapter 4

Axelrod, Morris and Charles F. Cannell—A Research Note on an Attempt to Predict Interviewer Effect. (1959-60) Pub. Op. Q. 23, No. 4:571-576.

Bucher, Rue, Charles Fritz and E. L. Quarantelli—Tape Recorded Interviews in Social Research. (1956) Am. Soc. Rev. 21, No. 3:359-364.

Bucher, Rue—Tape Recorded Research: Some Field and Data Processing Problems. (1956) Pub. Op. Q. 20, No. 2:427.

Cahalan, Don, Valerie Tamulonis and Helen Verner—Interviewer Bias Involved in Certain Types of Opinion Survey Questions. (1947) Inter. J. Op. Att. Res. 1, No. 1:63.

Campbell, R. K.—A Study of Interviewing Techniques. (1945) Applied Psychology Panel, NPRC. Project 116a, Memorandum No. 3.

Connelly, Gordon M.—Survey on Problems of Interviewing Cheating. (1947) Inter. J. Op. Att. Res. 1, No. 3.

Crossley, Helen M. and Raymond Fink—Response and Non-Response in a Probability Sample. (1951) Inter. J. Op. Att. Res. 5, No. 1.

Dornbusch, Sanford and Calvin Schmid—A Primer of Social Statistics. (New York, McGraw-Hill, 1955).

Dressel, Paul L., E. J. Shoben and Harold B. Pepinsky—Research in Counseling: A Symposium. (1953) Personnel Guid. J. 31:284-294.

Edwards, A. L.—Statistical Methods for the Behavioral Sciences. (New York, Rinehart, 1955).

Eysenck, Hans J. and S. B. Eysenck—A Factorial Study of an Interview Questionnaire. (1962) J. Clin. Psychol. 18:266-290.

Feldman, J. J., Herbert Hyman and Clyde Hart—A. Field Study of Interviewer Effects on the Quality of Survey Data. (1951) Pub. Op. Q. 15:738.

Fisher, Herbert—Interviewer Bias in the Recording Operation. (1950) Inter. J. Op. Att. Res. 4, No. 3.

Hanson, Robert H. and Eli S. Marks—Influence of the Interviewer on the Accuracy of Survey Results. (1958) J. Am. Stat. Assn. 53:635-655.

Harper, A. E.—Down With the Validity Coefficient. (1965) J. Voc. Ed. Guid. 11:75.

Hart, Clyde—Interviewer Bias. (Am. Soc. for Testing Mat., No. 117, 1951).

Jackson, Robert M.—Differential Value of the Mailed Questionnaire and the Interview in a Follow-up Study of High School Graduates. (Doctoral Dissertation, Univ. of Wisconsin) (D.A. XX, 923, 1960).

Jenkins, Kenneth F.—The Effectiveness of the Telephone as a Medium for Follow-up Interviewing. (Doctoral Dissertation, Univ. of Michigan, 1960) (D.A. XX, 4588, 1960).

82   Counseling in the United States

Lawson, Faith—Varying Group Responses to Postal Questionnaires. (1949) Pub. Op. Q. 13:114-116.

Lazarsfeld, Paul F.—Methodological Problems in Empirical Social Research. (1959) 4th World Cong. of Soc. 2:225.

Lenski, Gerhard E. and John C. Leggett—Case, Class and Difference in the Research Interview. (1959) Am. J. Soc. 65, No. 5:463-467.

Levine, Sol and Gerald Gordon—Maximizing Returns on Mail Questionnaires. (1958-59) Pub. Op. Q. 22:568-575.

Parker, Clyde E. and Wayne Wright, Jr.—Questions Concerning the Interview as a Research Technique. (1957) J. Ed. Res. 51:215-222.

Parry, Hugh J. and Helen Crossley—Validity of Responses to Survey Questions. (1950) Pub. Op. Q. 14, No. 1.

Parten, Mildred B.—Surveys, Polls and Samples: Practical Procedures. (New York, Harper, 1950) 624 pp.

The Questionnaire: A Reexamination. (1958) Hum. Org. 17, No. 3:1.

Saul, Leon J.—A Note on the Telephone as a Technical Aid. (1952) Psychoanal. Q. 20:287-290. Abs. Inter. J. Psychoanal. 33:506.

Schmidt, Lyle—Counseling Research in 1963. (1965) J. Counsel. Psychol. 12:418.

Smith, Harry L. and Herbert Hyman—The Biasing Effect of Interviewer Expectations on Survey Results. (Fall 1950) Pub. Op. Q. 491.

Smith, Henrietta T.—A Comparison of Interview and Observation Measures of Mother Behavior. (1958) J. Abnorm. Psychol. 57, No. 3:278-282.

Stember, Herbert—How Interviewer Effects Operate Through Question Form. (1949) Inter. J. Op. Att. Res. 3, No. 4.

Vaughn, C. L. and W. A. Reynolds—Reliability of Personal Interview Data. (Feb. 1951) J. Appl. Psychol. 35:61-63.

Chapter 5

Training For Counseling

Introduction

As pointed out in the previous chapter, we attempted a thorough survey of the law, medical and theological schools on all matters related to counseling (from selection of students to the actual training given and satisfaction with the training). We briefly compared this to training given in counseling for other specialties (marriage counseling, social work, etc.). Certain more or less expected results were verified but there were many more important observations for which we were not prepared. Theology turned out to have the most complete selection and training for counseling and yet recorded dissatisfaction with the training and a belief that it had been wrong in making psychiatric clinical training with abnormals the center of its instruction. Medicine drew the students of highest academic rating but those least interested in people or motivated by social service. Law rated next and was median on both dimensions. Theology accepted those with the lowest academic rating but through continuation of the concept of "the call" and by other means maintained a remarkably high motivation.

83

What We Were Trying To Find Out

Exactly what did we try to discover? How did we determine what factors might be worth analysis?

In a survey of already published material and in our own projection of areas of study we decided we wanted material on choice of this counseling profession, training, nature of each profession and achieving professionalism— according to the following outline (it can be seen that much of this material cannot be obtained from the professional school questionnaire but must be gathered from the practicing professionals or by combining the two). We used the same outline in collating published material in our *Counseling — A Bibliography*:

CHOICE OF COUNSELING PROFESSION—

Pre-profession and selection process:

1 Family before selection
2 Social status before selection; pre-profession education
3 Articulated values pre-profession—power, rectitude, respect, well being, wealth, skill, enlightenment, religion, affection, love, etc.
4 Articulated attitudes pre-profession
5 Core personality pre-profession
6 Factors for entering profession—socio-economic, self ideal, parent ideal, counselor guidance, IQ, intelligence, school achievement, helping or altruism rating, etc.
7 Tests for entering professional training not specifically related to counseling (intelligence, character, etc.)
8 Tests specifically for counseling (empathy, communication, etc.)
9 Validity or value of tests
10 Factors for choice of counseling or general job selection

TRAINING—Professional:

1 Professional training—general pattern
2 Counseling training, within profession—existence, absence, what
3 Training by whom—faculty, peers, self, method
4 Training curriculum—materials, subjects, "school" taught
5 Time at which counseling training received
6 Counseling abilities acquired—what abilities? Communication, sensitivity, intuition, observation, logic, ideation, skills and strategies, etc.
7 Psychoanalysis—relation to training, training in
8 Effect of training on values, attitudes, expectations, personality, etc.
9 Satisfaction with and successfulness of training; dropouts, rating

PROFESSIONAL AND PROFESSIONALISM

1 Definition and nature of profession
2 Empirical studies of professions
3 Status-rating of profession—social mobility, self, public or client rating, opportunities
4 Intra-professions: form of practice, mythology, relation to colleagues
5 Legal protections—license, confidential communications, etc.
6 Ethics and fees
7 Role of each profession
8 Type of problems handled, specialization
9 Counseling as separate, independent profession or specialty—marriage counseling

We also wanted to picture the professional school—its size, budget, standards. We sought to determine how students were selected and whether this related to counseling. We desired to know how counseling was viewed, its place in the profession, how teaching was and should be operating, what study materials were available or needed. Student opinion and the view of those out in the profession as to the importance of counseling, the nature of training and an evaluation of the available teachers and methods, rounded out our study. Insofar as possible we used open ended questionnaires, welcomed submission of supplemental material and filled in the data by extended interviews. We supposedly reached the Dean and the person on each faculty most interested in helping with our survey, most capable of full answers, and most committed to using any material which might result.

We also "threw our minds around" on questions which might properly relate to selection and training of the professional counselor and how the "profession" might control or be influenced by the training. We have previously pointed out that our "Series A-O" of open leads might or might not be determined or touched by questionnaire responses, yet served the purpose of assuring our attention to all possibilities. Series "A" "B" and "F" dealt in part with the subject of the present chapter, and can be examined in the Appendix.

To present the above three bodies of material we shall:

    a) Give a statistical summary of the questionnaire responses in the three schools: law (p. 89), theology (p. 92), medicine (p. 94), so that the reader may develop his own conclusions.

    b) Set forth *our* major conclusions coming from the questionnaires or interviews as to choice of students, training, professionalism: law (p. 97), theology (p. 103), medicine (p. 117), other (p. 120). Lest this list of conclusions get out of hand it has been decided to emphasize one or two major aspects best illustrated by each profession and allowing for comparison with other professions as follows: *Law* —Emphasis on student and school factors militating against adequate counseling training; description of professionalism and its effect. The legal outline is made most complete to suggest how a like catalogue could be constructed for each profession. Theology—Emphasis on the newly devised student selection process and theological pattern of training as adequate or inadequate.

Medicine—Emphasis on psychiatry as a specialty and coloration of "counseling" by health-illness dichotomy.

c) Take up the Series "A", "B" and "F" puzzlements which went beyond the strict questionnaires or original outline. (p. 122).

Survey Sample and Questionnaire

Law Schools were most cooperative (perhaps because your researcher was a law professor)—99 replies out of 132 schools. Theological schools came next—69 out of 122. Medical schools were least cooperative; the American Medical School Association refused its permission to the survey; we had questionnaire replies from less than 20%; without the help of a survey made by Dr. Ralph Heine and Dr. Friedman of Chicago and without personal visitation we would have been unable to make a meaningful survey.

The questionnaire used for all professional schools is as follows:

NAME OF SCHOOL..
ADDRESS ....
Persons teaching or interested in counseling................................
....
....

(If adequate space is not allowed for any question, use the other side of this paper.)
Number Students enrolled.................... Degree or training Prerequisite
Approximate school budget.................... to entrance....................
Tuition and fee charge per year................................
Number years for graduation................................
    What screening of prospective students is done?
    Academic ....
    Aptitude ....
    Personality-Psychological ....
    Other ....
    Would you feel your screening is concerned with the applicant's

interest or ability in counseling? How?...
....
....

How would you define counseling?..
....
....

Do you think that counseling is an important part of your profession? ....

Does the school have a theory or philosophy as to the place of counseling in the profession? What? ....

Do you believe that counseling can be taught in a professional school such as yours? How? ....

Are you satisfied with the teaching of counseling in your school?.............

What would you like to do to improve it?..
....

What more would you like to know about counseling for teaching purposes? ....
....

Do you believe there are adequate teaching materials available on counseling? ....

Do you believe materials from other disciplines should be used?.............

What materials? ....

What studies or preparation of materials would you like to see undertaken? ....
....
....

What training or experience in counseling do your instructors of counseling have? ....

Were they engaged in professional practice before teaching? ....

How long? .... In what capacity? ....
....
....

Do they engage in actual counseling at present in addition to teaching? .... What type of counseling? ....
....
....

With students only or with whom? ....
....
....

Approximate number counseled per year? ....

Have they written anything on counseling? ....What? ....

What courses does your school offer directly in counseling or preparative to counseling? ....

....

Which are optional, which required? ....

Approximate enrollment in each course? ....

....

Do your students take courses outside your school related to counseling? .... What? ....

What books or teaching materials do you use in counseling?......................

....

....

....

....

Do you use psycho-drama, taped interviews or like material? Please describe ....

....

....

Do your students run free counseling clinics or other practice procedures? Describe ....

....

....

The remaining space and the reverse side is for your general comment on my project to study counseling, on counseling generally or on any questions which may occur to you. I shall value as full communication as you feel you can make.

First   Statistics From Surveys of the Professional Schools:

Law

A coding of the questionnaire shows the following percentage of replies yielding the following data, set forth as the answer and percentage of replies giving the answer to questions on the questionnaire form:

Description of School

Number of students enrolled	336 average	
School budget per pupil	$970 average	
Tutition	$703 average	
Pre-law minimum training	3 years	40%
	4 years (degree)	60%
Number of years to graduate	3 years	98%

Selection of Students

Academic standard	chief reliance	73.3
Aptitude test	major part	70.7
Personality assessment	interview-recommendations	26.6
Psychological	tests	6.7
Counseling interest or ability	yes — 2.6; slight — 8.0	10.6
	no	65.3

Counseling and Place of Counseling in Curriculum

Define counsel	no answer	20.6
	giving advice type	24.8
	accepted suggested definition	37.3
	emphasis "whole man"	17.3
Important part of profession	very — 53.2 yes — 26.8	80.0
	no — 4.0; qualified no — 2.6	6.6
School as having theory on place of counseling	yes — 6.9; integral part — 29.1	36.0
	no	32.0
Can counseling be school taught	yes	56.6
	no	17.3
How teach (note % overlap)	blank	37.8
	don't know	26.5
	teach in other courses (gen. 10.6; prof. practice 5.7; legal aid 2.1)	18.4
	teach in special courses (gen. 12.3; socio-psycho materials 18.7)	31.0
Satisfied with teaching	yes	16.0
	no	41.3
	blank	42.7
How improve	teach ethics	2.6
	make non technicians	2.6
	improve pre-law	4.0
	inject into substantive	9.3
	enlarge legal aid	10.6
	educate the faculty	12.0
	teach counseling method separate	20.1
	nothing	10.6
	blank	28.2

What would you like to know	what other law schools do	24.0
	study what profession does	16.0
	technique and effectiveness of counseling courses	12.6
	how law-psychology or inter-disciplinary courses work	16.6
Are there adequate counseling teaching materials	yes	10.0
	no	37.0
	don't know	18.6
Would use material from other disciplines	yes	40.5
	yes-psychology	6.6
	no	6.6
	don't know	13.3
What materials would you like	like Freeman study	18.3
	new book materials	12.2
	syllabus, how to teach	12.0
	human problems in practice	12.0

Teacher Competence and Course Offering

What training or counseling experience in at least one member of faculty:

Excellent	4%	Use Psychology or Psychiatry Prof.	7.7
Good	14.6	"Law Practice or teaching training enough"	
Poor	20.0		20.1
None	36.0		

Have engaged in practice?

Yes	56%	1-2 years - 17.1; 3 years - 11.0; more - 27.3
No	12	
Blank	32	

Engage in counseling now?

Yes	46.6%	- With students - 30.6; with others - 16.0
No	10.6	
Blank	42.8	

Approximate number counseled   (average *15*):

Under	50	19.6%	100 or more 6.6%
	50-100	10.0	

Have written anything regarding counseling:

yes   6%   No   53.3

(Total of only 8 articles or books listed).

Courses are offered in the Law School in counseling?

None	54.6%	Special lectures	4.0
All courses are	8.0	Legal Aid Clinics	11.0
Legal Method	10.6	Law and Psychology (Psychiatry)	8.0
Negotiation	3.8		

Counseling courses optional   20.0%;   required   4.0;   blank   76.0
Enrolled under 50   13.3%   over 50   4.0
Books or materials used?

       None   35.0%   "Locally prepared"   6.3

       Tapes, etc.   4.5   "Recognized"   4.1

Do students take related courses outside?

       Few   8.9%   No   50.0   Blank   41.1

Operate free legal clinic?

       Yes   14.3%   No   48.6   Blank   37.1

Of the replies 36% added comments as requested; for 64% nothing was added.

Theology

We have already pointed out that Theology has gone far beyond law in recognizing the place of counseling, in selecting and testing students on a basis taking into account the counseling function, in offering counseling training, in systematically making personal counseling available to the students, in training materials developed, etc. It is not thought that we need to reproduce the same statistical table as that for law (we did use the same tables for all three professions). We believe more can be grasped by telling the predominance of counseling emphasis in the theology schools than by showing percentage of schools supporting a particular conclusion.

Theological schools subsidize students more (tuition $399), have fewer pupils (158), spend more per student ($3397), devote about the same period to training (4 years pre-profession 97%, 3 years professional 77%).

They have a lower academic rating for entering students than either law or medicine yet still primarily gear testing to academic-aptitude (69%-compared to law about 85%). They put greater emphasis on personality-psychological testing (59%-compare law about 25%) and counseling potential (45%-compare law about 6-8%).

     92% rate counseling important to the profession

     73% have a definite school policy accordingly

     92% are clear it can be taught in professional school

70% are still dissatisfied with counseling teaching

97% are united in what to do about it—more individual supervision, more courses, more clinical work, more time, more staff, more field work

37% (the largest) would like to know more on techniques

25% desired interdisciplinary studies and casebooks

85% would use materials from other disciplines

64% believe adequate teaching materials exist

52% listed faculty with doctorates in psychology and counseling

87% showed faculty having clinical or pastoral psychology training

70% had been practicing pastors

84% engaged presently in counseling (53% with non-students; 31% with students)

57% of the respondents had written articles and books on counseling (one over 50) and less than 30% had written nothing

69% gave a pastoral counseling course; 26% clinical counseling training; 30% psychotherapy, personality dynamics; 9% specialties like "the family"

74% require counseling courses; 12% optional (average enrollment 50)

53% show students taking courses outside theology school; 42% taking outside clinical training

75% had fairly high agreement on the standard books in the field, spanning psychology, psychiatry, counseling, pastoral specialties

72% used taped interviews, one way screens, psychodrama, like material

82% showed that students did not run free clinics but did clinical work in established clinics

38% added rather full comments

Medicine

Again we caution that the following statistics and percentages are the least supported or carefully cross-sectioned by sampling techniques of the three professions. The medical colleges subsidize students less than theology but more than law ($800 tuition), average about 325 pupils, take students with less cultural training (2-3 years), require more time for graduation (4 years) and more internship. They are most concerned with academic aptitude and get the highest standing students of the three professions. Increasingly they state a desire to test personality-psychological factors and ability in counseling—still less than theology. Their definition of counseling comes from three facets: wholistic medicine (treatment of the whole man), the medical specialty of psychiatry, and the interview as the means of diagnosis.

85% rate counseling important to the profession (mostly meaning the specialty of psychiatry, which they view as counseling)

40% have a philosophy as to its place (this centers on the diagnostic interview plus psychiatry as a specialty)

80% believe counseling can and should be taught (only 50% seem to mean taught to the general practitioner, GP)

48% teach some kind of psychiatry or interviewing-counseling as a part of general medicine [Note: The next 8 statistics are of this general practice, compared to specialized psychiatry, training].

60% of these are unsatisfied with their teaching; there is little agreement what to do about it, and like law they would "see what others are doing"

45% desire objective studies of counseling and other disciplines; 40% would like to see how much could be done by non-professionals; 10% want the validity of the psychotherapeutic process checked

75% think there is adequate teaching material available

50% would use materials from other disciplines and are particularly interested in case materials presenting similarities (the largest group wants new interdisciplinary studies and materials; others want improved tapes, recordings, etc.)

90% of instruction where it is given is by psychiatrists, 70% of these have had general practice and engage in private counseling practice

55% of the teachers have written something on counseling

75% of the answering schools offer some courses in general psychiatry, psychology, sociology and environment, medical interviewing. Most are required, use tapes, records, one-way screens, role playing, etc.

75% have student run (faculty supervised) free clinics

Immediately below we give some statistics as to the amount and type of psychiatric and interview training available to general medical trainees (non-psychiatrists) in the average good medical school. We treat this as counseling training, though no comparable material can be set forth from our data for law and theology. This comes about from the fact that some of our material for medical schools was collected through interview rather than questionnaire, from our use of the Chicago questionnaire replies on teaching psychiatry in general medicine, and from medicine's own view that psychiatry is the "counseling" specialty within medicine.

Time devoted to instruction in psychiatry—1st year, 30 hours; 2nd year, 47 hours; 3rd year, 107 hours; 4th year, 112 hours (most combine interviewing)

Method of instruction: 98% use supervised practice in
psychiatry (out patient or in patient), 83% theory
lectures-seminars, 78% practice lectures or seminars, 77% observation of skilled therapists, 60%
films, tapes, closed circuit TV, etc., 60% courses
in comprehensive medicine

In supervised practice the student handles an average
of 4 patients at a time, average 9 times, with 1-½
hours per week of supervision

65% training is in OPD (out patient); 16% in IP (in
patient) and about 15% in outside (county) hospitals

The theoretical climate of the psychiatry for GP's in
terms of instructors or departments shows 50%
classical psychoanalytic, 33% eclectic, 18% other
psychoanalytic with Sullivan predominating, 12%
biodynamic (Masserman) and lesser percentages
(note overlap) for psychobiological (Meyer), or-
ganistic (Maslow), existential (May)—actually
to make a list would show almost unlimited differentiation and emphasis.

The ten most often required or recommended books,
in addition to the APA Diagnostic and Statistical
Manual of Mental Disorders, are: Noyes & Kolbe-
Modern Clinical Psychiatry; Nemiah-Foundations
of Psychopathology; English & Finch-Introduc-
tion to Psychiatry; English & Pearson-Emotional
Problems of Living; Ewalt et al.-Practical Clinical
Psychiatry; Arieti-American Handbook of Psy-
chiatry; Goodrich & Ulett-A Synopsis of Con-
temporary Psychiatry; Henderson & Gillespie-A
Textbook of Psychiatry; Weiss & English-Psy-
chosomatic Medicine; Masserman-Principles &
Practice of Dynamic Psychiatry; Bracket-several
books: Colby-Primer for Psychotherapists; Bird
—Talking with Patients; Josselyn-Psychosocial
Development of Children.

Second: Conclusions Arising From Survey Materials
Law

Student Selection and Admissions: The law schools are not presently testing applicants or students to determine their qualifications for counseling. The Law School Aptitude Test (LSAT: supervised by Princeton and used by three-fourths of the Law Schools) is a logic, readng, comprehension, reasoning, aptitude test. It does not measure pre-law achievement, motivation, psychological adjustment, likely success or willingness to apply oneself. Though Princeton's Educational Testing Service has helped devise and check tests for theological students which do to some degree include counseling factors there has been no willingness to include these tests for law in LSAT. There are reasonably good tests available to determine counseling ability or potential; personality, attitudes, empathy, communication, tolerance of ambiguity, anxiety, etc. (See partial lists p. 111 and in Appendix, Series B''). The lack of use is due to lack of desire by the law schools to consider this factor. The proportion of students who have pre-law majors in psychology, sociology, social work, etc., is very low, perhaps 3-5%. Very few law students or lawyers have been psychoanalyzed or see any need therefor. Where "personality" tests are used they are to determine "success" personality rather than "counseling" personality. Admissions are based on academic and aptitude standing. No substantial group of students were discovered who had thought of "counseling" as the reason they came to law school or sought a particular law school. Any interest therein was post-admission created. There is a tremendous variation in intelligence-test ability, background and other factors from law school to law school but not so much within a given school. There are schools who take almost no student below LSAT 650, or others who rarely get one above 550. There are few where the whole scale appears. A school tends to select and maintain its own image lawyer.

Like most of the other professions, law is a man's world. Less than 3% women enroll. Law students are "rectitude" and "power" oriented. At some earlier point they seem to have come under or reacted to a strong authority figure (father), early discipline or intellectual and verbalization emphasis. A very small percentage of law students have lawyer parents but they do largely come from the professional and upper white collar class. Less than 10% come from manual worker homes. Fathers 65% of the time were of 3rd generation or older American stock. A stratification, both in the bar and law schools occurs, relating to originating parental background and practice into which students will go. Half of all law students come from homes with income over $15,000, with one or more parents college graduates, from metropolitan areas, having attended class A private schools and colleges, disproportionately Jewish. They consequently are seeking high income, professionalization, non supervision, high social status, reputation for service. The student whose parental background is Catholic or Jewish, manual or small entrepreneurial, of first to third generation American and ethnically non north-European will go to the smaller non-prestige schools and end up in solo private practice about 60-70% of the time. [The split was greater with the older lawyers, the younger lawyers showed larger percentage of Jews and Catholics graduating from the better schools and creating their own larger firms]. Our observations have been confirmed by the most recent NORC survey, *Lawyers in the Making,* Warkow and Zelon, Chicago, 1965.

Few law schools have any counseling service to aid law students in personality or emotional adjustment or in understanding and achieving good inter-personal relations. Their tendency is to look upon law students as mature and subject to no unusual emotional stresses or strains. They tend to deny admission or drop after admission those who are likely to or do develop emotional or psychological difficulties.

Place and Teaching of Counseling: Law school policy emphasizes "marks" and theoretical or "law review" concepts of law. The faculties are chosen on this basis and perpetuate the emphasis in entrants and students. The graduates, particularly the top graduates, of the better law schools go into large office practice; into large corporate, banking, tax matters rather than into human relations work or counseling.

The client and his personal and emotional problems are rarely thought of as "legal" concern. Yet it is generally recognized that counseling is an important part of the legal profession and can be taught. Most law schools are not attempting to teach it. Law schools are not satisfied in this regard. They blame lethargy and general faculty indifference. They do not believe adequate legal materials exist. They assume that there are materials in other disciplines which should be used—but they do not know what or where these are. With almost no exceptions, law schools are unaware of the development, outlined below and throughout this book, most useful and necessary to training the lawyer as counselor. Law schools generally do not have faculty adequately trained in interviewing-counseling theory, methods or teaching. There are in about 30% of the schools at most one or two persons per faculty interested in the field. Unlike medicine, law has never developed the clinic or outpatient work in which the specialist professional treats a client while students observe. There seem to be a number of serious obstacles to doing this and until these are overcome it is doubtful that legal clinics will serve as an acceptable teaching method. Among the hurdles to be overcome are these: practitioner lawyers do not respect law teachers as forefront practitioners, but view them as non-practitioners (due to our process of selection this may be an accurate criticism); there are insufficient "charity clients" to constitute subjects (again there is an objection by practicing lawyers to school-run charity clinics); a client's business and personal affairs are viewed as more confidential than his appendix or gall bladder; interviewing and advising are not as easily demonstrable as an open heart operation; the "book case method" has turned law away from the "live case method"; the lack of legal internship is a final handicap in this regard.

The present study shows that those practicing lawyers engaged in "counseling" come from the "lesser" schools—the night, factory, bar-exam schools. These are exactly the schools least interested in and least able to develop counseling training. It could be argued that the large, prestige schools who are the innovators and most likely to institute counselor training are the ones least in touch with counselors. In short, that if counseling training is given it is not likely to be much used. But, the large offices recognize that they in fact counsel and reforms in teaching always find a few interested at any school and trickle from the larger and more important law schools to others.

It may be that, until a lawyer has been out in practice and seen the raw material of living counseling cases, he neither has the concepts nor the motivation to acquire counseling skills. Much final teaching in this field may need to be done by law schools or others as part of the "continuing education of the bar". Our research shows, and Lortie's confirms this, that lawyers feel they are more influenced by what they learn in practice than in law schools. But it also shows that learning in practice always relates to something from law school and that the best learning and adjustment occur when early practice experience reinforces a view, skill or attitude explored in law school. The law schools should help to teach the student that law practice (even large office practice) involves personal factors—which are the same as would be taught and analyzed in a counseling course. Much lawyers' time involves: settlements, compromises, negotiations, personal problems, interpersonal relationships, interviewing, "selling oneself", internal office relationships, etc.

Our conclusions as to law schools may be summarized by saying that counseling must be recognized as an important part of law practice, that certain types of students make good counselors, that law schools should select such students, that counseling can be taught, that law faculties are now inadequately trained, that studies such as the present must reveal our difficulties and develop material usable in teaching counseling either in law schools or post-law schools. It would appear that the law schools can best serve the bar as to counseling in ways such as these: a) test and counsel their students as to those traits conducive or inimical to good legal counseling; b) give courses in interviewing, psychodynamics and counseling of an exploratory kind to alert the student to the field; c) develop further materials—book, pamphlet, audio-visual, articles—usable by any group or individual studying legal counseling; d) aid in continuing education of the bar projects to teach counseling to practicing lawyers; e) continue to conduct studies of lawyers and clients as to counseling and share these with students and practicing lawyers; f) improve the training of some faculty members in counseling; g) prepare lists and evaluation of potential referral facilities and make these generally available (Northwestern University Law School did this for Chicago); h) prepare bibliographies and articles on counseling and begin injecting this into the role concept of lawyers.

The Legal Profession and its Lesson for Trainee Selection and Counseling Training: Though judges rate almost at the top of socioeconomic profession scales, attorneys' ratings have slid well below doctors, clergymen, engineers. This, we found, is partly due to the lawyers' abandonment of the role of "counselor" or "helper". We need more clearly to determine the values or types of personality actually associated with law or included by the public in its image of this profession. Our study suggests that the public sees the lawyer and the lawyer views himself as characterized by power, wealth, social and political position, authoritarianism and rectitude; and also by logic, hard headed realism, intellectualism, verbalization, experience with all men's problems and vagaries, and able to manipulate power and compel people to act. It has been generally accepted that counseling requires different values or personality functions—respect, affection, well-being, love (agapé), sensitivity, intuition, observational ability, humanitarianism, optimism. (See Chs. 3 and 9). Almost any grouping of personality types would probably show lawyers as evidencing some patterns considered by psychology as least satisfactory in counseling. But law may be misled if it accepts this psychological standard as the proper total test for counseling lawyers.

We found much evidence, confirmed by other studies, that the "happy mean" is the best counselor and counseling pattern—on directiveness, involvement, personality, anxiety, psychological training, empathy and other dimensions. A non-specialist but trained person such as a lawyer might most adequately meet this standard. The responding lawyers sensed this, being critical of professions "too Freudian", "doctrinnaire", "soft headed or hearted", etc. They kept referring to their major asset as "rational", "in touch with reality", "aware of good and bad", "intuitive", "experienced". Recent suggestion by Wolpe, Eysenck Szasz, Sullivan, Fromm, Adler, Rogers, and others in the counseling or psychoanalytic field emphasize moving away from neo-Freudianism and strict psychiatry to other forms of counseling more appropriate to law teaching and practice. That is, they suggest manipulating the environment and other factors rather than depth analysis of the client. Lawyers recognize this kind of counseling as more appropriately theirs. The lawyers' professional image may thus appear unfavorable to counseling if his counseling is merely an apeing of psychiatrists-psychologists. Yet it may be adequate, in fact properly definitive, if he is performing a type of counseling which employs his own peculiar tools. One of the clear conclusions from our study of professional practitioners and clients was that a client selects a counselor (other than when due to casual chance, cost, lack of knowledge, etc.) by the way in which the client frames or is willing to face his problem or ask for help—as logical, legal, practical; or health, illness, cure; or moral, spiritual, absolutive. He may *need* another kind of counselor; the best available may be next door; but he will define his own need and seek out the counseling image likely to fulfill it. Therefore a given counselor may have to counsel outside his field and use referrals or he will leave the client unserved.

For purposes of law school teaching we should recognize that in the process of legal education the articulated values and personality patterns of the student are reshaped into the profession image. This applies to such factors as cynicism, humanitarianism, optimism; and also to ethics, goals, values, authoritarianism, conservatism, security, social and professional conformity and definition of the lawyer's role. The school can create a professional image unfavorable to the counseling role, or one favorable. Such attitudes of the lawyer as his being a "doer", a technician, a person whose legal know-how is a product to be sold for a fee, and his apologies for fees for general counseling or merely listening create an unfavorable image.

Theology

Student Selection and Admissions:

Clerical applicants are, like lawyers, 98% men. Unlike law they come considerably from ministerial families and almost wholly from those in which a parent (usually mother) has been very church active. They are of less academic rank, often younger, but more motivated by a sense of service and fairly uniformly by "a call". Whereas better law schools choose only one in 5 to 15 applicants most theology schools have a hard time finding sufficient applicants and have to choose one in 2 or 3 applying. A higher percentage of ministerial candidates than law students have had considerable previous psychology, sociology and social work training. A substantial number are psychoanalyzed prior to, or before leaving, theological school; about 60% of the students and younger ministers are favorable to psycho-analysis.

Psychological and other testing of applicants is more sophisticated than for the other professions and much of it relates directy to counseling in one of two ways: a) nearly all schools have a counseling *service* for students and the tests point out who can best use counseling and on what matters, b) students interested in and best qualified to train as counselors are directed into counseling training.

In 1960 the Ministry Studies Board* and Education Testing Service completed the formulation and testing of a Theological School Inventory (TSI) to be used in testing, selecting, evaluating and guiding ministerial candidates. The TSI answered the need to test abilities and motivations related to the actual types of functions performed in the profession, as found from a survey of clergymen. The results of TSI, school performance and performance out in the profession have been and are being correlated. Our present research was able to check both schools and practitioners on this.

This TSI is composed of 155 questions or sets of multiple choices in 4 sections, built so they will yield results on 12 scales. The first five scales are known as D, NL, SL, CC, FL and relate to *D* (Definiteness); *NL* (Natural Lead-ing); *SL* (Special Leading); *CC* (Concept of the Call); *FL* (Flexibility); the last seven are called AIFLERP and relate

---

*I am deeply indebted to the Ministry Studies Board, 1810 Harvard Boulevard, Dayton, Ohio, and particularly to Prof. Harry DeWire, Executive Director, for great assistance in my study and for permission to quote (as I do hereafter) from their Prospectus, Theological School Inventory (TSI) and Manual therefor (1964). Also to Dean John Bennett, Union Theological Seminary, Prof. James Dittes, Yale Theological School, Prof. John Vayhinger, Iliff School of Theology, Profs. Seward Hiltner, Samuel Blizzard, and Frederick Kling of Princeton Theological School.

to A (Acceptance by others); I (Intellectual concern); F (Self-fulfillment); L (Leadership success); E (Evangelistic witness); R (Social Reform); P (Service to Persons). Without reviewing all questions it may be said that a sizable number relate to the applicant's background—*italics* indicate the most important questions—(4, 5, 6, 11, 14, 17, 19, 26, 27, 28, 29, 31, 32); and interpersonal relations or emotional adjustment (20, 21, *22*, 23, *24, 30, 33,* 79, 89, 93, 95, 96, 99, 100). Another group deals with his intellectual interests or interest in other professions (7, 8, *9,* 10, *12, 57, 62,* 67, 70, *72, 73,* 74, 83, 120); a very large block covers the influences which directed him into the ministry (15, 18, 25, 34, *45, 46, 47, 48, 53, 54*) with great emphasis on the presence of a "call" (41, 42, 43, 44, *56,* 58, 59, 60, 63, 65, *66,* 68, 76, 78, 82, 84, 85, 87, 92, 94, 96, *101, 102, 103, 104, 105, 106, 107, 108, 109, 110).* Particularly pertinent to us are those related to emotional adjustment (supra) and those dealing specifically with counseling as a vocation (51, 52, 55, *89, 90, 91, 115, 116, 118, 122, 123,* 126, 127, 128, 129, 133, 139, 140, 145, 148, 151, 154, 155). It is worthwhile to briefly set forth a few of the questions or statements (multiple choice) relating to counseling:

> "89. A minister should try to counsel people who have problems by
>
> > A. impressing upon them the superiority of the Christian interpretation of life
> >
> > B. helping them find a solution through their own framework of thinking
>
> "90. I have found that the religious values which enable me to deal with life's problems
>
> > A. are the same ones I was taught as a child
> >
> > B. require continuing revision as I have become more mature
>
> "91. What I find satisfying about the ministry as a vocational choice

         A. is what it has in common with the help-
             ing professions
         B. is what makes it different from the
             helping professions
"118. I will work more effectively in a position
         A. in which I must be willing to work
             closely with people suffering from phy-
             sical and mental illnesses
         B. in which this is not one of the crucial de-
             mands determining my effectiveness."

[Note: 121-155 are 3 statement groups, the same statement appearing several times and being played off against
others in multiple choice; the following are devised to check
counseling interest].

"122 B. (also in 129B, 144C):
I felt I could give support to persons who were
adjusting to the crises, sorrows and demands of
everyday living.

"123 A. (also in 126C):
As a minister I could counsel with individuals at
the deepest levels of their self-understanding
and religious development.

"127 B. (also in 139C, 154A):
In aspiring to the ministry, I preferred to think
of myself as a friend, spending time in close and
patient relationship with those needing guidance
and encouragement.

"128 B. (also in 140C, 151A):
I wanted to share in the church's contribution
to people's emotional health and maturity.

"133 C. As a minister I could counsel with individuals at the deepest levels of their self-understanding and religious development.

"145 C. (also in 148B, 155B):
Entering the ministry was an outgrowth of my
interest in people and my apparent ability to
help them."

A very fine 125 page Manual comes with and explains the TSI. This can be used by any person of reasonable sophistication in counseling or guidance and testing. A few quotations will show its scope:

"The Theological School Inventory provides a description of the *motives* which a candidate for the Protestant ministry regards as instrumental in his vocational decision. It is a *self-report* psychological measuring instrument designed specifically for the *guidance* of students who are beginning professional preparation in a theological school . . . The test frankly deals with the nature of the "call" to the ministry.

"Motives: In measuring consciously perceived and reported motivation for the ministry, the TSI taps an aspect of personality different from that assessed by other tests. It is not meant to assess psychological *pathology* or the health of an individual, or the "normality" of his motives, as in some uses of the Minnesota Multiphasic Personality Inventory. It is not meant to measure basic *personality* characteristics or general psychological motives, as, for example, the Edwards Personal Preference Schedule may be used. It is not meant to assess ability or aptitude for the ministry or any of its aspects, as, for example, is the case with the Graduate Record Examination, the Miller Analogies Test, reading tests, speaking proficiency tests. The TSI is most closely related to the family of *interest* tests, but is intended to be narrower, deeper, and less "predictive" than such a test as the Strong Vocational Interest Blank. It does not assess the broad range of possible personal interests; it does attempt to make fine distinctions within the range of professional interest in the ministry . . .

"Motives are to be understood as conscious reasons, not psychological needs. Subconscious psychological processes and motives need not be ignored in interpreting results of the TSI (giving examples).

"*A self-report instrument*: Items on the TSI are intended to be taken at face value . . . It is also true of the scale designations . . . The scales have been derived from a content analysis of statements that ministers actually make about their motivation . . . The scales of the TSI are not defined and validated by reference to any external reference group . . . The greater maturity of the ministers whose statements were sampled to produce the TSI generally accrues to the advantage of the test . . . More serious, perhaps, is the possibility that the present form of the TSI may gradually become obsolete to the degree that conceptions of the ministry change, and with them motivational concerns and questions.

"*Primarily for guidance*: Either the taking of the TSI or the discussion of its results may become the starting point—or an adjunct, if discussion is occasioned later—for a franker and clearer discussion by the students—with himself, with friends, *or with a counselor—about ambiguities in his vocational planning* . . . The data which are presented in this manual, however, should be regarded as illustrative of two points: that there *are* meaningful and lawful patterns of subsequent behavior related in an expected way with TSI scores; and that these relationships are quite complex. The major contribution of the counselor ought not to be the attempt to make these decisions for the student, but to provide the atmosphere in which he can most honestly and forthrightly survey relevant considerations and reach his own decision. The qualities of the TSI contribute to the counselor's task at this point . . .

"*Who should use the TSI?* Any person who administers the TSI and reports its results to students must have the following characteristics: 1) Formal training and supervised experience as a counselor, and the readiness to devote the necessary time to a continuing counseling relationship . . . 2) A disposition and temperament consistent with the "open," mutually "respecting" mood . . . It is an important contribution of the TSI that it encourages a calm, matter of fact, trustful and open attitude toward the discussion of vocational planning, and this ought not to be undermined by contrary attitudes conveyed by its administrator . . . 3) Sufficient sophistication in the understanding of test construction so as to be able to understand fully the statements of this manual and to be able to interpret them to students . . . 4) Thorough familiarity with this manual." (Then follows some characteristic cases and uses: The boy preacher, suppressed turmoil, the intellectual rebel, the compelled theologian, etc.).

Of the several scales of the TSI, the *FL* (Flexibility), *A* (Acceptance by others), and particularly *P* (Service to Persons) scales are those most important to counseling interest. The following remarks taken from the *P* explanation will point this up:

"*Service to Persons* (*P*):

Range: 0-24

General mean: 14.6   Standard deviation: 4.2

"This scale records the desire to offer personal succor and support to individuals, especially at times of personal stress—the traditional concerns of pastoral care—as a motivation for entering the ministry. Emphasis is on personal, intimate involvement in the lives of others, as a friend and as a helper. The high *P* scorer is saying, I am in the ministry because I want to be close to people and to help them. Items especially call attention to problems of emotional health and maturity and to "adjustment" crises, and refer only obliquely and minimally to explicit "reli-

gious" needs or "religious" ministry. The motivation represented by P could presumably be regarded
as appropriate for other "service" vocations as for
the ministry. High P scorers tend to be confident
about their ability to "work with people" and "handle
personality differences," to minister to physical and
mental illness, and—at least as they leave seminary
—to minister to persons with restricted intellectual
interests, and to deal with social or racial antagonisms.
The higher P score obtained by females (see Appendix
II) may emphasize the maternal, solicitous nature of
P. If he has to choose between the dichotomy of
"people vs. ideas," the high P scorer seems to have
more interest in people. Among alternative vocations,
some social occupation is clearly his first choice.

"P is negatively correlated (RB 3:21; also RB 1:1,
2; RB 3:3, 9, 11, 13) with definiteness of commitment,
and with the more traditional conceptions of motivation implied by E (Evangelistic witness) and SL (Special Leading), and particularly with the vagueness,
irrelevance, or selfishness of purpose he finds implied
by F (Self-fulfillment). The higher P scorer is younger than the low scorer, more likely to be single, and
is particularly self-confident about his own emotional
health. He comes from a larger town, reports his
father as inactive in the church and not influential in
his own decision. He is not likely to have close friends
entering the ministry. He is more likely to criticize
his home and church religious training as inadequate.
He is somewhat more likely to enter a more supporting or peripheral form of the ministry, rather than
the parish ministry. During seminary, he may become
more involved in clinical training. P is loaded slightly
on the "liberal" side of the "conservative-liberal"
Factor 1 (RB 2:2). P tends to change during seminary as do "liberal" variables, i.e. increasing at
schools which draw the most "conservative" students

and decreasing at schools drawing more "liberal" students (RB 4:2). Faculty judgments of potential effectiveness are also correlated with increase of P during seminary (RB 4:9), so that presumably the P scorer upon leaving seminary would be most strongly correlated with faculty ratings of effectiveness—although this has not been specifically tested. P motivation itself tends to be stable, showing the least change during seminary of any $AIFLERP$ scales (RB 4:2). The suspicion may commonly be raised about service motivations that persons may be attracted to help others by attempts to solve stressful situation in their own lives. At worst, this may be a kind of sublimated aggression by the distraught. At best, it may be regarded as a sensitization toward the predicaments of others by one's own experience."

Both Theological schools and clergymen were critical that even these admissions tests are inadequate but on the whole recognized that they had tried more than other professions to devise and use valid tests. Nearly all good schools employ numerous tests other than the above TSI. The Szondi, Draw a Picture, Sentence Completion, MMPI, TAT, Strong Vocational, Rorschach, Wechsler Adult Intelligence, Bender-Gestalt and similar tests were those most frequently used at schools like Chicago, Drew, Garrett, Pacific, Princeton, Rochester-Colgate, Union, Yale. One school, for example [name withheld], uses the TSI and all of the following: MMPI; Ohio State Psychological Test; Locally devised pastoral information, personal evaluation, counseling aid; Wechsler Adult Intelligence; Draw-a-person and Draw-a-family; Rorschach; external evaluation and clinical observation; Gordon personal profile and inventory data.

Unlike law and medicine, the clergy early recognized counseling (often referred to as pastoring) as the very center of their function. As may be expected from the theological school statistics given earlier and from the above discussion of concern for counseling in admissions, the clerical schools are also more sophisticated and capable in training clergymen for counseling than are either law or medical schools as to their graduates. About 80% of the theological schools had an active service counseling their students, aiding them in psychological self knowledge and mental health. The faculties far outdistanced law or medicine in counseling training—over half the schools showing faculty possessing doctorates in psychology and counseling; two-thirds had written extensively on counseling; nearly 90% had clinical and pastoral counseling experience and were presently engaged in counseling practice. Whereas a good law school might show one to three faculty members seriously interested in counseling and socio-psycho dynamics, a third to half of the faculty in good theological schools were so characterized.

Consequently it turned out, as might be expected, that the definitions of counseling given by the replies on the theological school questionnaires were more sophisticated and experienced, witness the following samples:

> Counseling is the creation of a relationship and an atmosphere whereby a "disturbed person" feels that someone understands or is trying to understand, where he is free to be himself—and through such a relationship and in such an atmosphere he can develop insight and thus begin to redirect his life in new directions.

> An activity designed to establish meaningful personal contact between people (establish relationship, overcome isolation) and to make use of this new experience of relationship to unravel, work through and solve personal problems.

> Counseling is a process whereby a counselor and counselee establish a relationship characterized by acceptance and understanding, wherein the counselee is enabled to work through his problems toward greater wholeness.

Counseling is helping people to help themselves to find their way through stressful situations toward self chosen decisions. Through clarification of relationships and emotional responses growth in self understanding is made possible.

Assistance to people in their better understanding of their emotional and intellectual attitudes as well as their involvement with environmental circumstances.

An interpersonal relationship in which one person, more toward the "normal" end of the scale of "normal-abnormal" makes available to another (who seeks aid or help in counseling) to move in a more appropriate direction in his personal life including his total milieu.

A structured permissive relationship which encourages and permits the parishioner to understand himself and his conflicts and to overcome or to adjust to them creatively.

Next, it early appeared from the questionnaires and interviews that a great deal of instruction was offered in counseling, that this was taken by most students, that it used fairly sophisticated material and teaching methods and that it was clinical, personality-dynamics and psychotherapeutically oriented. The non-directive approach of Carl Rogers and the interpersonality theory of O. H. Mowrer had the greatest influence.

[Let us repeat the statistics: 69% gave a pastoral counseling course; 26% clinical counseling training; 30% psychotherapy, personality dynamics; 9% specialties like "the family"; 74% required counseling courses and 12% were optional (average enrollment 50); 53% show students taking courses outside theology school and 42% took outside clinical training; 75% had fairly high agreement on the standard books in the field, spanning psychology, psychiatry, counseling, pastoral specialties; 72% used taped interviews, one way screens, psychodrama, like material; 82% showed that students did not run free clinics but did clinical work in established clinics].

We might use Garrett Theological School in Chicago and Pacific School of Religion in Berkeley, California to show typical curriculum coverage. At Garrett there were in 1964 eighteen courses specifically designated "Pastoral Psychology and Counseling" and some 25 others on such related topics as principles of sociology, social psychology, the family and personality development, etc. The 18 designated courses were:

Personality and Pastoral Care
Psychology of Religious Development
Psychology of Religious Experience
Marriage and Pre-Marriage Counseling
Advanced Counseling and Pastoral Care
Group Approaches in Counseling
Clinical Course: Residence Training in Problems of Mental and Physical Illness
Pastoral Care and the Juvenile Delinquent
Supervised Field Study
Research Design with Religious Data
Reading Course in Psychology of Religion and Counseling
Seminar: Religion and Psychotherapy
Seminar: Anxiety and Guilt
Professional Seminar
Research in Psychology of Religion and Counseling
Clinical Training in Counseling
Religion and Health
Laboratory in Pastoral Counseling

At Pacific School of Religion (a smaller school) the pattern is much the same: 12 courses on personality, group therapy and mental health, pastoral counseling, interpersonal relationships, clinical training with the mentally ill, psychotherapy, marriage counseling; and about 10 more on the family, sociology, psychology and like topics; plus a free clinical Pastoral Counseling Service in which students train.

One overall criticism of theological school teaching in counseling that comes from our survey of schools, practicing professionals and clients is that it is too deferential to and centered on psychoanalysis—that this makes the clergyman a poor psychiatrist rather than a good pastor. In defense of the schools it may be pointed out that in small communities there are no or few available psychiatrists and in many communities people cannot afford those that there are, so the clergyman with his free counseling has had to become the poor man's psychiatrist.

About thirty years ago some of the theological schools in conjunction with psychiatrists and psychologists set up the first clinical training programs in counseling and psycho-dynamics for the clergy. Such organizations as the Institute for Pastoral Care, the Council for Clinical Training, the Clinical Training Program of the American Foundation of Religion and Psychiatry, the Menninger Foundation and others, provided pastoral training on an inter-school clinical basis, usually in a mental hospital, disturbed children's home or detention prison. This was essentially training with the insane, abnormal and mentally disturbed of the same type that a clinical psychologist or psychiatrist, who intended to work regularly with such mental patients, would take. The same clinical emphasis was reflected in the theology schools. Now comes *a revealing conclusion from the present study* (which has been relayed to several schools who confirm that they were beginning to suspect the same) : in-practice clergy who took this training believe it was ill fitted to the problems they face in pastoral counseling. Their reasoning is simple : a) they rarely work with seriously disturbed mental cases; b) the "normal" person who is jarred out of pattern by several unusual problems (death of relative, loss of faith, money, mate, etc.) is to be handled entirely differently from a mental patient; c) to be an amateur psychiatrist here is to be a poor pastor; d) clients who come to the clergy do not want a psychiatrist, else they could have gone to one; e) the pastor and the church have tools no psychiatrist can use —absolution, lifting of guilt, faith. They therefore believe, and many pastoral counseling teachers agree, that theological schools went down a blind alley in this mental hospital clinical training and that any training of counselors (religious, legal, otherwise) can best be given in clinics that cope with "normal" life people and problems. *Our study would confirm this, and it seems one of the most important conclusions in guidance of future professional training.* The theology colleges are dissatisfied with their teaching and know what they want to do (see statistics above). But this is not very imaginative, being essentially "more and better of the same."

There is some school and student stratification in theology as in law. Students from fundamentalist churches tend to go to fundamentalist schools, most schools are denominational, there is no real intermixing of Catholic, Jew and Protestant. Other than this, the major stratification is on the liberal/conservative or liberal/fundamentalist axis. This has some, but not extensive, effect on counseling. Liberal and better schools offer more and perhaps more modern instruction, but even conservative and smaller schools include substantial counseling training. Counseling training is central in modern Jewish schools. Catholics have undertaken much in counseling (see particularly the writings of Rev. Charles A. Curran), albeit they sharply distinguish between counseling and the confessional and are basically anti-Freudian.

Medicine

We have already documented that medicine attracts the most brilliant students, generally represents the highest social status and assures the highest average income (over 50% report net income above $25,000). We can further describe those chosing medical careers: 95% are white, 99% male, 90% native born; 65% Protestant, 18% Catholic, 13% Jewish;* 15-20% are sons of physicians, an additional 15% come from other professional families, and a further 25% are sons of business managers or owners; they are extremely conservative as shown by political, social and economic opinions and type of paper or magazine read. They are well satisfied with their choice of career, emphasizing financial rewards, attractiveness for marriage with desirable girls, and joy of working almost constantly with people in a helping relationship. Strangely, somewhat inconsistently with this last, psychiatry rates fifth as a specialty, well below internal medicine, surgery, pediatrics and obstetrics. Medical students are an "independent" group (90% expecting a non-salaried private practice). Yet they become "socialized"—that is, take on the expected social role of being a physician—more in the course of training than is true of the other professions; they really do come out like peas in a pod. Their values shift substantially during student years toward the professionally accepted.

Medical candidates (other than psychiatrists) show a high incidence of authoritarianism, paternalism and social restrictiveness—i.e. that they know best, play god and protect society against "health" and "mental health" hazards.

There are four professional assumptions that pretty well determine the training program of medical schools as this relates to interviewing and counseling: a) socio-psycho pathology is an illness like any other illness and is therefore

---

* Our actual questionnaire respondents in metropolitan areas showed somewhat different proportions, the younger and Jewish being more willing to reply and more interested in counseling.

a problem for medicine;* b) the psychiatrist is the specialist in this area and should be used by the G.P., as he uses other medical specialists; c) the diagnostic interview is a special type of interview and a specialty within medicine; d) the wholistic-homeostasis approach to medicine recognizes the treatment of the whole man and that disability comes from psychological as often as from physiological causes. To meet these assumptions, extensive training is given for psychiatry as a specialty; a psychiatrist must undergo analysis and follow a supervised clinical training in addition to his regular medical training and internship, so that one man has facetiously remarked that psychiatrists are those doctors who were themselves so maladjusted that they had to be analyzed and thus qualified for the mental "unhealth" profession. Other "counseling" than that of psychiatry tends not to be viewed as counseling in medicine and particularly by psychiatrists. The G.P. is not taught general counseling. Rather, as a part of "general" medicine or "comprehensive care" he is given an overview of psychiatry and psychiatry's answer to the problems beyond the strictly diagnostic. He is trained in the process of interviewing to be certain he gets a full case history and all the "facts" necessary for diagnosis; in this regard there is a frank recognition that what a patient says or doesn't say but shows may be more important to diagnosis than objective symptoms. The Comprehensive Care program is an extension of clinical training; clinical training deals either with the bed patient or the outpatient (that is with people seen only in the school or hospital environment). Comprehensive Care (for example as practiced at Cornell Medical) seeks to have the student follow the patient in his total environment, at home, in work,

---

* Whenever one attacks one of these assumptions, as Thomas Szasz (Syracuse Medical) has the concept of mental illness, or Edwin Lemert (UCLA) has the rating of socio-pathic, or Jerome Frank (Johns Hopkins) has the idea of extended therapy, he is somewhat ostracized by the profession.

marital and other problems (with the help of social workers, etc.). This is an attempt to introduce wholism, simulate the conditions under which he will practice and expose him to the socio-psycho dynamics involved. Medical training is fortunate in having available many "free" subjects for clinic and comprehensive care and to have encouragement rather than opposition from general practitioners in handling these charity cases. Finally, the doctor is introduced to the doctor-specialist (psychiatrist) referral route he will be expected to use in practice.

The teaching methods of medical schools are quite sophisticated (as they are in psychiatric training). Some of the best interview tapes, closed circuit television, one-way glass observation, clinical supervision, group therapy, occur here.

Much of what we have said about the professionalization of lawyers, their value structure, the possibility for their post graduate training, their willingness to accept counseling training as important, their use of their own special method (manipulation of power) to satisfy clients, their answering a client's particular way of framing his problem, their social status and acquisition of value syndromes, applies to doctor trainees. For example, the doctor early learns the use of drugs, pills and other overt "helps" as placebos in treating peoples' psychosomatic problems (much as the lawyer serves a complaint). Both correspond to the well known psychological principle of "do something, do anything—but *do*."

In terms of professionalism law and medicine differ. It has been said that in a profession status is determined by two judgments: that of clients and that of fellow practitioners. In law the judgment of clients is the more important; in medicine it is the rating of colleagues. This may be due to greater specialization and referral in medicine. It seems in part due to hospital affiliation for the doctor. The hospital, the number of hospitals and the rank at which you are affiliated is an important status symbol. On this scale the G.P. or general counseling doctor is near the bottom of the scale; 95% of all doctors have hospital affiliation; specialists are best affiliated and with the largest number of hospitals (5-10) ; G.P.s have lesser and fewer affiliations, 40% with only one hospital. It came as something of a surprise, in the light of the above low rating of counseling, that all doctors in our survey listed more "family problems" as coming to them than "physiological" ones. Your reporter believes that medical schools, like law schools, are beginning to realize that all doctors do and must counsel (whether they call it this or not), that this is different from psychiatry and ought to be taught independently and as such to all doctors.

Other Counselor Training Schools

We examined other counselor training programs and discussed with counseling psychologist-practitioners their effectiveness. These included training for clinical psychologists, social workers, marriage counselors, guidance workers. Our remarks here are not intended as a real analysis of these training programs or as directed to these disciplines. Our interest is in sharing with law, medicine and theological schools some generalized observations about other counseling training to encourage further inquiry at points which may seem particularly pertinent. We list the following suggestions as illustrative rather than definitive or statistical:

1. Almost no counseling training is undergraduate. The exception is "guidance" or lower school counseling which is often a part of the undergraduate teacher or testing training program.

2. Marriage counseling has few training centers (*e.g.* Merrill-Palmer, Detroit; University of Pennsylvania, Philadelphia). It relies on other professional training as qualification. The American Association of Marriage Counselors makes certification depend upon clinical training and advanced degrees in Psychology, Psychiatry or family service. The statutes, beginning to appear, make no independent test but accord the recognition to designated professional groups (see California Law, 1963).

3. Social Work training exists at the graduate level but is more concerned with casework, interviewing, processing and administration than it is with counseling.

4. These specialized "counseling" groups are constantly trying to achieve the professionalism, recognition and protections of the old line professions.

5. The academic, aptitude and personality standards for the admission of students to these specialties is generally below that for law, medicine and the clergy. Although there are notable exceptions (*e.g.* Menninger Clinic), there is little or no attempt to test or rate for potential counseling ability.

6. These new callings rate counseling as an even more important part of their activity than do any of the old-line professions, though it is not clear that both use the term in the same sense. They seem to be using "counseling" to say, "we do the same work as old line counselors (in a better or more modern way), why can't we have their protections" (particularly legal protection for confidentiality of communications).

7. Nearly all these training programs center their teaching in "case materials". Some use rather sophisticated methods of closed circuit television, one-way observation glass, tape recording, supervised field casework, clinics, etc.

8. On the whole these disciplines are more satisfied with available material and instruction methods than are the old professions. And an examination of their material tends to justify this satisfaction, in part because being new callings they are in response to the current socio-psycho movement and use new material as central to their work, compared to being peripheral as in the old professions, and partly because they have been less inhibited in developing material and in its use.

9. In terms of professionalism, these new callings are troubled most by being at the low end of the pecking scale; and they should like to be rated true professions. Some psychologists object to medics using the term "doctor" since they have no doctorate.

10. By way of compensating for their lower status, these disciplines tend to rope off a specialty (marriage counseling) and try to keep others out, or preempt the term counseling, or make use of a special technique (*e.g.* Rorschach or other testing) and insist that those who cannot use this are inadequate.

11. All these callings develop an ethic and a syndrome of values similar to the professions but unique to themselves.

12. Women have been accepted into and have found a place in these new callings which they have not been accorded in the professions.

13. Much of the training is geared to make the trainee an adjunct of one of the professions, *e.g.* psychiatric social worker.

14. There is such a need for persons in some of these fields that prospective employers make tuition-maintenance grants on the commitment of the trainee to come to work for the agency upon graduation.

15. Many of the training schools offer counseling guidance, psychoanalysis or other personal adjustment to their students who are believed to need it.

16. The training recognizes and the trainees show a greater willingness to work a) in community projects compared to private practice (*e.g.* Community Chest agencies) and b) in clinical cooperation with other callings (*e.g.* a marriage counselor attached to church, a social worker attached to a hospital, etc.).

17. The length of time required and the cost of training is not as great in these callings as in the professions.

Third: Some Observations on Series "A", "B"
and "F" Queries (See Appendix)

Series "A" in its first page asked the need and wisdom of studying counseling, jointly in these three professions, by subsidiary studies of school and professional and client, and laid out an outline similar to the present book. We can now say that most of our assumptions were confirmed by the research and that our experience in verifying this series of inquiries is recorded in Chapters 3, 5, 6, 7, 8.

Series "B" (Attraction, Recruitment, Education and Training of the Professional) concerned itself with the nature of a profession, the socio-economic rating, recruitment, tests relating to counseling ability, training, shifts in goals, values, personality or other factors during training, satisfaction with training. The following *observations on* admission and training, in addition to conclusions set forth in other parts of this manuscript, can be made:

Entry into a profession is largely a matter of interest and interest maturity. This changes little from age 16 on and can be measured (see interest tests in Series "B"). It is not significantly affected by High School or College guidance or teacher influence. It does not correlate with personality (though all three professions correlate positively with femininity scales), and is not changed by training or experience. Best prospects score high in their own and operationally related professions (*e.g.* law and journalism, surgery and mechanical engineering).

The emphasis on grades as the basis for admission is of increasingly doubtful validity. Satisfaction of employers and clients with those in the lower half of a professional class almost equals (and in relationships exceeds) the upper half. It is probable now that preliminary training has so improved that a person with a much lower academic ratio is capable of learning the professional material—in which event his attitude, adjustment and commitment may be more important.

The history of all professions seems to follow these patterns: 1) a social problem emerges, 2) it is treated by the most available unspecialized persons responding to the need, 3) a grouping of pertinent skills emerges, 4) recognized procedures and theoretical foundations are formulated, 5) some form of group consciousness and apprenticeship occurs,

6) education centers on theory and skills, 7) services become marketable and codes and standards develop, 8) specialization comes in, 9) a synthesis of specializations is devised, 10) the profession has to determine whether to surrender a part of its function to others or encompass a new social problem [whereupon the process repeats]. It is precisely at the break-point in this process that modern counseling stands. Our material would suggest that counseling is being reoriented into the old line professions and also emerging in new specialties (marriage counseling). There was an attempt after Freud (a medic) began systematizing psycho-dynamics to make psychological counseling a province of medicine by referring to this whole area as "mental health". Our study would conclude that this has passed its zenith and that counseling is being reoriented into all the professions as part of day-to-day adjustment and handling of problems, and is also becoming a separate profession with sub-professions.

As this reorientation occurs more attention is and must be given to the counseling aspect of professional candidate admission. This moves on three levels, it seems to the author: a) certain patterns which have proved likely to produce overall student failure, b) certain qualities associated with counseling ability which can be measured and predicted, c) the need to supply one who is going into counseling with counseling on his own problems.

The following are a few of the overall admissions cautions which emerge: Those who change schools frequently, who are consistently under-achievers, who are under pressure from parents or others to apply to specific schools or for specific professions, who seem to lack motivation or interest, whose financial need is greater than can be met, whose parents show discord of long standing, who evidence a history of ethical short cuts to gain desired ends, who reveal acted out behavior disorders or emotional illness, who have low grades and low test scores, who cannot handle pressure or anxiety—all these are poor bets for any of the professions, and particularly for counseling.

If we list in the order rated the twenty qualities most desirable in a counselor (those so rated by 75% or more of each of our professions), we have a satisfactory list of items to look for and test with applicants (the tests we should use —see Series "B" and TSI in this chapter—relate to these): (*Note*: There is some overlapping):

1) Possessing common sense
2) Good listener
3) Friendly
4) Patient
5) Mature
6) Tactful
7) Open minded (non-judgmental)
8) Kind
9) Tolerant
10) Liking people (ability to interrelate)
11) Sympathetic
12) Encouraging
13) Skilled in interpersonal relations
14) With humor
15) Intelligent
16) Objective
17) Handling pressures or anxiety
18) Warm
19) Well trained
20) Flexible

There was also general agreement among our respondents (confirmed by other studies) as to the areas of training desired for counseling: insight into typical problems of modern society and the socio-cultural factors involved, understanding of personality growth and dynamics of behavior, self knowledge and ability to therapeutically use the self without projecting oneself and one's ideas into what is observed or handled, components and techniques of interviewing, grounding in the counseling process, grasp of ethics of counseling and when and for what one may offer aid, how to deal with anxiety and fear and compulsion-aggression (the irrational), knowledge of all interdisciplinary helping resources of a community, knowing how to recognize the persons and problems this counselor cannot best serve and how, where and when to refer them. Finally, all professions must basically teach the professional how to learn from continuing professional experience. All this suggests more imaginative use of cases, interdisciplinary and continuing education. Our professions are becoming aware of the need but have not yet devised the means of meeting the demand.

Series "F" included nineteen questions aimed at defining the Image or Mythology or Professionalism in one's own profession. Nearly all the items as to professionalism generally (questions 2, 8, 9, 10, 11, 12, 13, 14, 16, 17) could be and have been adequately answered from the survey material Chs. 2, 5, 6); the similarities of the three ancient professions on all levels of recruitment, training, practice and professionalism were greater than the differences. We have to, and did, also define image differences (see Ch. 5 and Ch. 6). Law was authoritarian, directive, power oriented, somewhat unspecialized, offering itself as old, learned and servicing, objective and intuitive (1, 3, 4, 5, 6, 7, 15, 18, 19). Similar summaries have been made for medicine and religion (Chs. 5, 7). We can highlight some less expected points: medicine's image is of wealth and prestige above the lawyer; medicine is least service oriented and most conservative; it is the most specialized; it tried to claim most of counseling for itself (psychiatry).

We certainly found an overall and a separate profession mythology composed of general statements (doctrine), application of statements (formula) and jokes and stories (miranda) for each profession. We have examined the first two rather fully. The jokes-stories are interesting and also highly illuminating. There is more to the legal jokes about giving advice out of the big or little book or seeking the probate or reprobate lawyer than mere humor. As there is also in the patient or nurse on the doctor's knee, and the clergyman's reversed collar or his remark to other professionals "we are both doing God's work, you in your way and I in His." We cannot do it here, but a fascinating study of professionalism and the image of each professional, both from the professional's and the client's view, could be spelled out from jokes and stories.

Bibliography Chapter 5

See Freeman, Counseling — A Bibliography with Annotations
See Code B

Abel, Theodore M., S. Oppenheim and C. J. Sager—Screening Applicants for Training in Psychoanalytically Oriented Psychotherapy. (1956) Am. J. Psychother. 10:24-39.

Adams, Stuart—Trends in Occupational Origins of Physicians. (1953) Am. Soc. Rev. 18, No. 4:404-409.

Alaimo, Phillip—Factors Influencing Ministers' Vocational Choice. (Master's Thesis, Northwestern Univ., 1940).

Albee, George W. and Marguerite Dickey—Manpower Trends in Three Mental Health Professions. (Feb. 1957) Am. Psychol. 12:57-70.

Aldrich, C. K. and H. Bernhardt—Evaluation of a Change in Teaching Psychiatry to Medical Students. (1963) Am. J. Orthopsychiat. 33:105-114.

Allen, Philip J.—Childhood Background of Success in a Profession. (1955) Am. Soc. Rev. 20:186-160. Rep. in M.L. and N.R. Haimowitz, eds.—Human Development. (New York, Crowell, 1960) pp. 736-742.

American Psychological Association, Education and Training Board— Doctoral Training Programs in Clinical Psychology and in Counseling Psychology. (1961) Am. Psychol. 16:312-313.

American Psychological Association—Internships for Doctoral Training in Clinical Psychology Approved by the American Psychological Association. (1961) Am. Psychol. 16:25-29.

Anderson, D.—Enrollment and Production of Physicians. (Dec. 1950) Today's Health 28:13.

Anderson, Hugh—Some Impressions of Theological Education in America Today. (1959) Expos. Times 70:356-360.

Anderson, Robert P.—Tape Recordings and Counselor-Trainee Understandings. (1955) J. Counsel. Psychol. 2:189-195.

Appel, K. E., et al.—Training in Psychotherapy: The Use of Marriage Counseling in a University Teaching Clinic. (Feb. 1961) Am. J. Psychiat. 117:709-712.

Arbuckle, Dugald S.—The Learning of Counseling: Process not Product. (1963) J. Consult. Psychol. 10:163-68.

Arnold, Magda B.—Screening Candidates for the Priesthood and Religious Life. (Loyola, 1962).

Ashbrook, James B.—Clinical Training for What Kind of Ministry? (1962) J. Past. Care 16:139-148.

Atkin, I.—Psychotherapy and the Trainee Psychiatrist. (1950) Am. J. Psychother. 4:85-89.

Bachrach, Paul B.—The Relationship Between Social Identification and Attitudes Toward Occupational Expectancies. (Doctoral Dissertation, Columbia Univ., 1955) 85 pp.

Baird, J. Arthur—Pre-theological Training: An Empirical Study. (1959) J. Bible Rel. 27:303-310.

Balinsky, B. and A. Dispenzier—An Evaluation of the Lecture and Role-playing Methods in the Development of Interviewing Skills. (1961) Personnel Guid. J. 39:583-585.

Balint, Michael—Method and Technique in the Teaching of Medical Psychology. II. Training General Practitioners in Psychotherapy. (1954) Brit. J. Med. Psych. 27:37-41.

Balint, Michael—Training Medical Students in Psychotherapy. (1963) Lancet 2:1015-1018.

Ball, D. H. and H. H. Wolff—An Experiment in the Teaching of Psychotherapy to Medical Students. (1962) Lancet 1:214-217.

Barnes, F. W.—Graduate Clinical Education. (1962) J. Med. Ed. 37:192-200.

Bauder, George E.—The Preparation of the Minister for Counseling. (Doctoral Dissertation, Stanford Univ., 1956) (D.A. XVII, 89, 1957).

Beale, Lathrop V. and Louis Kriesberg—Career Relevant Values Among Medical Students. (Surveys 387, 414 NORC). Also, Preferences and Expectations Concerning Individual Practice Among Medical Students. (Nov. 14, 1959) J.A.M.A. 171:1447-1448.

Becker, Howard—Medical Education. In Freeman, H. E., ed.—Handbook of Medical Sociology (Englewood Cliffs, P-H, 1963).

Becker, H. S., et al.—Boys in White—Student Culture in Medical School. (Chicago, Univ. of Chicago Press, 1961) 470 pp.

Becker, Howard S. and Blanche Geer—The Fate of Idealism in Medical School. (1958) Am. Soc. Rev. 23, No. 1:50-56.

Becker, Russell J.—Can Seminaries Train Pastors? Yale Divinity Schools' In-parish Pastoral Studies Program. (April 26, 1961) Christian Cent. 78:513-15.

Bellak, Leopold, et al.—Psychiatric Training for Non-Psychiatric Physicians. (1963) J.A.M.A. 184:470-472.

Benton, John Keith—The Place of Clinical Training in the Theological Curriculum as Theological Educators See It. Seward Hiltner, ed. —In Clinical Pastoral Training, Commission on Religion and Health, Federal Council of the Churches of Christ in America, 1945.

Berblinger, K. W. and D. G. Langsley—Student-patient Interviewing as a Method of Teaching Psychiatry to Sophomore Medical Students. (1962) Dis. Nerv. Syst. 23:191-198.

Berdie, Ralph F. and Theda Hagenah—A Training Program in Counseling. (1950) Am. Psychol. 5:140-142.

Berlin, Irving N.—Training in Community Psychiatry (1965) Comm. Mental H. J. 1:357.

Bieber, Irving A.—Training of Medical and Non-medical Personnel in Psychotherapy. (1951) Bull. World Fed. for Mental Health. 3:285-288.

Bier, William C.—Practical Requirements of a Program for the Psychological Screening of Candidates. (1954) Rev. for Religious 13:13-27.

Bier, William C.—Psychological Testing of Candidates and the Theology of Vocation. (1953) Rev. for Religious 12, 291-304.

Billinsky, J. M.—An Inquiry Into Procedures of Admissions of Students in Theological Schools. (Doctoral Dissertation, Harvard Univ., 1952).

Blizzard, Samuel W.—The Training of the Parish Minister. (1956) Union Sem. Q. Rev. 11, No. 2:45-50.

Blocksma, D. D. and E. H. Porter, Jr.—Short-term Training Program in Client-centered Counseling. (March 1947) J. Consult. Psychol. 11:55-60.

Bonacker, R. D.—Clinical Training for the Pastoral Ministry: Purposes and Methods. (Spring 1960) J. Past. Care 14:1-12.

Booth, Gotthard—Unconscious Motivation in the Choice of the Ministry as a Vocation. (Dec. 1958) Past. Psych. 9:18-24. Reprinted in W. W. Oates, ed.—The Minister's Own Mental Health. (Great Neck, N. Y., Channel, 1961) pp. 76-85.

Boyd, Richard W.—The Use of Group Psychotherapy in the Professional Training of Ministers (Doctoral Dissertation, Boston Univ., 1952).

Bridgeman, R. P.—Lawyer and Marriage Counselor Paripassu-Partners in More Effective Service to Ailing Marriages. (May 1956) Kan. L. Rev. 4:546.

Brosin, Henry W.—Role of Training in Clinical Psychology in General Medical Education. In Transactions of Conference on Training Clinical Psychologists Mar. 27-28, 1947. (New York, J. Macy, Jr. Foundation, 1947) pp. 46-54.

Brown, Coleman B.—Theological Students Today: A Student's Perspective. (March 1959) Union Sem. Q.R. 14:32-6.

Brown, Louis M.—The Educational Aspects of Preventive Law. (Dec. 20, 1949) Harv. L.S. Rec.

Brown, R. N.—The Training of the Doctor for his Work in the Community. (1962) J. Med.

Bruder, Ernest E.—Clinical Pastoral Training in Preparation for the Pastoral Ministry. (1962) J. Past. Care 16:25-33.

Bruder, Ernest E.—Present Emphasis and Future Trends in Clinical Training for Pastoral Counseling. (April 1960) Past. Psych. 11:33-43.

Bucher, Mary R.—Conflicts and Transformations of Identity: A Study of Medical Specialists. (Doctoral Dissertation, Univ. of Chicago, 1960-61).

Burke, Edward M.—The Legal Profession in Regard to Separation and Divorce Cases. (Oct. 1955) Juris 15:422.

Cahalan, Don, Patricia Collette and Norman Hilmar—Career Interests and Expectations of U.S. Medical Students. (1957) J. Med. Ed. 32:557.

Cahalan, Don and Patricia Collette—Career Preferences of Medical Students in the United States. (1956) Survey 387 NORC. See outline 2184.

Calhoun, J. R.—By These Paths; Avenues of Pre-theological Study. (Spring 1957) Encount. 18:174-81.

Cannon, Mary A.—Recommended Standards for the Use of the Practician in Graduate Training Programs for College Personnel Workers. (Doctoral Dissertation, Univ. of Colorado) (D.A. XXII, 3481, 1962).

Cantrall, Arch M.—Law Schools and the Layman: Is Legal Education Doing Its Job? (Nov. 1952) A.B.A.J. 38:907-910.

Caplovitz, David—Student-faculty Relations in Medical School: a Study of Professional Socialization. (Doctoral Dissertation, Columbia Univ.) (D.A. XXII, 666, 1961).

Carkhuff, Robert R. and Charles B. Truax—Training in Counseling and Psychotherapy: An Evaluation of a Integrated Didactie and Experimental Approach. (1965) J. Consult. Psychol. 29:333-36.

Carrier, Blanche—Counseling Pre-ministerial Students. (1951) Past. Psych. 2, No. 18:21-25.

Carstairs, G. M., H. J. Walton and P. G. Fawcett—General Practitioners and Psychological Medicine. Their Views on a Postgraduate Course. (1963) Lancet 2:397.

Cash, William L.—Relation of Personality Traits to Scholastic Aptitudes and Academic Achievement of Students in a Liberal Protestant Seminary. (Doctoral Dissertation, Univ. of Michigan) (D.A. XIV, 630, 1954).

Cavers, David F.—Legal Education and Lawyer-made Law. (1952) W. Va. L. Rev. 54:177.

Caves, Jack W.—An Evaluation of Growth and Change During a Guidance and Counseling Institute. (Doctoral Dissertation, Univ. of Texas) (D.A. XXII, 3517, 1962).

Challinor, R. H.—Student Evaluation of Clinical Training. (1949) J. Past. Care 3, Nos. 3-4:36-8.

Change in Emphasis Seen in Medical Education. (July 19, 1958) Sci. N.L. 74:38.

Chesler, Julia A.—Teaching Medical Students the Principles of Mental Health. (1959) J. Med. Ed. 34:674-679.

Christie, Richard and Robert Merton—Procedures for the Sociological Study of the Values Climate of Medical Schools. Chapter 6 in Ecology of the Medical Student (1958). Book also appeared as Part 2 of (1958) J. Med. Ed. 33: No. 10.

Clark, Charles E.—How Far Can Professional Competence and Responsibility Be Taught? (1961) J. Legal Ed. 13, No. 4:472-479.

Clinical Pastoral Training as a Religious Experience. (1951) J. Past. Care 5, No. 1:31-5.

Clinical Pastoral Training Programs and Centers and Member Seminaries by Regions (Council for Clinical Training, Inc.). (1961) J. Past. Care 15:225.

Cockrum, L.V.—Personality Traits and Interests of Theological Students. (Jan. 1952) Rel. Ed. 47:28-32.

Cockrum, L. V.—Predicting Success in Training for the Ministry. (1952) Rel. Ed. 47:198-202.

Cohen, Louis D., Ivan Mensh, G. K. Yacorzynski—The Teaching of Psychology Courses in Medical Schools. (1953) J. Med. Ed. 29:42-43.

Coker, Robert E., Norman Miller, Kurt Back, Thomas G. Dennelly—The Medical Student: Specialization and General Practice. (1960) N. Car. Med. J. 21, No. 3:96-101.

Coker, Robert E., Jr., et al.—Patterns of Influences: Medical School Faculty Members and the Values and Specialty Interests of Medical Students. (1960) J. Med. Ed. 35, No. 6:518-527.

Conference on Motivation for the Ministry. (Louisville, Southern Baptist Theological Seminary, 1959).

Continuing Legal Education for Professional Competence and Responsibility, The Report on the Arden House Conference, Dec. 16-19, 1958. (1959).

Coon, Gaylord P.—Psychiatry for the Lawyer: The Principal Psychoses. (March 1946) Cornell L.Q. 31:327-362.

Cotner, John H.—An Evaluation of Academic Status and the Methodological and Ideological Orientation of Psychology of Religion and Pastoral Counseling in American Seminaries. (Doctoral Dissertation, Univ. of Southern California, 1952).

Coville, W. J.—Personality Assessment of Candidates to Seminaries. In S. W. Cook, ed.—Research Plans. (New York, Religious Education Association, 1962) pp. 175-188.

Cowell, D. J.—Selection for Universities; Assessment of Medical Students. (March 1951) Times Ed. Sup. 1873:227.

Crabb, John—On Integrating Law With the Academic World. (1962) J. Legal Ed. 14:329.

Crofoot, Kenneth S.—A Survey of Programs of Clinical Pastoral Education in the Protestant Denominations of the United States as a Preparation for Pastoral Counseling. Ed. Dissertation, George Washington Univ., Washington, D.C., 1959; (1959) Geo. Wash. U. Bull. 59, No. 2:70-74.

Cryer, Newman S., Jr. and John M. Vayhinger—Casebook in Pastoral Counseling. (Nashville, Abingdon, 1962).

Curran and Cockevill—Widening Horizons in Medical Education: A Study of the Teaching of Social and Environmental Factors in Medicine. (New York, Commonwealth Fund, 1948).

Curriculum for Teaching Psychiatry in Medical Schools. (Feb. 1956) J. Med. Ed. 31:115-128.

Currie, Brainerd—The Materials of Law Study: Part Three. (1955) J. Legal Ed. 8:1-78.

Darling, Harold Wm.—A Comparative Study of Persisting and Non-persisting Ministerial Candidates in Evangelical Colleges. (Doctoral Dissertation, Purdue Univ., 1958) (D.A. XX, 586, 1960).

Davis, D. and W. Ponsar—A Field Trip Program in Psychiatry for Senior Medical Students. (1962) J. Med. Ed. 37:211-216.

Dellis, Nicholas and Herbert Stone, eds.—The Training of Psychotherapists; a Multidisciplinary Approach. (Baton Rouge, Louisiana State Hospital, 1961) 195 pp.

Dewan, John G.—Psychiatric Illness in Medical Students. (1960) Stud. Med. 9, No. 1:50.

DeWire, H. A.—Psychological Testing in Theological Schools. (April 1962) Ministry Studies Board Newsletter No. 1:2-4.

Dickel, Herman A.—The Physician and the Clinical Psychologist. A Comparison of Their Education and Their Interrelationship. (1966) J.A.M.A. 195-365.

Dodge, E. F.—Preparation of Physicians for Their Role in Parent Education. (1963) J. Am. Med. Wom. Assn. 18:289-292.

Douglas, W. G. T.—Predicting Ministerial Effectiveness. (Doctoral Dissertation, Harvard Univ., 1957).

Dricker, James M.—An Interview Study of the Counseling Responsibilities of Protestant Ministers With Implications for Professional Preparation. (Doctoral Dissertation, Univ. of Denver, 1956).

Dugan, W. E.—The Impact of N.D.E.A. upon Counselor Preparation. (1960) Personal Guid. J. 39:37-40.

Eaton, Joseph W.—The Social Science Content of a Medical Curriculum. (1956) Am. Soc. Rev. 21, No. 5:614-617.

The Ecology of the Medical Student—Report of the 5th Teaching Inst. (1958) Assoc. of Am. Med. Colleges, Evanston. (1958) J. Med. Ed. 33, No. 10 (2nd part of Journal has whole book).

Enelow, A. J., D. L. Forde and R. H. Gwartney—Psychosomatic Medicine: An Avenue for the Psychiatric Education of Medical Practitioners. (1962) Dis. Nerv. Syst. 23:565-567.

Eron, Leonard D.—The Effect of Professional Education on Attitudes. (1955) 4 Nurs. Res. 24.

Eron, Leonard D.—The Effect of Medical Education on Attitudes. (1955) J. Med. Ed. 30:559.

Eron, Leonard D. and Robert S. Redmount—The Effect of Legal Education on Attitudes. (1957) J. Legal Ed. 9:431-443.

Establish Mental Health Curriculums for Theological Students. (Sept. 5, 1956) Christian Cent. 73:1038.

Fairweather, Paul D.—The Appropriateness of Field and Level of Vocational Choice as Related to Self-Concepts, Intelligence, School Achievement, & Socio-Economic Status. (Doctoral Dissertation, Univ. of Southern California, 1960) (D.A. XX, 4032, 1960).

Fine, Xenia F.—In-Service Education for Teachers of Family Living. (1963) Marr. Fam. Liv. 25:111-113.

Farris, Norman J.—Reality Practice as a Procedure in Counselor Training. (Doctoral Dissertation, Stanford Univ., 1953) (D.A. XIII, 203, 1953).

Finkenstein, D. H.—A Study of College Seniors Who Abandoned Their Plans for a Medical Career. (1961) J. Med. Ed. 36, No. 8:924-933.

Fox, H. M.—Psychiatric Consultation in General Medical Clinics. An Experiment in Postgraduate Education. (1963) J.A.M.A. 185:999-1003.

Fox, Henry M., et al.—Applicants Rejected for Psychoanalytic Training (1964) J. Am. Psychoanal. Training 12:692-716.

Frank, Lawrence K.—Psycho-cultural Approaches to Medical Care. (1952) J. Soc. Issues 8, No. 4:45-55.

Frank, Jerome—A Plea for Lawyer-Schools. (Sept. 1947) Yale L.J. 56:1303.

Freedman, Monroe H.—Testing for Analytic Ability in the Law School Administration Test. (1958) J. Legal Ed. 11, No. 1:24-42.

Freedman, Howard E. and Geo. G. Reeder—Medical Sociology: A Review of the Literature. (1957) Am. Soc. Rev. 22, No. 1:73-81.

Freyhan, F.A.—On the Psychopathology of Psychiatric Education. (1965) Comp. Psychiat. 6:221.

Garland, Joseph and Joseph Stokes—The Choice of a Medical Career: Essays on the Fields of Medicine. (Philadelphia, Lippincott, 1961) 231 pp.

Gazda, George M.—The Effects of Short Term Group Counseling on Prospective Counselors. (Doctoral Dissertation, Univ. of Ill., 1959-60).

Gee, Helen H. and John T. Cowles, eds.—The Appraisal of Applicants for Medical Schools. (Evanston, Ill, Association of American Medical Colleges, 1957).

Gee, Helen H.—Learning the Physician-Patient Relationship. (1960) J.A.M.A. 173:1301-1305.

Gilmer, V., and Haller, Ivan N. Mensh—Psychology in Other Professional Schools. (Dec. 1956) Am. Psychol. 11, No. 12:676-679.

Ginzberg, E.—Occupational Choice. (New York: Columbia Univ. Press, 1951).

Golden, M. M., M. Brody and H. S. Lichtman—Psychiatric Education of Physicians. The Brooklyn Institute for the Psychiatric Education of the Private Practitioner. (1961) N.Y.J. Med. 61:3799-3782.

Goodling, R. A. and S. C. Webb—An Analysis of Faculty Ratings of Theological Students. (1959) Rel. Ed. 54:228-233.

Gordon, I. J.—Role-Playing as a Technique for Teaching Medical Students. (Aug. 1960) J. Med. Ed. 35:781-785.

Goshen, C. E.—Psychiatric Training and its Relation to Medical Education. (April 1960) J. Med. Ed. 35:360-368.

Gough, Galal A.—An Exploratory Study of Counseling Responsibilities of Nazarene Pastors with Implications for Professional Training. (Doctoral Dissertation, Michigan State Univ., 1963). (D.A. XXIV, 2561, 1963).

Gounley, M. E.—Needed: A Scholastic Psychiatry. (1960) The Priest 16, No. 8:686.

Gary, Robert M.—The Relationship of Medical Students Attitudes of Cynicism and Humanitarianism to Performance in Medical School. (1962) J. Health Hum. Beh. 3:147-151.

Greenacre, Phyllis—A Critical Digest of the Literature on Selection of Candidates for Psychoanalytic Training. (1961) Psychoanal. Q. 30:28-55.

Greenfield, Norman—A Brief Appraisal of the Role of Clinical Psychology in Medical Education. (1960) Am. Psychol. 15:624-625.

Griswold, Erwin N.—Educating Lawyers for a Changing World. (Nov. 1951) A.B.A.J. 37:805-808.

Griswold, Erwin N.—Law Schools and Human Relations. (Feb. 1956) Chi. B. Rec. 37:199; (June 1955) Wash. U. L. Q. 1955:217.

Gynther, Malcolm D. and J. Obert Kempson—Personal and Interpersonal Changes in Clinical Pastoral Training. (1958) J. Past. Care 12:210-219.

Hamilton, James D.—An Evaluation of Professional Preparation for Pastoral Counseling. (Doctoral Dissertation, Univ. of Denver, 1959).

Hammond, Kenneth R., et al.—Teaching Comprehensive Medical Care; a Psychological Study of Change in Medical Education. (Cambridge, Harvard, 1959) 642 pp.

Hammond, Philip C., Jr.—A Study Concerning the Use of Psychological Testing in 66 Accredited Graduate Professional Schools of Theology in the United States. (Drew Univ., 1951).

Hand, William J.—Principles and Techniques for Counseling Students in a Protestant Theological Seminary. (Doctoral Dissertation, Temple Univ., 1959-60).

Harms, Ernest and Paul Schreiber—Handbook of Counseling Techniques. (New York, Pergamon, 1963) 492 pp.

Harrower, Molly—Selection of Personnel for the Clergy. In H. C. Meserve, ed.—Significant Areas for Research in Religion and Health. (New York, Academy of Religion and Mental Health, 1962) pp. 117-132.

Head, Murdock—Education for the Professions in the United States— A Basic Challenge. (Spring 1959) Mercer L. Rev. 10:263.

Heckel, R. V. and M. J. Brennan—A Summer Externship in Psychology for Medical Students. (1963) J. Clin. Psychol. 19:363-364.

Herr, Vincent V.—Mental Health Training in Catholic Seminaries. (1962) J. Rel. Health 1:127-152.

Heston, Joseph C.—Standards of Selection of Pre-ministerial Candidates. (Co-operative Study of Pre-ministerial Education, Protestant Council on Higher Education, 1950).

Hiltner, Seward and Jesse H. Ziegler—Clinical Pastoral Education and the Theological Schools (1961) J. Past. Care 15:129.

Hiltner, Seward, ed.—Clinical Pastoral Training. (Commission on Religion and Health, Federal Council, 1945). 176 pp.

Hiltner, Seward—The Literature of Pastoral Counseling—Past, Present, and Future. (1951-52) Past. Psych. 2:21-28.

Hiltner, Seward—A Program in Religion and Psychiatry. (May 1960) Past. Psych. 11:12-14, 16-18.

Hiltner, Seward—Psychological Tests for Ministerial Candidates. (1957) J. Past. Care 11:106-108.

Hiltner, Seward—Psychoanalytic Education in the United States. (Oct. 1961) Past. Psych. 12:22-26.

Hodgsen, Leonard—Training of the Clergy. (1953) Ch. Q. Rev. 154, No. 3:282-91.

Hofman, Hans—The Ministry and Mental Health. (New York, Association, 1960).

Hollander, I. Fred—Mental Health Teaching Materials for the Clergy. (1962) J. Rel. Health 1:273-282.

Hollyer, Stewart G.—Social Status Factors and Achievement Needs as Related to Entry Into a Professional Field. (Doctoral Dissertation, Univ. of Nebraska, 1961) (D.A. XXI, 3844, 1961).

Hoon, Paul W.—Training for the Parish Ministry. (1958-59) Rel. Life 28:13-24.

Hoppe, Nancy H.—A Descriptive Study of Concepts, Attitudes, and Functions of a Selected Number of Physicians, Attorneys and Religious Leaders—Relative to Their Training and Efforts in Marriage Counseling as Related to Suggested Professional Concepts of Marriage Counseling. (Master's Thesis, M.A.. Brigham Young Univ., 1961).

Houston, Marietta and David Allen—Clinical Experience in a Psychiatric Setting for Sophomore Medical Students. (1957) J. Med. Ed. 32:483-492.

Howard, Judson D.—Interpersonal Group Seminar: A Training Method In the Pastoral Care of Groups. (1960) J. Past. Care 14:160-166.

Howe, Reuel L.—Institute for Advanced Pastoral Studies, A New Development. (Winter 1957) J. Past. Care 11:226-28.

Howe, Reuel L.—The Role of Clinical Training in Theological Education. (1952) J. Past. Care 6:1-12.

Hoyer, Louis B.—Theory of Ego Identity with Reference to the Young Pastor in Clinical Training. (Doctoral Dissertation, Boston University School of Theology, 1962) (D. A. XXIII, 1809, 1962).

Hughley, J. N.—Theological Education: Its Problems and Tasks. (1952-3) J. Rel. Thought 10, No. 1:44-55.

Hyde, Robert W. and Robert C. Leslie—Introduction to Group Therapy for Graduate Theological Students. (Summer 1952) J. Past. Care 6:19-27.

Hylbert, Kenneth W.—A Survey and Analysis of College and University Programs for the Professional Preparation of Public School Counselors. (Doctoral Dissertation, Penn. State Univ., 1954).

Jalkanen, Ralph J.—The Personality Structure of Seminarians: The Use of Available MMPI Norms for Diagnosis. (Master's Thesis, Roosevelt Univ., 1955).

Johnson, G. K.—Psychological Testing at the Seminary. (1952) Augustana Sem. Rev. 4, No. 2:18-20.

Johnson, Paul E.—Clinical Pastoral Training at the Crossroads. (1962) J. Past. Care 16:65-71.

Johnson, Paul E.—A Training Course in Pastoral Counseling. pp. 352-354. In Helen I. Driver—Counseling and Learning Through Small Group Discussion. (Madison, Wisc., Monona, 1958) 464 pp.

Johnston, Gordon W.—Sociological and Non-Legal Courses, (Summer 1950) Rocky Mt. L. Rev. 23:71-74.

Jones, Marshall R. and David Levine—Graduate Training for Community Clinical Psychology. (1963) Am. Psychol. No. 4, 18:219-223.

Jorjorian, Armen—Some Reflections on the Future of the Summer Quarter of Clinical Pastoral Training. (1959) J. Past. Care 13:155-159.

Kahana, R. J.—Teaching Medical Psychology Through Psychiatric Consultation (1959) J. Med. Ed. 34:1003-1009.

Kalvin, Harry, Jr. and Ralph W. Tyler—Palo Alto Conference in Law and Behavioral Science. (1957) J. Legal Ed. 9:366.

Kandel, Denise B.—The Career Decisions of Medical Students: a Study in Occupational Recruitment and Occupational Choice. (Doctoral Dissertation, Columbia Univ., 1960) (D.A. XXI, 985).

Katz, Jay—Law and the Behavioral Science Program at Yale: A Psychiatrist's First Impressions. (1959) J. Legal Ed. 12:99.

Katz, Robert L.—Aspects of Pastoral Psychology and the Rabbinate. (1953) Jewish Soc. Serv. Q. 29:367-373; also in (1954) Past. Psych. 5:35-42.

Kelley, A. D.—Dean Looks at Clinical Training. (1951) J. Past. Care 5, No. 1:61-7.

Kelley, Paul—Rorschach Measures of Affect-adjustment in Candidates to the Religious Life. (Master's Thesis, Catholic Univ., 1951).

Kemp, C. Gratton—Influence of Dogmatism on the Training of Counselors. (1962) J. Counsel. Psychol. 9:155-157.

Kendall, Patricia—Impact of Training Programs on the Young Physician's Attitudes and Experiences. Bureau of Applied Social Research Reprint No. 324. From (1961) J.A.M.A. 176:992-997.

Kienast, A. W. and H. J. Erwin—Teaching Psychiatry to Non-Psychiatric Residents. (1961) J. Nat. Med. Assn. 53:610-614.

Kim, Lester E.—A Critical Study of Selected Changes in Protestant Theological Students with Clinical Pastoral Education (Univ. Southern California, Los Angeles, 1960) (March 1962) Past. Psych. 13:39-40.

King, F. R.—Teaching Psychiatry to G.P.'s—An Early Experience. (1962) Ment. Hosp. 13:27.

Kinzer, John R.—The Educated Counselor. (1961) J. Counsel. Psychol. 8:14-16.

Kirk, Barbara A.—Techniques of In-Service Counselor Training. (1955) Personnel Guid. J. 34:204-207.

Kirkendall, Lester A.—A Reading and Study Guide for Students in Marriage and Family Relations. (Iowa, William C. Brown, 1960).

Kleinschmidt, H. J., et al.—Experiences in Teaching Basic Psychiatry to Medical Practitioners at the Mt. Sinai Hospital, New York. (1963) J. Mt. Sinai Hosp., N.Y. 30:384-400.

Kling, Frederick R.—The Motivations of Ministeral Candidates. Research Bulletin 59-2. Princeton, N.J., Educational Testing Service, 1959 (a).

Kling, Frederick R.—A Study of Testing as Related to the Ministry. (1958) Rel. Ed. 53:243-248.

Knoff, Irwin Jr.—Summary Report on the Conference on Psychology in Medical Education. (1956) Am. Psychol. 11, No. 12:684-685.

Knopf, J. and R. L. Stubblefield—Contributions of Psychology to Medical Education. (1960) Tex. St. Un. Med. 56, No. 2:93-97.

Kobler, F. J., N. J. Webb, V. V. Herr, W. J. Devlin—Loyola University NIMH Project on Religion and Mental Health. Report on Research Procedures. (Feb. 1959) Past. Psych. 10:44-46.

Kohut, H.—The Psychoanalytic Curriculum. (1962) J. Am. Psychoan. Assn. 70:153-163.

Kriesberg, Louis and Lathrop Beale—Career Specification Among Medical Students. (NORC, 1961, mimeo).

Kubie, Lawrence S.—The Impact of Modern Psychiatry on Medical Education, Medical Practice and Hospital Organization. (1947) Bull. Johns Hopkins Hosp. 80:348-360.

Kubie, Lawrence S.—Medical Responsibility for Training in Clinical Psychology. (1949) J. Clin. Psychol. 5:94-100.

Kubie, Lawrence S.—Problems of Psychoanalytic Training (Report of Panel). (1948) Bull. Am. Psychoanal. Assn. 4:29-36.

Law and Behavioral Science Program at Yale: Symposium. (1959) J. Legal Ed. 12:83.

The Law and Behavioral Science Project at the University of Pennsylvania: Symposium. (1958) J. Legal Ed. 11:74-99.

Law and Divorce: Symposium. (Winter 1953) Law Contem. Prob. 18:1-106.

Law and the Behavioral Sciences. Symposium. (Spring 1959) B.U.L. Rev. 39:157-187.

Law and Social Work: Symposium. (March 1957) Kan. L. Rev. 5:363-392.

Law-Medicine and Professional Responsibility: Symposium. (Dec. 1960) La. L. Rev. 21:128-167.

Law School Admission Test: Summary of Validity Studies. (Princeton, N.J., Educational Testing Service, June 1961).

Lawyers Need Psychiatric Training to Detect Mentally Ill Clients. (Jan. 1959) Sci. Digest 45:29-30.

Leon, R. L. and J. P. Friedman—Method of Orienting Medical Students in Community Social Services. (1962) Pub. Health Rep. 77:752-754.

Leslie, Robert C.—The Therapeutic Group Experience as a Course in the Theological School Curriculum. In Helen I. Driver, ed.—Counseling and Learning Through Small-Group Discussions. (Madison, Wisc., Monona, 1958) pp. 346-349.

Lesse, S.—The Physician and the Psychotherapist—A Problem in Medical Education. (1963) Am. J. Psychother. 17:569-578.

Lester, B. K., J. Gussen, J. Yamamoto and L. J. West—Teaching
    Psychotherapy in a Longitudinal Curriculum. (1962) J. Med.
    Ed. 37:28-32.
Levine, Maurice A. and H. D. Lederer—Teaching of Psychiatry in
    Medical Schools. In Silvano Arieti, ed.—American Handbook of
    Psychiatry. (New York, Basic Books, 1959) Vol. 1 p. 1923.
Liberty, Paul G.—Value and Trait Comparison of Clinical and Counsel-
    ing Students. (1965) Psychol. Rep. 17:157.
Lidz, Theodore—The 1951 Ithaca Conference on Psychiatry in Medical
    Education. (1955) J. Med. Ed. 30:689-697.
Lief, H. I., et al.—A Psychodynamic Study of Medical Students and
    Their Adaptational Problems. Preliminary Report. (July 1960)
    J. Med. Ed. 35, No. 6:696-704.
Lifton, Walter M.—A Study of the Changes in Self-Concept and Con-
    tent Knowledge in Students Taking a Course in Counseling Tech-
    niques. (Doctoral Dissertation, New York Univ., 1950) (Mic.
    Abs. XI, 1, 55, 1951).
Lortie, Dan C.—Layman to Lawmen: Law School, Careers and Pro-
    fessional Socialization. (Fall 1959) Harv. Ed. Rev. 29, No.
    4:352-369.
Lubin, B.—A Symposium: The Psychologist in Undergraduate Medical
    Education. (1961) J. Ner. Ment. Dis. 133:108-109.
Luborsky, Lester, et al.—Interim Report of the Research Project on
    the Selection of Medical Men for Psychiatric Training. (1950)
    Bull. Menn. Clinic 14:92-101.
Macartney, E.E.N.—The Making of a Minister. (Great Neck, N. Y.,
    Channel, 1961).
MacDonald, John M., and H. Weihofen—Teaching of Psychiatry in
    Law Schools. (Nov.-Dec. 1958) J. Crim. L. 49:310.
McDonnel, Kilian—Psychiatry and Pastoral Psychology: The Experi-
    ence of an Institute for Mental Health. (1957) Lumen Vitae
    12:253-259.
McIntyre, John—Structure of Theological Education. (April 1959)
    Expos. Times 70:210-5.
Maguire, John D.—Theological Appropriations of Psychoanalytic Con-
    cepts: A Critical-descriptive Study in Theological Method. (Doc-
    toral Dissertation, Yale Univ., 1959-60).
Martin, S. H.—A Twenty-Year Survey of the Functional Aspects of
    Methodist Theological Education. (Doctoral Dissertation, Boston
    Univ., 1954).
Masserman, Jules H. and Ralph T. Palmer—Psychiatric and Psycho-
    logic Tests for Ministerial Personnel. (March 1961) Past. Psych.
    12:24-33.
Masserman, Jules H., ed.—Psychoanalytic Education. (New York,
    Grune and Stratton, 1962).

Matarazzo, Joseph D.—Comprehensive Medicine: A New Era in Medical Education. (1955) Hum. Org. 14, No. 1:4-9.

Matarazzo, Joseph D., R. S. Daniel—The Teaching of Psychology by Psychologists in Medical Schools. (1957) J. Med. Ed. 32:410-415.

Matching Plan of Selecting Candidates for Medical Schools. (Nov. 27, 1953) Science 118:646.

Meadow, Lloyd—Toward a Theory of Vocational Choice. (1955) J. Counsel. Psychol. 2, No. 2:108.

Medical College Admissions Test. (New York, Psychological Corporation, 1946-1961).

Mehler, Irving M.—Medical Education: A Guide for the Law Schools. (1958) A.B.A.J. 44:869.

Meissner, W. W.—Psychiatric Training for Theology Students: A Report. (1961) Psychiat. Q. 35:720-725.

Menninger, Karl A.—Changing Concepts in Medicine and Their Effect Upon Medical Education. (1947) J. Kansas Med. Soc. 48:353-355.

Mensh, Ivan N.—Psychology in Medical Education. (1953) Am. Psychol. 8:83-85.

Merton, Robert K., George G. Reader, and Patricia L. Kendall, eds.— The Student Physician. (Cambridge, Harvard Univ. Press, 1957) 360 pp.

Merwin, J. C. and F. J. DiVesta—A Study of Need Theory and Career Choice. (1959) J. Counsel. Psychol. 6:302-308.

Miller, Caroll H.—Occupational Choice and Values. (1956) Personnel Guid. J. 35:244.

Million, E. G.—Psychological Testing in the Seminaries. (1954) Bull. Am. Assoc. Theol. Schools 21:85-99.

Minor, C. A. and R. G. Neel—The Relationship Between Achievement Motive and Occupational Preference. (1958) J. Counsel. Psychol. 5:39-43.

Morgan, Mildred I.—Course Content of Theory Courses in Marriage Counseling. (Aug. 1950) Marr. Fam. Liv. 12:95-99.

Moses, Darrell L.—The Relationship of Self-concept Discrepancies to Vocational Choice, Intelligence, School Achievement, and Socio-economic Status. (Doctoral Dissertation, Univ. of Southern California, 1959-60).

Mudd, Emily, Hilda Goodwin, Donald Young—Mental Health Teaching in Professional Education. (School of Medicine, Univ. of Pennsylvania. 1961).

Munger, P. F. and C. A. Johnson—Changes in Attitudes Associated with an NDEA Counseling and Guidance Institute. (1960) Personnel Guid. J. 38:751-753.

Murray, J. B.—Training for the Priesthood and Personality and Interest Test Manifestations. (Doctoral Dissertation, Fordham Univ., 1957). Also in (1959) Hom. Past. Rev. 59:443.

National Council on Legal Clinics—Project for Law School Education in Professional Responsibility. (Chicago, American Bar Center, 1962).

National Opinion Research Center: Great Aspirations—Career Plans of American June 1961 College Graduates. 33,982 graduates of 135 colleges, June 1961.

Nelson, John Oliver—Vocation, Theism and Testing. (Dec. 1958) Past. Psych. 9:33-40.

New York Academy of Medicine, Course Syllabus-Emotional and Psychiatric Problems in Medical Practice.

Nisi, W. F.—A Study of Dependency as a Dominant Personality Factor in Ministerial Students and Its Implications for Theological Education. (Master's Thesis, Princeton Theological Seminary, 1962).

Oldenburg, Cornelius—An Analysis of Pastoral Counseling Needs and Training in Two Church Denominations. (Doctoral Dissertation, Michigan State, 1954) (D.A. XV, 766, 1955).

Oren, Anne W.—The Construction of an Instrument for the Measurement of Social Worker Attitudes Associated with Aptitude in Interpersonnel Relationships. (Doctoral Dissertation, Univ. of Minnesota, 1957) (D.A. XVIII, 325, 1958).

Ornstein, Paul—An Experiment in Teaching Psychotherapy. (1961) J. Med. Ed. 36:154-161.

Owen, Llewelyn A.—An Evaluation of Field Work Guidance at the Oberlin College Grad. School of Theology. (Doctoral Dissertation, Boston Univ. School of Theology, 1956) (D.A. XVI, 1515, 1956).

Page, Howard E. and George E. Passey—The Role of Psychology in Medical Education. (1949) Am. Psychol. 4:405-406.

Paterson, D.—A Note on the Training of Clinical and Counseling Psychologists. (1960) Am. Psychol. 15:365-366.

Pfouts, J. H. and G. E. Rader—Instruction in Interviewing Technique in the Medical School Curriculum: Report of a Trial Program and Some Suggestions. (1962) J. Med. Ed. 37:685-686.

Pittenger, R. A.—Training Physicians in the Psychological Aspects of Medical Practice. (1962) Penn. Med. J. 65:1472-1474.

Plotmick, Harold L.—The Relation Between Selected Personality Characteristics of Social Work Students and Accuracy in Predicting the Behavior of Clients. (Doctoral Dissertation, Columbia Univ.) (D.A. XXII, 1259, 1961).

Poehler, W. A.—An Appraisal of Two Types of Pre-ministerial Training Programs of the Lutheran Church—Missouri Synod. (Doctoral Dissertation, Univ. of Minesota, 1954).

Proctor, Robert A.—A Study of Attitude Changes in Theological Students During One Year of Seminary Training. (Doctoral Dissertation) (D.A. XXII, 343, 1961).

Psychiatric Education of Physicians: Management of Emotional Problems Encountered in Private Practice. (1961) N. Y. J. Med. 61:3783-3801.

Psychiatry for Pastors; Omaha Ministers' Clinic. (Oct. 26, 1953) Time 62:67-71.

Psychological Testing in American Seminaries, Department of the Ministry of the National Council of the Churches of Christ in the U. S. A. (Mimeographed, New York, 1954).

Queener, Llewellyn—The Psychological Training of Ministers. (1956) Past. Psych. 7:29-34.

Ralph, R. B. and C. W. Taylor—Role of Tests in the Medical Selection Program. (April 1952) J. Appl. Psychol. 36:107-111.

Ramsey, Robert R., Jr.—Law School Admissions: Science, Art, Or Hunch? (1960) J. Legal Ed. 12, No. 4:503-520.

Rauner, Therese M.—Occupational Information and Occupational Choice. (Dec. 1962) Personnel Guid. J. 41, No. 4:311.

Reader, George G.—Comprehensive Medical Care. (1953) J. Med. Ed. 28:34.

Reader, George G.—Development of Professional Attitudes and Capacities (Chapter 8 of The Ecology of the Medical Student, 1958). The book also appeared as Part 2 of (1958) J. Med. Ed. 33, No. 10.

Regensburg Jeannette—The Curriculum Study: Implications for the Practice of Social Casework. (Jan. 1960) Soc. Casework 41, No. 1:13-18.

Rex, Ronald G.—A Theory of the Internship in Professional Training. (Doctoral Dissertation, Michigan State Univ.) (D.A. XXIII, 557, 1961).

Rice, Otis R.—Opportunities for Study, Training and Experience in Pastroal Psychology. (1956) Past. Psych. 6:23-49.

Riesman, David—Law and Sociology: Recruitment, Training and Colleagueship. (July 1957) Stan. L. Rev. 9:643.

Robbins, F. C.—Special Responsibilities of the Medical School in the Education of Physicians to Serve the Individual and the Community. (1962) J. Med. Ed. 37, No. 12:221 226.

Roe, Anne—Early Determinants of Vocational Choice. (1957) J. Counsel. Psychol. 4:212-217.

Roe, Anne—The Psychology of Occupations. (New York, Wiley, 1956).

Romano, J.—Teaching of Psychiatry to Medical Students. (1961) Lancet 2, No. 7193:93-95.

Rosenberg, M., et al.—Occupations and Values. (Glencoe, Free Press, 1957) 158 pp.

Ross, Sherman—APA-approved Doctoral Programs in Clinical and Counseling Psychology: 1964. (1965) Am. Psychol. 20:91-2.

Ruth, David N.—An Analysis of the Graduate Degree Programs in Pastoral Psychology. (B.D. thesis, Union Theological Seminary, New York, 1955).

Sacks, Howard R.—Human-Relations Training for Law Students and Lawyers. (1959) J. Legal Ed. 11:316.

Sacks, Howard R.—Special Legal Clinic Program, Course Syllabus, 1961.

Samler, Joseph, Jr.—Professional Training. (1952) Personnel Guid. J. 31:15-19.

Schneiders, Alexander A.—Proceedings of the Institute for the Clergy on Problems in Pastoral Psychology. (New York, Fordham Univ., 1956).

Scholefield, Harry B.—Psychoanalysis and the Parish Ministry. (1963) J. Rel. Health 2:112-127.

Schorr, Martin M.—Conformity Strength and its Relationship to Personality Characteristics of Ministerial Candidates. (Doctoral Dissertation, Univ. of Denver, 1960-61).

Schroeder, C. E.—Personality Patterns of Advanced Protestant Theology Students and Physical Science Students. (Doctoral Dissertation, Michigan State Univ., 1956).

Schwartz, Richard D.—Law and Behavioral Science Program at Yale. (1959) J. Legal Ed. 12:91.

Seeman, Melvin and John W. Evans—Apprenticeship and Attitudes Change. (Jan. 1962) Am. J. Soc. 67, No. 4:365-378.

Selecting Ministers for Tomorrow. (June 1956) Nat. Coun. Outlook 6:22.

Sells, S. D.—The Purposes of Psychology Curricula in Medical Education. (1956) Am. Psychol. 11, No. 12:679-683.

Shapiro, D., R. Robertson and L. Mahalic—Training Ministers for Mental Health Work. (1962) J. Past. Care 16:145-156.

Sharat, Myron R. and Daniel Levinson—The Quest for Omnipotence in Professional Training: The Case of the Psychiatric Resident. (1964) Psychiatry 27:135-149.

Shatin, L., et al.—A Behavioral Science's Teaching Program for First Year Medical Students. (1963) J. Med. Ed. 38:839-851.

Shepherd, M.—Postgraduate Psychiatric Education. (1963) Postgrad. Med. J. 62:301:302.

Shepard, William P. and James Roney, Jr.—The Teaching of Preventive Medicine in the United States. (1964) Milbank Mem. Fund Q., 42:7-31.

Skolnick, Jerome H.—Articulated Values of Professional Students. (56th Ann. Am. Soc. Assn., St. Louis, Sept. 1, 1961).

Small, Leonard—Personality Determinants of Vocational Choice. (1953) Psychol. Mono. 67:1-21.

Smyth, F. S.—The Place of the Humanities and Social Sciences in the Education of Physicians. (1962) J. Med. Ed. 37:495-499.

Sprinkle, Ronald L.—Permanence of Measured Vocational Interests and Socio-economic Background. (Doctoral Dissertation, Univ. of Missouri) (D.A. XXII,, 3527, 1962).

Stainbrook, Edward—The Place of the Behavioral Sciences in the Medical School. (1956) Psychiatry 19:263-269.

Stalnaker, John M.—Validation for Professional Apitude Batteries: Tests for Medicine. Proc. 1950 Conference on Testing Problems. (1951) Ed. Test Service.

Steele, Eleanor A.—The Problem of Teaching Psychological Attitudes to Medical Students. (1949) Am. J. Psychiat. 106:59-64.

Stephenson, Richard R.—Occupational Choice as a Crystallized Self-Concept. (Fall 1961) J. Counsel. Psychol. 8, No. 3:211.

Stockin, B. C.—An Empirical Investigation of Two Basic Assumptions of a Theory of Vocational Choice. (Doctoral Dissertation, Univ. of Buffalo) (D.A. XXII, 2469, 1962).

Strange Role for Univac: Probing Motivation of Ministers. (April 11, 1960) Newsweek 55:84.

Strong, Edward K., Jr. and A. C. Tuckey—Use of Vocational Interest Scales in Planning a Medical Career. (Am. Psychol. Assn., 1952).

Strong, Edward K., Jr.—Interest Scores While in College of Occupations Engaged in 20 Years Later. (1951) Ed. Psychol. M. 11: 335-348.

Strong, Edward K., Jr.—Vocational Interests 18 Years After College. (Minneapolis, Univ. of Minnesota Press, 1955).

Strunk, Orlo, Jr.—Clinical Pastoral Training: Experiment in Theological Education. (May 26, 1956) Sch. and Soc. 83:183-186.

Strunk, Orlo, Jr.—Interest and Personality Patterns of Preministerial Students. (1959) Psychol. Rep. 5:740.

Strunk, Orlo, Jr.—Theological Students. A Study in Perceived Motives. (Jan. 1958) Personnel and Guid. J. 36:320-322.

Strunk, Orlo, Jr.—Training Empathic Abilities: A Note. (1957) J. Past. Care 11:222-225.

Super, Donald E. and John O. Crites—Appraising Vocational Fitness by Means of Psychological Tests. Rev. ed. (New York, Harper, 1962) 688 pp.

Sutter, Cyril—A Comparative Study of the Interest and Personality Patterns of Major Seminarians. (Doctoral Dissertation, Fordham Univ., 1961) (D.A. XXII, 328, 1961).

Swanson, Paul Reginald—Some Effects of Clinical Pastoral Education on a Group of Theological Students and Pastors. (Doctoral Dissertation, Boston Univ. School Theology 1961) (D.A. XXIV, 1812).

Szasz, Thomas S.—Psychoanalytic Training. (1958) Inter. J. Psychoanal. 39:1.

Szasz, Thomas S.—Three Problems in Contemporary Psychoanalytic Training. (1960) A.M.A. Arch. Gen. Psychiat. 3:82.

Szurek, S. Z.—Teaching and Learning of Psychoanalytic Psychiatry in Medical School. (1957) Psychoanal. Q. 22:387-396.

Tageson, Carrol F.—The Relationship of Self-Perception to Realism of Vocational Choice. (Doctoral Dissertation, Catholic Univ. of America, 1959-60).

Taggart, Morris—A Study of Attitude Change in a Group of Theological Students. (Doctoral Dissertation, Garrett School of Theology, 1961).

Terry, Frank—Expected Changes in a Pastoral Clinical Training Program. (Iliff School of Theology, 1960).

Theological Education; Annual Review of Current Issues, Books and Seminary Programs. Christian Cent.

Thielens, Wagner, Jr.—Some Comparisons of Entrants to Medical and Law School. (1958) J. Legal Ed. 11, No. 2:153-167.

Thomas, Rose E.—Psychiatric Social Work in a Medical School. (1952) Ment. Hygiene N. Y. 36:286-293.

Thorne, Frederick C.—Training the Student in Medical Psychology. (1952) J. Med. Ed. 27:253-257.

Thornton, Edward E.—A Critique of Clinical Pastoral Education. (Doctoral Dissertation, Southern Baptist Theological Seminary, 1961).

Towle, Charlotte—The Learner in Education for the Professions: As Seen in Education for Social Work. (Chicago, Univ. of Chicago Press, 1954) 432 pp.

Training for a More Meaningful Ministry: Clinical Pastoral Training. (Feb. 1959) Nat. Coun. O. 9:24-26.

Traynor, Roger J.—Who Should Be A Lawyer, But Why? (1960) J. Legal Ed. 13:157.

Turner, E. L.—The Facts about Medical Students (Medical School Facilities, Standards, Students and Graduates, 1910-50). (March 12, 1955) Am. Med. Assn. J. 157:903-906.

Turrell, E. S.—Psychiatry: A Problem in Medical Education. (1963) Marquette Med. Rev. 29:61-63.

Union Theological Seminary—A Program of Teaching, Counseling and Research in the Interrelations of Psychotherapy and Religion at Union Theological Seminary. (1952).

Walcott, Dorothea K.—Field Work Experiences with Children and Youth—Seminary Training for the Ministry. (1958) Rel. Ed. 53:285-289.

Wanberg, Kenneth W.—The Expectations and Realizations of Clinical Training. (Doctoral Dissertation, Illiff School of Theology, 1961).

Watson, Andrew S.—Teaching Mental Health Concepts in the Law School. (1963) Am. J. Orthopsychiat. 33, No. 1:115-22.

Weiner, H.—Behavioral Science Courses, Their Function and Relevance in Medical Education. (1961) Arch. Gen. Psychiat. 4, No. 3:307-315.

Weiskotten, Herman G.—Lasting Values in Medical Education. (1957) J.A.M.A. 164, No. 4:533-537.

Werkman, Sidney L.—The Role of Psychiatry in Medical Education. (Boston, Harvard, 1966) 187 pp.

Werner, H. D.—Training Social Work Students for an Expanding Mental Health Clinic Program. (1963) Ment. Hygiene 47:103-107.

West, Louis J.—Behavioral Sciences in the Medical School Curriculum. (1959) J. Med. Ed. 34:1070-1076.

Whitcomb, John C.—The Relationship of Personality Characteristics to the Problems of Ministers. (1957) Rel. Ed. 52:371-374.

Whitlock, Glenn E.—The Choice of the Ministry as an Active or Passive Decision. (March 1961) Past. Psych. 12:47-53.

Whukhovn, et al.—Psychiatry and Medical Education: Report of Ithaca Conf. 1951 (Am. Psych. Assn.) (Baltimore, Lord Balt. Press, 1952).

Wilson, H. D.—A Study of Policies, Procedures and Practices in Admissions to Medical Schools in N. Y. State. (Albany, N. Y. State Univ., June 1953) 70 pp.

Wirtz, W. W.—Training for Professional Competence and Responsibility. (1961) J. Legal Ed. 13:461.

Wise, Carroll A.—The Call to the Ministry. (Dec. 1958) Past. Psych. 9:9-17.

Wise, Carroll A.—Education of the Pastor for Marriage Counseling. (Dec. 1959) Past. Psych. 10:45-48.

Wise, Carroll A.—The Place of Clinical Training in the Department of Pastoral Theology. (Spring 1951) J. Past. Care 5:46-52.

Withrow, Carlos Q.—A Study of the Possible Correlation Between Theological Orientations and Certain Variables of Personality. (Doctoral Dissertation, Univ. of Southern California, 1960) (D.A. XXI, 1651, 1960).

Wood, Leland F.—The Training of Ministers for Marriage and Family Counseling. (1950) Marr. Fam. Liv. 12:46-47, 50.

Woodroofe, Robert W.—Selection of Candidates for the Ministry. (1952) J. Past. Care 5, No. 4:23-28.

Wynn, John C. and James J. Hunt—Experiment in the Use of a Family Casework Agency as a Training Source for Pastoral Counseling. (Nov. 1962) Marr. Fam. Liv. 24:381-383.

Zane, M. D. and R. J. Campbell—Course on Psychiatry for Physicians. (1962) N. Y. J. Med. 62:3430-3434.

Zimmerman, J. S.—Christian Theological Approach to Clinical Pastoral Training. (1953) J. Past. Care 7, No. 2:59-76.

Chapter 6

The Practicing
Professional (Counselor)

Introduction: General Observations

Although, as we have stated, our research project originated in a desire to improve the teaching of counseling for the professions, it early became clear that a very significant part of our study must center on the counselor (this chapter) and the client (Chapter 7). To a considerable degree the professional school could not rightly chart what to teach and how to teach it until it understood the actual practice of the professional and the felt needs of the counselor and his counselee.

In early interviews and in shaping the questionnaires we found that to study a professional person one must gauge for each (and the questionnaire-interviews and coding were so planned): 1) Training of professional, 2) Composition of practice, 3) Self image, 4) Mythology or professional image, 5) Counseling practice, 6) Attitude and relation to other professions, 7) Definition of counseling, 8) Client relation and satisfaction, 9) Psycho-socio dynamics involved.

It can easily be seen that portions of even the counselor's questionnaire-interview responses do not primarily belong in the present chapter. Those relating to (1) and (4) have appeared in Chapter 5; the definitions of counseling (7) are

149

in Chapters 3 and 5; client relations and satisfaction (8) enter into Chapter 7; the attitude and relation to other professions (6) are in Chapters 2 and 8; and socio-psycho dynamics (9) constitute Chapter 9. This means that practice composition (2), self image (3) and counseling practice (5) make up the bulk of the present chapter.

It is considered that an exact statistical analysis of the IBM cards prepared from the questionnaires and interviews and checked to chi-squares for significant correlation is not so important for present purposes as drawing the picture of the modal lawyer, clergyman or doctor, from this data. This is partly due to our failure to get replies from as large a percentage of practitioners as we should like for an adequate sociometric pattern and also to the lack of clear proof or rejection of many hypotheses. In the Appendix is the questionnaire form and the coding device we employed to score both the questionnaires and interviews. The order, number and exact wording of the questions differed slightly from profession to profession, and even for different groups in a profession. They all contained the same content and effect and we have used only one sample form, set of questionnaire numbers and code in this chapter. Reference in this report will not use the code numbers but will refer to the question numbers when it is believed desirable for checking the point made. (As pointed out in Chapter 4 on method, two IBM cards were used per subject; the card punch square numbers were correlated with the questionnaire question numbers, card one not being *italicized,* card two being *italicized, e.g. 35*). Many observations will be an amalgam of several questions or the interplay of several answers.

How Question Interplay Yields Valuable Insights:

We have previously noted that interplay of questions often will produce major insights—conflicts, uncertainties, defenses, anxieties, unconscious processes. Some of these will be discussed as they are evidenced in a particular profession. For example, one of these will be inconsistencies between questions #2, 3, 4, 5, 25, 33, 33a, 33b, 21a, and #9 on training.* Another will be between questions #30, 31a and #8, 8a, 8b, 20b, 20f, 24, 35, 9b, 10a, 22, 23, 23a, etc., on psychology and religion.

A few samples will now be given of interplays of questions which proved rewarding (we have IBM'd thousands of interplays and by actuarial formula there are upwards of 150,000 that might be useful; most of these will in fact turn out to show *nil* correlation and therefore be unimportant). We checked our correlations not only statistically but by interviews:

> Positive answers to questions #8, 10, 22, 24b, 24c, 33a were correlated to a favorable attitude to psychology and psychiatry. Negative replies did not adequately correlate with negative attitude except that #22 showed a high correlation.

> Positive replies to #8, 20c, 24b, 24c, 33a, 33b and negative to #7, 29, 33 coincided with a non-directive orientation.

> A combination of various questions (here illustrated by 30-35b) showed a continuum of response which marked a person as viewing himself as narrow "technician", balanced "professional", or broad "imperialist":

Question	Technician	Professional	Imperialist
30	Agree	Agree	?
30a	Agree	Disagree	Disagree
31	Disagree	?	Agree
31a	Disagree	Disagree	?
32	Agree	?	Agree
32a	Agree	Disagree	Disagree
32b	Agree	Disagree	Disagree
33 (see below)			

Note: Where it is important to identify subdivisions of questions, we use a), b), c), etc.; otherwise we use only the question number to identify the whole question.

34	Agree	Agree	Disagree
35	Disagree	Disagree	Agree
35a	Disagree	Disagree	Agree
35b	Disagree	Disagree	Agree

Similarly, questions 33, 33a, 33b could be made to show a directive to non-directive continuum:

Question	Directive	Non-directive
33	Disagree	Agree
33a	Agree	Disagree
33b	Agree	Disagree

(It can be seen how this permits comparison of doctors, lawyers, psychiatrists, clergymen, others).

We also constructed continuums from question interplay and open ended replies on how one views himself as to items like these:

1. Efficiency, Energy, Forcefulness, Seriousness, Industry.
2. Maturity, Sureness, Egocentricity, Tenseness, Submissiveness.
3. Judgment, Can be counted on, Trusts others, Gullibility.
4. Interesting, Clever, Awkward, Suspicious, Angered.
5. Warm and close relations with others; Feels common ties and basic goals with others; Recognizes and considers feelings, intentions, motives of others; Too conscious of own problems—tries to get ahead by belittling others; Can't stand to be wrong; Distant and cold relations with others; Left out of things, doesn't belong.

Still another interplay of questions testing a hypothesis can be used by way of illustration. We hypothesized that those showing authoritarian, managerial-administrative, wealth orientations would basically accept societal mores and institutions and line up with authority. They would not be largely involved in counseling, in criminal, family, or adjustment matters, or with the "weak" in society. On the other hand the reform, change, sensitive types would seek out counseling, live through the criminal's rebellion against society, aid and counsel the weak, feel for the family, etc.:

> An interplay of questions #3, 4, 5, 6, 12, 20f, 26, 29c, 31a, 33b and cases A,B,C, seemed to substantiate this hypothesis.

Again, we were able to trace the effect of training and general human interest on counseling attitudes:

> The greater the training in counseling the more aware was the counselor of his limitations as shown by #8, 9, 10, 11, 21, 22, 26, 28, cases "A" and "B".

> Those who accept counseling as a major part of their role (#2-5) are more accepting of and adequate with emotionally disturbed patients (#9, 11, 30, 33), are sympathetic to psychiatry and psychology (#10, 20, 22, 29c, 35) and do not worry about cost and time (#6-7).

> Positive replies to #20c, d, e, 35, 35a, b, and negative #32, 32a, 32b almost invariably indicated an integrative or "whole man" approach and the opposite responses a particularistic one.

> Those showing a yes-yes and thought out answer to the "why" of #21, 22, 23, appeared open and non-defensive to the whole human side of counseling; the yes-no answer indicated willingness to be taught, some questioning of psychiatry; the no group checked out as most defensive and closed.

> The professional indicating more outside and community interests (#12) did more general counseling (#30, 31, 35, 35a) and took a more active role (#24, 25, 27).

Preliminary Observations as to Responses
of the Professionals:

Who are our repliers and non-repliers and what does their overall handling of the questionnaire show? Regretfully we have to report that try as we would our repliers are not a cross-section. They are the younger men, practicing in smaller offices (or parishes) or the older men in non-metropolitan practice (we got the extremes, not the middle). Jews, proportionate to their number were our best respondents and most sophisticated. Those most interested in psychology and counseling tended to reply. The better established (firms, business lawyers, preaching ministers, "Park Avenue" psychiatrists), did not respond and substantially denied counseling when interviewed. In spite of this, through interview, spot checking and extensive discussion with those most knowledgeable on counseling in the communities, we did get an accurate picture of the whole scale.

Little effort went into some questionnaire fill-outs. On the mechanics of the profession—time spent, type of client, fees, etc.—the responses were extensive. Questions that went deepest were more often left blank, or on a few occasions caused incoherent or over-responsive answers. Each profession strongly resented another profession or calling invading its field of competence, while admitting no clean cut division in problems presented. The respondent became defensive when any question implied lack of competence or omniscience. Certain responses, on time devoted, free work, questions of advice, seemed stereotyped. The tentative definitions of counseling were often accepted without much discrimination; some redefined counseling (the clergy did most often). There was a tendency of respondents to a) separate themselves from the questioner and b) from counseling. Expressed or implied in many instances was the concept that the only counseling was "marriage counseling"—an indication of how a popular and stereotype view can preempt the field. A whole series of escapes, evasions, defensive attitudes appear —emphasis on free work, apology for fee or pressure of time, pride in not charging, etc. Even those conscientiously trying to answer most questions started out strong and gradually weakened: *strong* on training and composition of practice; *reducing* on self, his profession or other profession image; *strenghtening* again as to client relationship and satisfaction. The lawyer was aware of traps set for him in the questionnaire and frequently wrote over answers in an attempt to keep logical consistency, the clergy and doctors less so.

We are cognizant that our survey and questionnaire have only scratched the surface at many points. Take the relation of some of the questionnaire items, which Talcott Parsons would call "social system variables" or alternate rules of societal interpersonal behavior. "Religion" may be used to demonstrate what we mean. Even the very roughest category of religious affiliation showed a correlation with counseling and counseling practices. But "religion" is a very nondiscriminating category. Where we could (interviews) we tried to expand it into sub-topics like religious orientation, practices, role, belief structure (reason, will, judgment, ethics, moral laws, nature of man, spiritual reality, human and divine, etc.). Religion, wherever we found it and in whatever detail, revealed much. For example, the Catholic lawyer is more universal, Protestant less so, Jewish most humanitarian. The religious lawyer's (and to some extent, doctor's) referral route is to minister-priest rather than psychiatrist-marriage counselor. The variations from the modal or characteristic response patterns are more frequently due to religion than to any other factor (except sex). Christian professionals seem more optimistic about success (question 11) than do Jewish professionals. Even where the professional answers that religion of counselor and counselee are *not* important, he demonstrates that they are in fact important as to orthodoxy, puritanism, liberalism, optimism, individualism, activism, emotionalism, inevitability, predestination, marriage, money, work, other values, in the process of giving the rest of his answers. We use this to illustrate the extensive amount of research needed on the professions and counseling. We really examined only the Protestant-Catholic-Jewish-None breakdown of data, and this as to only some factors of counseling. Yet we found great significance. Further study is needed as to the other religious subtitles set forth above—and many more.

A similar research dimension is sex. We correlated only the most obvious interrelations of sex of counselor and counselee. We could determine that both men and women clients preferred male counselors (even in the case of doctors and clergy) but our questionnaire was too explorative to determine finer variables and why. We also found that though news articles and their own "counseling" journals emphasized the role of doctors and clergymen as counselors and few lay people mentioned lawyers as counselors whom they sought, the fact was that lawyers were the chief counselors of men and were seen by them as more nearly fulfilling the requirements of reality counseling (as compared to psychoanalysis) and therefore performing an essential role. In pragmatic, hard-headed consideration of all the multiple factors the lawyers rated high, though relatively unsophisticated psychologically and needing additional training.

At the end of this chapter as a "Supplement" are set forth a few typical quotes, for each profession, from answers to the open ended questions of the questionnaire, so that the reader may more fully appraise the approach of our respondents and the type of questionnaire material in addition to straight question answers which we had available.

We have already cautioned that our questionnaire data was limited and reflected a self-selection process. We tried to correct this in all communities and for each profession by two processes: interviews and check out for the most obvious factors (age, sex, type practice, rating, etc.) through professional lists. In the statistics which follow we have primarily reflected our questionnaire-interview data but have corrected it from the other sources where found inaccurate due to the selective process.

The Modal Lawyer

In vital statistics the modal lawyer is male, 48.4 years old (questionnaire lawyers averaged 39 years old—true

cross-section about 48 years old), married, with young and
teenage children, Protestant. His sports-hobbies are active,
his organizations social, his intellectual interests limited. He
practices in urban-metropolitan areas, rates himself as a
"general" practitioner, devotes 1/3 of his time to counseling,
primarily with married business men and housewives in the
35-40 year age group and on business-financial and family
problems. His normal charge is $20-25 per hour but he does
about 1/5 of his work free. His sessions average 1/2 to 1
hour and he sees each client 3 to 5 times per year. Almost
without exception he prefers to work with the group he does
in fact work with and feels he has the greatest success in
such group. He has less success with young and more success with older people. His appraisal of his own success in
counseling is far from modest: 60-70% of his cases solve
the problem, 20-30% show some improvement, 10-20% remain unchanged and only 5-10% get worse; he is confident
they would not do as well on their own.

Few lawyers (less than 5%) have had any training in
counseling or have undergone psychoanalysis. It is precisely
in the recognition of the ideal or norm in counseling and
thereafter in revelation of his own attitudes and practices
that the lawyer shows his greatest ambivalence. He refuses
to be a mere technician, allowing others to do the counseling
and then tell him what to do (#32a, 32b).* He states that
he does (#2, 3, 4, 5) and should (#25, 33, 33a, 33b) counsel,
that one should have professional training in counseling
(#21a) and be different from a "friend" (#28b), that
counseling is best defined as one with superior competence
advising a less competent (#20a), and he reacts favorably
to a series of questions dealing with trained competence in
the field (#8, 20e, 24, 25, 26, 27, 29, 29b, 29c, and the series
30-37); yet he admits having no such training (#9) and reveals by his answers that he does not know what such train-

* This is the form in which reference to questions on the questionnaire, from which our conclusions are drawn, will appear.

ing would be. He sees no need for psychoanalysis (#22) and has not been psychoanalyzed (#10). Our lawyer entered counseling because it is "a part of the profession" (#12), rates simple professional training and experience (#9b, 12), interest in others and empathy (#12) as his best counseling qualifications. The modal lawyer feels capable of handling emotional (#30)** or moral (#31) problems, attempts to ascertain the unconscious process at work in clients (#8a) and self (#8b), acts as an adviser on human relations (#20f), and judges that lawyers do give psychological and extra-legal aid (#20b, 24, 35). Nevertheless, his attitude toward psychology is distinctively negative (#9b, 10 22). He does not feel lawyers should practice *any* psychology (#35***cf. 35c), he relies heavily on "intuition" (#29b), and does not refer to psychological principles in getting at the unconscious (#8c). He sees no relationship of religion to counseling (#23, 23a)—but immediately reveals in his own answers how central religion is.

The ideal counselor is described as actively interested (#25), emotionally uninvolved (#26), fitting counseling to the client (#29), possessing flexibility, tact and understanding (#20e), different from a friend (#28b). Yet the lawyer is quite uncertain about the matter of emotion: emotional involvement destroys objectivity (#26b) but he does become emotionally involved (#26c); he thinks clients expect more than objectivity and he responds (#27a, b);

** Astonishingly, after answering yes to #30 for "emotional disturbances . . . . I feel competent", most of our respondents agree in the very next question #30a that "emotionally disturbed clients need more help than I can give." Psychologists would call this second guessing or delayed defensiveness. Realizing that he has gone too far in trying to measure up to a role he would like to meet but cannot, the hang-over of ambivalence shows itself in the next answer.

*** Again here in #35 he sees it as wrong for the lawyer to practice psychology but by the time he has been conditioned by four gradation questions, at #35c he recognizes that problems are so intertwined as to render psychological counseling necessary.

emotional problems do not disappear with time (#30c);
he does not know whether to handle emotional problems or
not (#30, 30a, 30b); he sees nothing difficult in counseling
a friend (#28).

The modal lawyer is fairly directive: active interest
gets more votes than professional detachment (#25); the
largest number limit themselves to advice requested but a
substantial group give unsolicited advice and probe beyond
the stated problem (#24a, b, c), often cross-examining the
client (#8); our lawyer favors definitions of counseling
involving "advice" and shies away from "helping the client
to develop his own pattern or orientation" (#20a-f); he
does not favor merely listening with interest (#33) but
wants to *discuss* cause and effect and to *reassure* the client
(#33a, 33b); he is convinced the client selects him for his
superior knowledge (#29a).

The lawyer is quite defensive of his own profession:
law problems are too difficult for any but lawyers (#32)
yet he tries to picture lawyers as capable in other disciplines
(see above). He might himself be willing to be interviewed
but he would not tape a counseling session, even with client
permission (#38a, b). He is unwilling to be classed as a
technician (#32b). He is resistive of the questionnaire as
a whole, structured, rather than open, fails to answer open
ended questions (#1, 5c, 8, 10, 12, 29c, 36—one exception is
#23). He is apologetic for counseling (#1-7) and for
training in counseling (#9, 21, 29c), while recognizing its
profound importance.

Lawyers do little referring (#34), though recognizing its
theoretical place (Case "A"), and are basically anti the
two other professions (#30-36). In case "A" most lawyers avoid the problem and say they would refer the client
to a psychiatrist, yet, because case "B" sounds in business
terms, nearly every respondent tries to handle it (as though
fully covered by legal rules).

Just as we did in the report on law schools it is important that we now free ourselves from the questionnaire

form and set forth some further observations about lawyers derived from the overall study:

A most interesting insight developed from the lawyer's view of counseling and its relation to fees and time. Counseling is viewed by the lawyer as what keeps his a "helping" profession. He can see taking fees for his legal skill or "performance." But is it proper to take pay for "helping"? The lawyer does have a "buy and sell" orientation and has always found it harder to charge for a conference than for a deed or will. But the lawyer needs to go back to the old legal saw that "advice is worth what you pay for it." The proof is now convincing that this is good counseling theory. The client who is charged for a therapy session feels he has received something: the non-fee session is forgotten. Even social agencies are therefore charging for sessions. The "fee" question has another aspect. How much you can charge is a test of rating in the profession. The lawyer respondents stated a high fee to show high rating. Then he seemed ashamed of his money grasping and gave an estimate of the free work he performed which checked out in interview as too high. Thus he satisfied his "high rating" and also an "altruistic" image.

Lawyers differ as to the form of practice. The "firm" lawyer worries less about where the next case comes from, seeks advancement in the firm and prestige in the profession. He finds it less desirable and profitable to counsel. He gets his status and satisfaction from colleague rating. The "solo" lawyer does those things that will cultivate contacts (e.g. politics), seeks clients and fees, tends to take an active interest in clients' affairs and do more counseling.

So also, lawyers' counseling practices vary with the social class counseled. As we have pointed out, we assumed that, being part of the upper classes, it would be easier therein for the lawyer to establish the rapport necessary to "shared" or "interrelational counseling" according to psycho-social theory. But for some reason most lawyers of upper-class clients seem to abrogate this role and become mere representatives or legal interpreters for decisions these clients have already made. There appears to be a great deference for or desire to be a part of this upper class. With clients from the lower class, in theory it should be hard to establish rapport. But the lawyer does almost without exception as he counsels in a directive, advice giving, persuasive, power-yielding way. It almost seems that a parent-child, authority-subordinate relationship is expected and meets the need. The above observation indicates in part why lawyers are authoritarian, directive, parental in their counseling image, and in the image that most of our client respondents had of them.

Lawyers are greater manipulators of social persons and power than doctors and clergymen. As power-holders they have more alternatives open to them in counseling and moving in and out of counseling to bargain, reconcile, force (sue), etc. On the whole, lawyers seem to achieve in a large proportion of cases a realistic resolution of conflicts. They draw on community resources for domestic pacification and contribute to the stability of expectations which people have about one another.

Law has long recognized the great lawyer not as the one bound by stereotyped rules but as the one who senses all of the subjective-intuitional factors bearing on the application of the law. He is, above all, pragmatic. He is middle-of-road. He is a student of multiple cases of unique shadings. The lawyer responses on the questionnaires and in interviews show this. He has less extremes than the clergyman or the psychiatrist. He relies heavily on intuition, which was defined as unverbalized or semi-conscious knowledge and accumulated learning, used in sorting out facts, evaluating problems and counseling. It rounds off the sharp corners, is skeptical about the too pat, the absolute. Current theories and research on counseling show that it is the "happy mean" that assures best counseling. One can discover this on the questionnaire. The hypothesis would be that use of intuition should increase from facts, to problem evaluation, to counseling. It does for the *non*-extremists, whereas the extremists do not show this. The total questionnaire responses show that lawyers recognize the best lawyers as those who are learning that intuition does operate, who seek to bring its use out of the semi-conscious to the conscious, who systematize and use intuition in a creative fashion, who thus become neither wild intuitionists nor "compulsives," hiding behind repetitive rules—in short, who become the "happy mean." [In fact, one can see much of the frustration the lawyer shows in answering the questionnaire as precisely because of this attempt to be pragmatic. He rebels at the ideal, the expectations, the assumed need for training, the very absoluteness of the questionnaire].

The lawyer having lost out in wealth, prestige or social status to religion and medicine (and engineering, business and the sciences), clings to legal counseling for its professional "oldness" and "learned" quality. For the three old professions were the ones the public looked to for general, not merely technical, knowledge. The lawyer's outlet tends toward social service, the doctor's toward psychiatry, the clergyman's toward pastoring. The self claim of the legal profession, in which counseling plays a large part, is very extensive: that it is a way of harmonizing all values in society—correcting overindulgence of one value (*e.g.* wealth) or overdeprivation of another (*e.g.* affection in marriage).

Lawyers indicated that they knew little of the literature on interviewing and counseling, yet surprisingly they showed a sensitivity to many of the recognized indices of facilitators and inhibitors of good interviewing, counseling and interrelating. They mentioned: *sex* of client and counselor; *biography*, personal history, class, economics, socio-economic variables of each; variety of *motivation; expectancies* clients bring to interviews and reshaping these; degree to which the counselor holds actual client up to an "ideal" client: extent and effect of feeling *boredom*, folly of client or client's problem; client's *distortion* of data; *voice* and *verbal* clues, semantic difficulties and differences; *levels of anxiety*, hostility, defensiveness, dependency, guardedness, openness, resistance, etc., and the degree to which one communicates these back and forth; frequency with which client or counselor causes change in topic; ambiguity of counselor and client "behavior" and perception of behavior; interpretive compared to supportive aid; etc.

The attorney has often been thought of as paying much attention to his office and other physical settings for interviewing and counseling. But, we found both in questionnaire and interview that the lawyer placed nowhere near as high as emphasis on this as did doctors, psychiatrists and particularly clergymen (one psychologically bent lawyer who explained the meaning and effect of his coat-of-arms behind his desk to the contrary notwithstanding). Many did not even have their diplomas or certificates of admission to the bar framed.

It is increasingly clear that counseling and ability therein is a function of personality more than of the "school" of counseling to which one belongs or the pattern and techniques one employs. Psychology has established types of personality and has posited that the acceptive, non-directive, non-authoritarian makes the best psychological or psychiatric (psychoanalytic) counselor. Much difficulty, we believe, has arisen from an assumption that all counselors should be in the mold of psychiatrists. Theology, we have pointed out, made this error by going all-out in training clergyman-counselors in mental hospitals and under psychiatrists. Our study and that of some others show that there is (and should be) a different function of counseling and a different ideal counselor in each profession, the characteristics of a good general counselor being: personally function effectively, accurately perceive himself and others, be reality oriented, hold a recognized leadership position, possess broad subject matter coverage and adaptability.

Lawyers may very well, therefore, have to define their counseling competence, their approach, their type of personality within the total pattern of good counseling but differing from the other professions. The following observations are taken from the questionnaires and interviews as suggestive:

a) Lawyers are generally skeptical, extroverted, authoritarian, tough-minded, directive. Psychologic counselors are often defined as tender, open minded, introverted, flexible, altruistic. Legal *counseling* may be the area of overlap.

b) Our lawyer respondent shows no desire to and should not become an amateur psychiatrist. He wants to stay away from psychiatric disorders—they make bad clients. He seeks the unconscious, but no one of the respondents suggests using dream analysis, projection tests or free association. Exposure to psychiatry is only to increase awareness and remove blocks.

c) There are acceptable and unacceptable topics for legal counseling. The lawyer keeps insisting he is a counselor *at law,* not just any old counselor. He is "legalistic," not "moralistic" or "healthistic." A client who frames his problem in legal, right, logical terms, he will serve. One who wants Freud can go to a head-shrinker.

d) The lawyer tends to measure success by this one case or problem—not the overall movement of the client (unresolved problems, adjustments). He seeks a short range, compassable goal.
Because of his training with "cases" a lawyer responds well to any problem that can be laid out as a case. The response of lawyers to cases "A" and "B" on the questionnaire revealed this compared to the other professions. If he is to be a good counselor he needs to frame a "case" out of the typical rambling remarks of counselees. He

tends to start where the client is, with his stated problem and expectations—not to assume that getting deeply beneath the stated problem is necessary. This fits well with certain modern psychological theory (Wolpe, Eysenck) that treatment of symptoms sets conditions in operation which tend to remove the deeper causes.

e) The lawyer fits well into some modern theories that counseling is different from therapy—that mere listening is unsatisfactory, that ventilating solves nothing and leaves the client more depressed, that the client wants something *done*, that the lawyer's tendency to *do* something (almost anything) is good counseling.

f) Yet the attorney is not taken in by the client. He does not look at the problem solely through the client's eyes. He examines it from the perspective of the third party, judge, society. Far more than the other professions he interviews others and makes external investigations.

g) The lawyer is often criticized for his "one interview" or few interview technique. Yet this may be a strength of legal counseling, for much modern research (Frank) has indicated that even therapy can achieve astonishingly good results in a few sessions if this expectancy is communicated to the patient.

h) Unlike psychiatrists and clergymen, lawyers do not specialize on the counseling dimension (only 2 lawyers listed themselves as counseling specialists). They engage in counseling, if at all, for whatever problems they handle otherwise.

i) The lawyer maintains a peculiar balance between remaining aloof and participating in the client's affairs. He insists he is a professional and separates himself off from the client even more than a psychiatrist (treats the client as a "case," "*they* want sympathy," "*they* want advice"). Yet he is traumatized at deep levels by the client (the cases which the respondents submit so show). David Riesman, on seeing how some of the lawyers handled the cases, entitled his observations "Beyond the Call of Obvious Duty," see Freeman, Legal Interviewing and Counseling, p. 65.

j) Even the above indicates a nice attempt to merge the counselor and counselee approaches. Other studies, as well as ours, show the counselor prefers ideation or content, the counselee usually wants emotional-interpersonal relationship.

k) There is much indication that lawyers primarily counsel men and as such meet a need; clergy and doctors (psychiatrists) mainly counsel women. The reasons for this are many.

l) Within the legal field counseling has varied characteristics based on the nature of the problem (business, marital, criminal, neurotic), and on the type of client. Lawyers represent more and different "images" in the client's eyes than do doctors, psychiatrists, marriage counselors, social workers or clergymen. The lawyer may have to play the role of "heroic leader," "parental substitute," protest absorber, confessor, comforter, law enforcer, champion, facilitator.

m) Lawyers do undertake a role generally criticized by psychiatrists—the "cast all on me," "go home and forget it" reassurance of the client. In terms of counseling, of people who are "normal" and not sick this checks out as a legitimate position. True, this avoids deep analysis, yet it may relieve anxiety and support the client on a problem that seems huge to him, but easy to handle for the lawyer.

The Modal Clergyman

Because some of the general observations with regard to lawyers have drawn comparison with the clergy, because certain approaches are revealed by our study to be common to the several professions and because a section comparing the counseling of these professions follows the separate analysis of law, theology and medicine, this section will be much shorter than that on law.

The modal clergyman is urban, male, about 45 years of age (the repliers averaged 38), married, Protestant, with a medium sized family of young children. [Few Catholic clergy replied—far smaller percentage than Catholic lawyers and doctors]. The clergyman's organizations are church and community, his hobbies active, his interests social and international issues. He entered the ministry because of "altruism," a "calling," or "interest in and relationship with people."

The clergy were the most spontaneously cooperative with the questionnaires. A high percentage would be interviewed or tape a session. They responded most to open-ended questions. They re-defined counseling and outlined improvements in training they would like to see. It was primarily from the practicing clergy that we got the insight (which we shared with theological schools) that training with mentally sick (mental hospital) persons was not the best preparation for counseling normal or near-normal persons in the stream of society.

The clergyman's percentage of counseling is high (45% of his time). It is even higher when we consider the percentage of ministers who do substantial amounts of counseling (90-95%). The minister has few men clients; sees, prefers and has greatest success with 25-50 year old women. His is the only profession to list special (adequate) training in counseling (about 50% did) and to rate this and empathy his highest counseling qualifications. The problems he deals with are predominantly family, marital, spiritual, but one

is impressed with the extreme variety of problems he reports. He does about half his counseling in his study and
half elsewhere (homes, hospitals). His sessions average
over 1 hour, he sees counselees about 6-7 times in a year.
He has five client attractions which neither the lawyer nor
doctor have—(1) he is known never to charge a fee (note:
some of the new church counseling centers do, to give the
same client seriousness found in psychiatric clinics); (2)
it is acceptable professional ethics—in fact it is expected—
that he seek out or "visit" his parishoners; (3) some form
of "confessional" with the therapy of ventilation and forgiveness is a recognized adjunct of much of the church.
(4) His job requires him to be involved at precisely the
points where counseling may be needed: at marriage, child
birth, death, in the home, upon moving to new location, etc.
(5) Sermons touch off or raise questions in parishioners'
minds and thus encourage seeking out the counselor.

Ministers revealed the most realistic appraisal of their
counseling success: problem solved 30%, some improvement
30%, remain unchanged 20%, become worse 20%. [It
should be *noted* that our study of counselees showed that
clergymen were client-rated highest in contribution to problem solution].

The average clergyman's practice is more closely in
harmony with his counseling ideal than is true in the other
professions. He would fit counseling to the client, remain
actively interested, recognize the unconscious in himself and
the client—and do this by accepted psychological techniques.
He is not ready to accept a "no-involvement" generalization,
though his general orientation is Rogerian or non-directive.
He goes to some length to point out the differences between
unconscious or improper over-involvement (to satisfy one's
own needs) and proper religious, love, agapé involvement
which meets the clerical image of spiritual concern each-in-
the-other and the "church family" giving support and assurance. Within this re-definition he keeps himself reasonably professional. He seems to know his limitations on

medical, emotional and legal problems and maintains an active and fairly unstereotyped referral service.

Our study confirmed one point raised in several articles —that clergymen use their sermons for "group counseling." There are strong doubts on the part of many whether this is proper, or therapeutically sound. There is some attempt to fit counseling into the total concept of the church—to establish the abundant life, create a community of believers, achieve societal concern, lead youth, even the outside community, preach the good news, etc. The clergy speak of their continuing problem of properly interpreting their counseling function to the church community, which often doubts the propriety of this psychological work.

Your researcher was not prepared for another conclusion which came from the survey material. The minister does not seem to include as a proper part of counseling the aiding of parishioners to get a total or religious orientation for life or to cause a person's religious beliefs and faith to grow and mature. He does not, in short, view counseling as teaching. He leaves this to sermons, literature, "religious education," work with youth in classes, etc. Only the handling of a specific set of problems is treated as counseling. There is a tendency to distinguish between pastoral care (pastoral calls, officiating at weddings, funerals, help in finding a job, ministration in normal situations) and pastoral counseling (a more direct, intensive attempt to change behavior, focused on specific problems and scheduled for specific hours). One is impressed how specialized and compartmentalized the ministry has become.

A clergyman's clientele is stratified, but perhaps not so much so as attorneys'. The stratification comes about more from the location of the parish than from self selection. In the average to large city about one-half are blue collar. There is more diversity in the middle bracket church than in a comparable law office. In smaller communities both lawyers and clergymen tend to serve a cross section. The counseling clergyman is less free than others to select his counselees, to terminate his relationship, to devote his full time to a few individuals, to isolate counseling from religious terminology and association (which may themselves be part of the counselee's problem).

The clergyman is more cognizant of his part in the network of doctors, lawyers, social agencies, police, etc., which constitutes the social or deviant control system of the community than would have been expected. He works out matters with, takes referrals from and sends referrals to all these.

This profession has a high "acceptance of others" tolerance related to its philosophy of the nature of man that is a positive factor in empathy and counseling. It also possesses one of the highest catharsic factors—confession before a higher power; the element of pre-existing general faith (whereas the psychiatrist has to struggle through many sessions to create faith in himself); and a general optimism or expectation of success. All these were recognized as important pluses for counseling. The clergy is partcularly successful with those who take a non-rational, emotional, and often supernatural approach, *e.g.* lower social class frequently in dealing with inability to secure necessities (job, good marriage, education, money, food). However, it still remains true that the minister, like other therapy or counseling media, gives less time and less full service to the lower economic person.

Partly because the clergyman is a continuing pastor of his flock and his schedule calls for periodic seeing of each other, he tends to give more extended and continuous counseling and therapy than does the lawyer or doctor (except psychiatrist).

In the more sophisticated church counseling service greater steps have been taken toward an interdisciplinary clinic than by any of the other professions. A large church marital or general counseling service will surely have social caseworkers, clinical psychologists and psychiatrist attached, and probably have a consulting attorney. Many counseling clergymen now hold advanced psychology, social work or psychiatry degrees and do engage in diagnosis and psychotherapy.

The cleric is most charitable to the other professions. He ranks them higher in prestige (but not in contribution to society); and, while his other answers show that he has reason to admit his own superior counseling training, he judges all three professions as equally delinquent in doing competent counseling.

On the whole, it would seem that the clergy constitute a good case-study in what can be achieved by professional schools assuming the obligation of testing for counselor potential and for training in counseling. I would rate the clergy as the best counseling profession.

The Modal Doctor

We developed one of our most difficult problems of reporting on a profession with regard to medicine. We found the doctors least cooperative, most baffled by the "why" of our research. Psychiatrists, who presumably knew most about the matters in which we were concerned did not rate themselves merely "counselors," though they objected to others less trained holding themselves out as such and though other doctors and patients considered them counselors. We early saw how much counseling the general practitioner (GP) did, but we noted it also in the internist, gynecologist, pediatrician and other specialists. How could we interrelate all these and tell a faithful story. General practitioners responded well; therefore the report is frankly dominated by GP's. We decided that this was fair and to let the statistics stand in total as giving predominance, with some overtones for psychiatry, to the general counseling we were examining in the other professions.

Our doctor is then 53.7 years old (respondents were 46.8), 93.6% married, 95.3% male, 94.2 religious (29% Protestant, 24% Catholic, 40% Jewish among our repliers). The GP accounts for 55% of the profession, works longer hours than the specialist (70% over 50 hours, 25% over 70 hours), sees more patients (20% more than 200 a week, 60% more than 100). All doctors concentrate on patients with above average income, the specialist more so. Two thirds of all doctors are age 40-60, 20% over 60 (the GP being in the low and high extreme).

To return to describing our modal doctor, he spent 3.2 years in undergraduate college, 4.0 years in medical school, 2.4 years in internships. He sees patients 9.3 times per year, gives about 25 minutes per session and charges (and collects) about $11.00 per call. He claims to do 30% free work. He lives and works predominately in an urban area (20-75,000 persons); a sizable 20% are in areas under 20,000. He entered the profession because he liked its image and is satisfied with his choice. More specifically family tradition, socio-economic standing, academic achievement and challenge, drive to be needed, liking to deal with people— these are what account for the choice. His sports and hobbies are sedentary, his children teenage and grown, his organizations professional, his other interests travel.

The counseling picture is something like: 35% of the doctor's work is viewed as counseling ("verbal or non-verbal advice, direction or guidance by a trained physician to a less knowledgeable person presenting a problem"). The doctor considers himself not specifically trained in counseling; he rates psychiatry as general professional training; he has not been psychoanalyzed and while giving a high rating to the total profession tends to be contemptuous of psychiatry (the psychiatrists to the contrary of course); general experience is his chief component of counseling. His counselees are predominantly women (twice the number of men) in the age bracket 25-50 (more than other ages combined); he prefers to work with women younger than himself and believes this is where he has success. He serves a predominantly middle class clientele. He, like the lawyer, has confidence in his ability—that 35% solve their problems, 45% show improvement, 15% remain unchanged and only 5% get worse—he admits that 15-20% might do as well on their own.

The doctor handles more "psychosomatic" than "physiological" ailments by nearly 10% and his counseling problems are mainly "personal," "family" and "marital." One senses in the answers a good deal of psychological jargon: "don't project own prejudices," "a good listener," "the healing profession is a supportive role," "helping the patient develop his own orientation," "treating the whole man," yet his attitude toward psychology and psychiatry is distinctly negative. The modal doctor says he does and should counsel. He should have professional counseling training (88%), but feels that he does not have (80% as to counseling, 65% as to interviewing). Strangely, the younger men did not seem better trained than the older ones. What training they have came from the army, psychiatry, post graduate psychology.

The doctor's ideal is to remain uninvolved (98%), for involvement destroys objectivity (90%), yet 50% do become involved against their will; 35% consider their actual attitude "detached," 50% "friendly sympathy" and 65% "active interest;" few would merely listen, and a large percentage (90%) see their role as one of reassurance. They try to meet the patient's expectation for something more than objective interest. They make less use of intuition than lawyers (though perhaps they use the word "experience" more). Seventy per cent say they attempt to recognize the unconscious in themselves and clients. How? In order the answers are: by questioning, experience, intuition, other means, psychological method.

Doctors are strong on referral (72% take active charge of referrals). They refer to psychiatrists more than to the clergy or lawyers or any other type counselor. Most feel (60%) incapable of dealing with emotionally disturbed patients, but 70% view themselves as competent to deal with moral-ethical problems (they think the religion of counselor-counselee is unimmportant). Doctors look upon clergymen as counselors (they believe that most people seeking counsel go to a clergyman or doctor), but they view lawyers as merely technicians. They are ambivalent as to their own operation in several fields: 25% thought they should counsel on non-medical problems, 45% thought they did, 50% believed they must (problems are so inter-twined). The medics hesitated to give their opinion on the sample cases; where there was a reply, referral was what was suggested; almost no doctors submitted typical cases of their own.

The psychiatrist group, as might be expected, showed an extremely high degree of training; defined the ideal in most accepted psychological terms; and showed their practice as conforming thereto. An unusual development was that the psychiatrist did not view what he was doing as counseling (it was therapy) and yet he thought of himself as the only one trained to counsel. Actually, when one studied the psychiatrist replies and the client responses, the problems actually taken to the private psychiatrist (compared to those attached to mental hospitals and clinics) were much the same as those taken to lawyers, clergymen. The psychiatrist was generally working in the same field of "normal" or near normal people and in the same upper income group as the lawyer or clergyman. The psychiatrist's method was different. And the end sought was more the adjustment of the individual to himself than adjusting him to society. It seemed to this researcher, however, more nearly counseling than true psychoanalysis. The psychiatrist group averaged a later age for entering the specialty; few had chosen it originally; a large percentage had emotional disturbances of their own and, having been analyzed, shifted to psychiatry.

On the whole, the ambivalence and contradiction of the doctors was about the same nature as that of lawyers. The doctors had their own clientele (more women), their own approach (sugar pills and placebos), their own method out of the problem (referrals to psychiatrists) and their own attraction and competence in counseling. They, like their professional schools, were more resistive to the study and questionnaire than any of the other professions, and were particularly defensive to any suggestion of lack of competence (yet, strangely, their answers showed the highest feelings of inadequacy and lack of success).

General Comparisons Between the Modal Lawyer, Doctor, and Clergyman

There are a great number of striking similarities between the responses of the three professions. All are overwhelmingly male, married, Protestant, without psychoanalysis, treat the middle class and middle aged (law predominates with men, clergy and doctors with women), show little energy in responding to open-ended questions, feel that very few clients show slight improvement, become worse, or remain unchanged. All try to get at the unconscious in their clients, agree that emotional problems need more help that they are capable of giving, but feel able to handle moral problems, while opining that a counselor ought not to practice in an area outside his specialization. They believe that the counselor should demonstrate active interest without becoming emotionally involved, that counseling should be fitted to the client, that counselors should have professional training in counseling, that the counselor should be different from a friend. All would counsel a friend, would help in selecting someone more competent, agree that the counselor helps re-orient the client, feel that emotional involvement destroys objectivity, agree that clients expect more than objective interest and that flexibility, tact, and understanding are important to the counselor. All three professions admit that each counsels in fields primarily other than his own (but, from other statements, imply that this is not a desirable situation), feel that emotional problems do not disappear in time, and are most clear about leaving legal problems to lawyers.

Our study shows an interesting circle of cause and result. The more counseling done, the more the professional feels at home in counseling, the more experience he acquires, the more counseling he will undertake or retain. Legal protection of confidentiality of communications is still one of the major counseling advantages of law, medicine, religion. Definition of the protection and knowledge of its limits were usually fuzzy.

In a very broad general sense our respondent professional sensed that to be successful in counseling he had to articulate: a) *who am I,* the counselor? — really what kind of a person in the eyes of others and in my own eyes; b) *who is my client?* as I see him, as others do, as he sees himself; c) *what do I do?* advise, inform, decide, take over, implement; d) *how do I do it?* what skills. The lawyer seemed weakest on items (a) and (b). The clergyman seemed stronger on (a) and (b) and least certain on (d). The doctor seemed to concentrate on (b) and (d) and be weak on (a) and particularly (c).

There was general agreement that of necessity the counselor "intervenes" and is the "active" one—setting the appointment and time, terminating, questioning, recommending, advising. The more sophisticated well gauged their time patterns in the interviewing-counseling process—that 15% of interview time was empathizing, 35% information getting, about 15% appraisal, 20% advising, guiding, applying, 5% hypothesizing, planning and 10% terminating; that the largest block composed "understanding." They were aware that personality and behavior was content to be analyzed, that unconscious values impinged on counseling and that the counselor was lopsided in having only his own memory of an interview instead of a verbatim report.

A number of important and revealing dissimilarities between the professions must also be noted. The residency of the three types is different. The clergy are the youngest group, the doctors are oldest. Only the clergy reply that they have had special training in counseling, and they actually do the most counseling. While it is reasonable that the clergy should list a predominance of spiritual problems, and lawyers a predominance of business problems, it is surprising that doctors list family problems as more frequent than physiological. The clergy appear to give the most time to their clients, the doctors least. Only the clergy were willing to tape an interview, although about the same proportion in each profession agreed to be interviewed.

It is interesting that while doctors and lawyers state that they are most successful with the type of client that comes to them most frequently, this is true to a somewhat less extent for the clergymen. This could imply a greater contentment and feeling of accomplishment for the lawyers and the doctors. It could also mean that lawyers and doctors are satisfied because they select their clients while the clergy's clients are assigned to them as part of the job. Lawyers are by far the most optimistic concerning their successes. It could be speculated that legal problems are more readily solved than medical or spiritual-moral ones. Finally, while the lawyers give no age difference for type of client with whom they are most and least successful, both the doctors and clergy suggest they are more successful with younger than older people (this may be interrelated to the male-female client dimension).

We may also note the tendency for each profession to be somewhat egotistical concerning the value of its own services. All three show a strong distaste for psychology, and particularly psychoanalysis despite the fact that they admit to counseling beyond mere advice, etc. The modal lawyer, interestingly enough, is the only counselor to disagree with the statement that a lawyer should be consulted only after other interests of the client are determined. On the other hand, the modal clergyman is the only counselor to give a strong "yes" to the importance of the counselor's, and client's religion. Again, he is the only counselor to agree that all problems have moral-religious issues, and it would not be unlikely if he would object strongly to the statements of the other counselors that they feel able to handle moral problems, just as it would not be improbable for the lawyer to object to any legal advice the others might give. [Note: A psychologist might shake his head sadly at the home-made "probings" of all three professions]. Each profession rates itself as first in its contribution to society; but drops itself lower (sometimes below the objective ratings) regarding prestige; and still lower on wealth or economic well-being.

What other short comparative generalizations should be made?

1) There is a clear referral route within a profession, medical GP to psychiatrists; general lawyer to marital lawyer; general clergy to counseling clinic. There is also an interdiscipline route; it is M.D. to lawyer; clergy to psychiatrist; lawyer to clergy.

2) Such items as religion, age, type of school attended, community in which practice, class of clients, have more to do with counseling than the usually mentioned factors.

3) Almost all secular professional counselors— lawyers, doctors, psychiatrists, marriage counselors—compete for the same middle class clients. Clergy also serve here.

4) Clergy and special charities (social workers, legal aid, etc.) serve the lower economic groups to same degree.

5) It is quite clear that the counseling professions are rated differently by the professionals themselves and by clients. The professions use these tests: societal status, monetary rewards, security, service opportunities, social and activity pattern, professionalization or colleague cohesiveness, time spent and freedom possible, happiness, roots in the community. A good check is whether they would want their children to enter the profession. The client tests a professional by availability, social distance, emotional concern, time

accorded client and interest shown, competence, empathy, acceptance, and to some degree fees.

6) "Counseling" has unfortunately been so used in guidance and marriage counseling that our three old professions are apologetic for their counseling segment.

7) The counselor, in all professions, probably unconsciously sets the pattern of the relationship, and even the "facts" that come out, more than the client does. If a Freudian counselor, the client will gradually talk sex, libido, etc. If legalistic, the client shakes down to "provable" facts. If a minimum of 20 hours of "treatment" are scheduled, the client will see they are all used.

8) The counseling process is mainly relationship. Communication, motivation, the unconscious, transference and countertransference operate in all cases—whether recognized or not.

9) It tends to appear that the important elements in counseling by these professions are: similarities of counselor-counselee, formulation of client's problem, degree of motivation or stage of client as to his problem, expectations (role expectations) of client, acceptance and empathy, communication, commitment (length of time and and primacy to problem), and movement or change.

10) The evaluation of the client and the counselor will be different. Neither is to be wholly relied upon.

A Note on MARRIAGE COUNSELORS.

Although we studied marriage and other counselors for comparative purposes only, and have treated of these in Chs. 2 and 5 on developing professions, we shall not try to give a "modal" picture of any of these. We could point

out such data observations as these on marriage counselors
as a typical illustration:*

> Marriage counselors' basic "professions" appeared
> in this order—psychology, social work, religion, edu-
> cation medicine-psychiatry, sociology. Law was
> hardly mentioned.
> Most practiced solo (55%).
> About half (52%) would like to expand their marriage
> counseling, while 45% would not.
> The median amount of time devoted to marriage coun-
> seling was less than half time—15 hours per week.
> Marriage counselors placed great emphasis on the
> Masters' or PhD degree.
> Counselors were very ambivalent as to fees.
> They believed marriage counseling was a profession
> and should be given confidential protection.
> They considered themselves adequately trained.
> They did not view law, medicine (other than psy-
> chiatry) as adequate. They grudgingly recognized the
> clergy's right in marital and premarital counseling.
> They bemoaned their lack of social and economic
> status.
> They did not want more marriage clinics but wanted
> to achieve profitable private practice.
> In other regards they showed many of the features
> generalized as to counseling, above. They believed
> colleges should give marriage counseling training—
> emphasizing psychology, sociology and counseling
> method first, and then religious, medical, legal con-
> siderations. They strongly approved apprenticeships.
> They, like the three professions, would take charge of
> interviews.
> They were stronger on listening, not judging, helping

---

* Our general survey here was supplemented by a national study
of marriage counselors within the American Association of Marriage
Counselors.

the client solve his problem than the three professions, and avoided giving advice, information, issuing directives and making decisions.

They were far less moralistic or inclined to require religious orientation or happy family life as a prerequisite to counseling compared to the clergyman but more so than lawyers and medics.

Women were struggling for a place here and rated women as preferred counselors (though our client statistics were to the contrary).

Marriage counselors, in short, were most interesting to study as typical of an emerging specialty.

There are many other possible generalizations, both as to the three professions and other counseling services, which are suggested by our material. Many are omitted because adequately treated elsewhere in this book or in other publications and pieces of research, some of which we list in the annexed bibliography. Certain it is that more accurate and detailed studies of the professions and particularly the counseling function of each are seriously needed.

SUPPLEMENT

We have selected at random, 10 open ended replies for each profession, summarized these and paralleled them in three areas: (a) life, hobbies, etc., (b) counseling and training, (c) handling the "A" hypothetical case. The numbers in the left margin identify the respondents.

LAWYERS

Life, Hobbies, Associations, etc.

(1) Age 31 - Protestant, married: Born and happily raised in a small town. Now located in another. Happily married, 4 children. Enjoy hunting, fishing, camping—family sports. Active Rotary, Chamber of Commerce, Church.

(2)   36 - Jewish, single: Drama, local democratic party, cooking, jazz, skiing. Service clubs. Being single is a handicap.

(3)   43 - Protestant, married: 12 years district attorney, wonderful wife, Rotary Club, Red Cross, Community services, golf, politician, read extensively in philosophy, poetry, history, warden of church, work with local ministers in counseling.

(4)   50 - Protestant, married: Live on farm, 4 children, recreation family type (skiing, picknicking, swimming), absolutely bar TV, Chairman Rotary, Red Cross, Community Chest, Better Business Bureau, Church Board.

(5)   51 - Protestant, married: Live just outside large city, wife and 3 children. Leader in Boy Scouts, YMCA, Community Chest, Church. Active sports.

(6)   37 - Jewish, married: We have 3 young children, close family, belong to most civic and social clubs. Many hobbies from golf and fishing to reading and music.

(7)   50 - Protestant, married: Have splendid family, wife and 3 children, chose law as good life. Active in all civic projects. Active, forest conservation, hunting.

(8)   47 - Jewish, married: My hobbies are helping people and sports of all kinds. Served as children's court judge; lawyers better counselors than clergy who do not experience full life.

(9)   49 - Protestant, married: Interests—politics, ornithology, music, math, photography; Community Chest, YMCA, local and state bar, Masonic; married to head of Family Service Agency.

(10)   44 - Protestant, separated: cards, poker, golf.
Just my law is a place to make money.
Rotary, Red Cross, Chamber of Commerce.
Two children, wife has them.

Counseling, Teaching

(1) Age 31 - Protestant, married: Our letterhead says
"Counselors at Law", could be taught, can
be obtained through experience. Too much
"counselng"; people use us in the professions. Ministers better trained. Counseling should be frank, objective, not self
serving.

(2)   36 - Jewish, single: Counseling is a joke. Clients
seldom want to take steps to improve their
situation. They want sympathy—endow
layers with mystical abilities we don't
have. Counseling derives from human
experience.

(3)   43 - Protestant, married: Ministers are still
tied to puritanic concepts, medics see only
the physical. Lawyer has become the true
spiritaul adviser of modern man, broader
gauge. Teach counseling (philosophical,
psychological, social) and by supervised
experience.

(4)   50 - Protestant, married: There is a century
old office tradition against charging for
counseling. Important part of work, comes
from experience.

(5)   51 - Protestant, married: Counseling is in-
cidental; I do it free as part of lawyer's
obligation. Chief motive to help others
achieve happy life. Can teach (psychology
and sociology) but prefer new and well
trained full-time profession. Law School
stresses academic, need practical, and ethics,

moral pragmatic. Learn from social work methods teaching case counseling.

(6)   37 - Jewish, married: Counseling because I like peope. Am told I am good at analysis and making people feel they decide. Haven't the heart to charge; they don't think you do anything.

(7)   50 - Protestant, married: Law and medicine must counsel. Clergy better trained. Suggest same for law.

(8)   47 - Jewish, married: Counseling not to be taken lightly. Requires: mutual trust, moral integrity, flexibility, understanding, objectivity, all the facts, no rigid rules, absolute confidentiality.

(9)   49 - Protestant, married: Teach law student that legal processes can wait until human factors determined and clarified; apply common sense. Clients want assurance, objectivity, competence, involvement.

(10)   44 - Protestant, separated: This is hogwash; the questionnaire is stupid; it discusses the unimportant and rediscovers the obvious. I work in estate planning, don't counsel.

Handling The Specific Case "A".

(1)   Call both parties into the office. Is there basis for keeping this marriage together. Call doctor, medical attention required.

(2)   Needs psychological help. Refer. Don't accept case.

(3)   Get facts, get premarital and marital situation from spiritual adviser, determine cause, work out by semi-religious methods an appropriate solution.

(4)   Either early menopause or depressive paranoid. If not advanced, take vacation, get

away from mama. If advanced, psychiatric treatment. Anyway—alert the husband.

(5)   Handle only to point sell parties need for psychiatrist.

(6)   Advise on legal rights. Refer to Family Service.

(7)   Would not take case. Religious and psychiatric counseling. Refer to Dr. at once. Could jar her loose.

(8)   Take the case; get her to psychiatrist; problem not incompatibility, problem beyond marriage; should save marriage. Draw woman out, session with husband, then joint session.

(9)   Act, you can't wait for someone to be killed. Get tests and treatment. Talk to husband, suggest he see psychiatrist or psychologist also.

(10) Take case "A"; here is $200,000 involved. Advise her to stay away from husband. Get psychiatric examination.

MEDICAL

Life, Hobbies, Associations, etc.

(1) Age 54 - None, married: Medicine only hobby, only societies medical, only books medical except 2-3 popular novels a year. Second in family of 7, always looked to for advice. Two children "lack of direction" "lost in uncer-certainties".

(2)   50 - Jewish, married: Happy marriage and 3 sons. Sail 3-4 afternoons a week, fish, mountain hiking. Few clubs, go to synagogue.

(3)   57 - Protestant, married: Golf, Rotary, School Board, politics, medical societies; 3 children, 3 grandchildren; prefer scotch whisky and young brunette women.

(4)   62 - Protestant, married: Two sons, 2 foster sons; gardening, achitectural drawing, church affairs, local clubs, travel, learned 3 languages.

(5)   36 - Protestant, married: Interested in history, photography, skiing, Lions, Chamber of Commerce, 3 children.

(6)   59 - Protestant, married: Interested in music, hi-fi, logic; clubs, VFW, etc. Own background working way through college plus army experience in Pacific taught what people like. Basis of all counseling.

(7)   62 - Catholic, married: Travel, coin and bottle collecting, politics, 5 children graduated from college.

(8)   40 - Catholic, married: Great suffering, 8 surgicals, gives deep empathy with suffering. Now happily married to well balanced, beautiful woman, 4 children. Only medical societies.

(9)   46 - Catholic, married: Divorced twice, remarried. Music, group psychotherapy, travel.

(10)   53 - Protestant, married: Jewish-Christian marriage, 3 children, 5 grandchildren, stamp collector, Boy Scouts, medical associations, early desire to serve humanity.

Counseling, Teaching.

(1)   54 - None, married: We lack time and training. Start training in college, extend post graduate.

(2)   50 - Jewish, married: Counseling quixotic. Helps adults little, can't harm much. Real help where one problem breaks life's normal routine. Education, experience, liking are important.

(3)   57 - Protestant, married: Experience   more important than training.

(4)   62 - Protestant, married: No real training in college. GPs gain by experience. We refer to psychiatrists.

(5)   36 - Protestant, married: Need training and experience. Intensive psychology; clergy now receive it, doctors do not.

(6)   59 - Protestant, married: Greatest difficulty to lower self to other's level. Establish trust, confidence.   Help them work out, use "why" and "so that's it", etc.

(7)   62 - Catholic, married: Counseling usually poor because of lack of time and "too professional". Knowledge of life and great common sense needed.

(8)   40 - Catholic, married: Counseling should be attempted only by a well rounded, educated individual well grounded in philosophy, morals, religion and his profession, without unsolved personal problems.

(9)   46 - Catholic, married: Experience important. Sex problems to doctor. Difficult decisions for Catholic.   Realities more important than religious dogma.   Poor training in medical school.

(10)   53 - Protestant, married: Could profit from college and post college training. Involves being alive, alert, active, accepting people as irrational, cowardly, destructive, etc.

Handling The Specific Case "A".

(1)   Refer to psychiatrist. No one else should take.

(2)   Put her under psychiatric treatment.

(3)   Should be referred to a psychiatrist who might explain her obsession or compulsion.

(4)   Probably no organic brain damage; psychiatrist a must; psychogenic, possibly early schizophrenic.

(5)   Needs shock treatment, drugs, supportive therapy.

(6)   Compulsion pathological and deep rooted; grave responsibility; needs full psychiatric care in hospital.

(7)   Definitely psychotic; should be institutionalized.

(8)   May be case non specialist can handle. Save marriage. Ask opinion psychiatrist (Catholic one); refer to priest.

(9)   Needs psychiatric workup and therapy.

(10)   Do complete medical, check menstrual history and hormonal balance. Then use hypnosis for hypno-analysis. Interview husband.

CLERGY

Life, Hobbies, Associations, etc.

(1)   37 - Protestant, married: Collecting stamps, sea shells, swimming, fishing; 4 children; wife invaluable help.

(2)   51 - Protestant, married: Carpentry, choral music, gardening, church history; welfare, hospital, ministers association.

(3)   35 - Protestant, married: Kiwanis, Boy Scouts, swimming, boating, etc., 2 children.

(4)   54 - Protestant, married: Active in sports and community affairs, 2 children (one married).

(5)   36 - Protestant, married: Reading, spectator sports, golf, Council of Churches, Planned Parenthood, 3 children, family sports.

(6)   49 - Protestant, married: Married children, good students, self *magna cum laude,* wood-

working, reading, swimming, teacher.

(7)   44 - Protestant, married: Reading, bowling, music; no clubs outside of church activities, 2 children, PTA.

(8)   45 - Protestant, married: Hi-fi, photography, reading, stamps, pool, cards, no clubs.

(9)   38 - Protestant, married: Originally musician, like pageantry.

(10)   60 - Protestant, married: Taught school but didn't like, liked people. Jolly. Reading classics. All clubs, optimist, etc.

(11)   36 - Protestant, married: Issue hobbies, race relations, underprivileged, family shared sports. Work with Negroes in south, projects with slum children. Great wife, 4 enjoyable children. Little time for clubs.

(12)   38 - Protestant, married: Foreign cars, travel, philosophy. Wife and 3 children. Near college and act as Chaplain. Pacifist.

Counseling, Teaching.

(1)   37 - Protestant, married: Psychologists and psychiatrists do wrong in minimizing religion as integrating force. Find college training in counseling too psychiatric oriented.

(2)   51 - Protestant, married: Urge in-service training at parish level rather than institutional work.

(3)   35 - Protestant, married: Counseling requires acceptance, diagnostic ability, empathy, patience to listen, acceptance of confession without judgment. Need interaction between professions, group seminars.

(4)   54 - Protestant, married: Greatest asset compassion for people. Don't like marriage counseling, untruths, time consuming. Doc-

tors need higher ethic (sex) and appreciation of religion. Not aware lawyers do
much counseling.

(5)   36 - Protestant, married: Great advance in
clerical counseling, treat person as whole,
need professional cooperation, avoid guilt
and advice, help individual to work out.

(6)   49 - Protestant, married: Courses in mental
health and counseling in seminary; use
sermons to counsel; interest in what makes
people as they are. Counseling not a cult
or deep analytic—is objectivity, sympathy,
understanding

(7)   44 - Protestant, married: Being married, visit-
ing in homes, maturing experience most
important.

(8)   45 - Protestant, married: Group and social
dynamics, clinical training needed. Effort
to minimize his share in "therapy", refer.

(9)   38 - Protestant, married: Counseling needs
improvement. Value of sacramental confession high. Doctors and lawyers should
recognize this.

(10)   60 - Protestant, married: Regard counseling
as center of work. Do it across desk and
by letter to former parishioners (3 hours a
day). Keep in touch, be available, good
listener, non shock, common sense.

(11)   36 - Protestant, married: Trained at Chicago;
good Rogerian-Hiltner training. Need in
community for people to counsel those with
problems, not psychotic. Need both skill
(lawyer, clergy different) and general
therapy counsel.

(12)   38 - Protestant, married: Spend 30% of time
counseling. More than giving advice; pastor
has advantage of "calls"—can go where

not invited, see parishioners everywhere go, stop to talk. Counseling is handling problems, not therapy; people need help in thinking.

Handling The Specific Case "A".

(1)   Need for cooperative help; doctor for physical, clergy for spiritual, perhaps law.

(2)   No psychiatric help available here. Take case. Do something. She needs to talk. Talk to husband. Be ready to refer to hospital.

(3)   Refer her to mental hospital, call in social worker for family.

(4)   Try to convince her of inanity of her fears, next complete medical check up, finally if needed "competent" psychiatrist (not one seeing sex in everything).

(5)   Believe myself competent to handle early interviews. Get psychological opinion if needed.

(6)   See a doctor about sleepless nights, then psychiatrists as to knife; my task to keep in touch with family and break "fortune-teller" aspect.

(7)   Afraid of this. Psychotic. Refer at once.

(8)   Take case if parishioner. Encourage to talk out. See husband.

(9)   If they permit, refer to psychologist (good one in church). Some case. Beyond me. Perhaps husband should be jailed.

(10)   Listen, dispel guilt, assure of covenant of forgiveness, consult doctor, advise husband to be alert, schedule time to talk and talk.

(11)   Religious overtones. I've got to see it through. Don't jump to refer to psychiatrist (lack religious sense).

(12)   Would handle jointly with good marriage counselor in town; better than psychiatrist; only as last resort visit mental hospital with her.

Bibliography Chapter 6

Bibliography for Chapter VI
See Freeman, Counseling — A Bibliography with Annotations
Particularly Code D.   See also B-6; C-2; 7, 8; H; I; J.

Arbuckle, Dugald S.—The "Self" Shows in Counseling.   (1954) Personnel Guid. J. 33:159-161.

Aronson, Manuel—A Study of the Relationships Between Certain Counselor and Client Characteristics in Client-centered Therapy. (Doctoral Dissertation, Penn. State, 1951) (P.S. XIV, 423, 1951).

Balint, Michael (Translator)—The Analyst's Attitude to His Patient. In Sandor Ferenczi—Final Contributions to the Problems and Methods of Psychoanalysis.   (New York, Basic Books, 1955).

Bandura, A.—Psychotherapists' Anxiety Level, Self-Insight, and Psychotherapeutic Competence.   (1956) J. Abnorm. Soc. Psychol. 52:333-337.

Barnes, Edward J.—Psychotherapists' Conflicts, Defense Preferences and Verbal Reactions to Certain Classes of Client Expressions. D.A. XXV, 618-619, 1964.

Bartelme, Kenwood F.—Relationships between Certain Personality Characteristics of Psychotherapists and their Characterization of Patients.   (Doctoral Dissertation, Univ. of California, Berkeley, 1958-59).

Berdie, Ralph F., ed.—Roles and Relationships in Counseling. (Minneapolis, Univ. of Minn. Press, 1953) 37 pp.

Berdie, Ralph F.—Counselor Attitudes.   (1951) Ed. Psychol. M. 11:349-354.

Berg, I. A., Harold B. Pepinsky, Seth Arsenian, Joseph C. Heston— Age, Income, and Professional Characteristics of Members of the APA's Division of Counseling and Guidance.   (1952) Am. Psychol. 7:125-127.

Betz, Barbara J.—How Do Personal Attitudes and Interests Influence Psychotherapeutic Effectiveness?   In Proceedings of the Sixth Annual Psychiatric Institute.   (Held Sept. 17, 1958 at the New Jersey Neuro-psychiatric Institute, Princeton) pp. 14-28.

Blaustein, Albert P. and Charles O. Porter—The American Lawyer: A Summary of the Survey of the Legal Profession.   (Chicago, Univ. of Chicago Press, 1954).

Blizzard, Samuel W.—The Parish Minister's Self Image and Variability in Community Culture.   (Oct. 1959) Past Psych. 10:27-36.

Blizzard, Samuel W.—Role Conflicts of the Urban Protestant Parish Minister.   (Sept. 1956) The City Church No. 4:13-15.

Bohn, Martin J.—Relationship of Counselor Dominance and Experience to Counseling Behavior. D.A. XXV, 5380, 1965.

Borgatta, Edgar F., David Fanshel and Henry J. Meyer—Social Workers' Perceptions of Clients. (New York, Russell Sage Foundation, 1960) 92 pp.

Borresen, Ann M.—Counselor Influence on Diagnostic Classification of Client Problems. (1965) J. Counsel. Psychol. 13:252.

Bradway, John S.—Legal Hazards of the Marriage Counselor. (May 1949) Marr. Fam. Liv. 11:62.

Brams, Jerome M.—Counselor Characteristics and Effective Communication in Counseling. (1961) J. Counsel. Psychol. 8:25-30.

Brigante, T. R., D. P. Haefner and W. B. Woodson—Clinical and Counseling Psychologists' Perceptions of Their Specialties. (1962) J. Counsel. Psychol. 9:225-231.

Brough, James R.—Sources of Student Perceptions of the Role of the Counselor. (1965) Personnel Guid. J. 43:597-599.

Cahoon, Richard A.—Some Counselor Attitudes and Characteristics Related to the Counseling Relationship. D.A. XXIII, 3472-3473, 1963.

Campbell, Robert E.—Influence of the Counselor's Personality and Background on His Counseling Style. (Doctoral Dissertation, Ohio State Univ.) (D.A. XXII, 3739, 1962).

Carlin, Jerome—Lawyers on Their Own: A Study of Individual Practitioners in Chicago. (N.J., Rutgers University Press, 1962).

Carlin, Jerome—Metropolitan Law Office Study, 1964 Progress Report.

Clarkhuff, Robert R. and Charles B. Truax—Lay Mental Health Counseling. (1965) J. Consult. Psychol. 29:426.

Conner, John D.—Coming: A Survey of the Legal Profession in Wisconsin. (Dec. 1960) Wis. B. Bull. 33:47.

Cottle, William C.—Personal Characteristics of Counselors. Part I. (1953) Personnel Guid. J. 31:445-450. See III (1954) J. Counsel. Psychol. 1:74-77.

Cumming, Elaine and Charles Harrington—Clergyman as Counselor. (1963) Am. J. Soc. 69:234-243.

Curran, Charles A.—Personality Factors in Counseling. (New York, Grune and Stratton, 1947) 287 pp.

Cutler, Richard F.—The Relationship Between the Therapist's Personality and Certain Aspects of Psychotherapy. (Doctoral Dissertation, Univ. of Michigan, 1954) (D.A. XIV, 709, 1954).

DeHaan, Nancy—Patients' and Therapists' Definitions of Therapist's Role. (Paper read at American Psychological Association, Washington, D. C., Sept. 1958).

Devereux, G. and F. H. Hoffman—Non-Recognition of the Patient by the Therapist: An Analysis of a Counter-transference Distortion Related to the Therapist's Professional Stance. (1961) Psychoanal. Rev. No. 3, 48:41-61.

Drakeford, John W.—The Dilemma of a Woman Counselor in a Church Situation. (June 1962) Past. Psych. 13:37-42.

Drucker, A. J. and H. H. Remmers—The Validity of University Counselor Self-ratings. (1949) J. Ed. Psychol. 40:169-73.

Durnall, E. J., E. Moynihan, and C. Wrenn—Symposium: The Counselor and His Religion. (Jan. 1958) Personnel Guid. J. 36:326-34.

Ehrenwald, Jan—Family Diagnosis and Mechanisms of Psycho-social Defense. (1963) Fam. Process 2:121-131.

Ellis, Albert—Report on the Survey of Members of the Division of Clinical and Abnormal Psychology Who are Presently Engaged in Paid Private Practice. (1951) Newsletter, Div. Clin. & Abnorm. Psych. A.P.A. 4, No. 6: supp.

Ellmann, James I. and E. B. Ellmann—Counseling and Counseling Fees. (March 1954) Detroit Law, 22:37-41; (Jan. 1955) Com. L.J. 60:13.

Evans, Theodore Q.—The Brethren Pastor: Differential Conceptions of an Emerging Role. (Doctoral Dissertation, Ohio State Univ., 1960) (D.A. XXI, 257, 1960).

Fanshel, David—A Study of Caseworkers' Perceptions of Their Clients. (1958) Soc. Casework 39:543-551.

Fiedler, F. E.—The Concept of an Ideal Therapeutic Relationship. (1950) J. Consult. Psychol. 14:239-245.

Fiedler, Fred E.—Quantitative Studies on the Role of Therapists Feelings Toward Their Patients. In O. Hobart Mowrer—Psychotherapy—Theory and Research. (1923).

Fromm-Reichmann, Frieda—Notes on the Personal and Professional Requirements of a Psychotherapist. (1949) Psychiatry 12:361-378.

Fuller, Frances F.—Influence of Sex of Counselor and of Client on Client Expressions of Feeling. (1963) J. Counsel. Psychol. 10:34-40.

Garfield, S. L. and D. C. Affleck—Therapists' Judgments Concerning Patients Considered for Psychotherapy. (1961) J. Consult. Psychol. 25:505-509.

Gilbert, Norman S.—When the Counselor is a Disciplinarian. (1965) Personnel Guid. J. 43:485-491.

Grant, C. W.—The Counselor's Role. (1954) Personnel Guid. J. 33:74-77.

Grimes, Walter—A Study of the Differences in Role Perception Between Physicians and Their Clientele. (Cornell Univ. Department of Sociology—Doctoral Dissertation, 1960).

Halkides, Galatia—An Investigation of Therapeutic Success as a Function of Four Therapist Variables. (Doctoral Dissertation, Univ. of Chicago, 1957-58).

Harper, Robert—Neurotic Interaction Among Counselors. (1958) J. Counsel. Psychol. 5:33-38.

Harrington, Charles and Elaine Cumming—The Clergyman as He Reports His Place in the Counseling System. (Syracuse, 1962, mimeo.).

Hedahl, Beaulah M.—A Study of the Role Expectations of Counselors in Three University Student Counseling Centers. (Doctoral Dissertation, Univ. of Minnesota, 1958) (D.A. XIX, 1291, 1959).

Hiltner, Seward—The Counselor in Counseling: Case Notes in Pastoral Counseling. (New York, Abingdon-Cokesbury, 1952) 188 pp.

Hiltner, Seward—The Role of the Clergyman as a Counselor. In Social Work in the Current Scene. (New York, Columbia Univ. Press, 1950).

Hoffman, Abe—An Analysis of Counselor Subroles. (Doctoral Dissertation Ohio State Univ. 1956) (D.A. XVII, 177, 1957).

Holland, Robert E.—An Exploratory Study of the Counselor Variable. (Doctoral Dissertation, Univ. of S. California, 1956-57).

Hudson, Roland V.—A Study of Counseling Techniques as Used by the Clergy. (Doctoral Dissertation, Purdue Univ., 1950) (D.A. XV, 2294, 1950).

Kadushin, Charles—Social Distance Between Client and Professional. (March, 1962) Am. J. Soc. 67:517-531.

Kagan, Henry E.—The Role of the Rabbi as Counselor. (1954) Past. Psych. 5:17-23.

Kahn, Robert K.—Therapist Discomfort in Two Psychotherapies. (Doctoral Dissertation, Penn. State Univ.) (D.A. XVII, 1118, 1957).

Kargman, Marie W.—Lawyer's Role in Divorce Reconciliation. (March 1960) Prac. Law. 6:21.

Karmiol, Edward—The Effect of the Therapist's Acceptance of the Therapeutic Role on Client-Therapist Relationship in a Reflective and a Leading Type of Psychotherapy. (Doctoral Dissertation, Penn State Univ., 1957) (D.A. XVII, 1119, 1957).

Kenney, Raymond C.—An Analysis of Self-Perceptions in Counselor Trainees. (Doctoral Dissertation, Univ. of Texas, 1959) (D.A. XX, 2677, 1960).

Klausner, Samuel Z.—Role Adaptation of Ministers and Psychiatrists in a Religio-Psychiatric Clinic. (Bureau of Applied Social Research, Columbia University, New York, 1957).

Kling, Frederick R.—Value Structures and the Minister's Purpose. (March 1961) Past. Psych. 12:13-23.

Kumar, Usha and Harold B. Pepinsky—Counselor Expectancies and Therapeutic Evaluations. (1965) Proc. 73rd Ann. Convention Am. Psychol. 357-358.

Kuhn, Manford H.—Self-Attitude by Age, Sex, and Professional Training. (Jan. 1960) Soc. Q. 9:39.

Kutner, Bernard—Physician-Patient Relationships: A Theoretical Framework. In Platman, John G. and Eugene L. Hartly, eds.—Festschrift for Gardner Murphy. (New York, Harper & Bros., 1960) 399 pp.

Laidlaw, Robert W.—The Psychiatrist as Marriage Counselor. (1950) Am. J. Psychiat. 106:732-736.

Lantz, Herman R.—Counselor Hopelessness as an Obstacle in the Marriage Counseling Relationship. (1959) Marr. Fam. Liv. 21:367-368.

Lawyers Earnings and Prestige Shrinking Because They Fail to Counsel Their Clients Personal Problems? (May 1960) Current Med. 7:45.

Lefton, Mark, et al.—Status Perceptions of Psychiatric Social Workers and Their Implications for Job Satisfaction. (1961) Am. J. Orthopsychiat. 31:102-110.

Lerman, Hannah—A Study of Some Effects of the Therapist's Personality and Behavior and of the Clients' Reactions in Psychotherapy. (D.A. XXV, 1339, 1964).

Levine, David L.—Teacher-Counselor: Role and Qualifications. (1953) Marr. Fam. Liv. 15, No. 3:313-315.

Lieberman, E. James—Preventive Psychiatry and Family Planning. (1964) J. Marr. Fam. 26:471-477.

Luborsky, L.—The Personality of the Psychotherapist. (1952) Menn. Q. 6:3-8.

McClelland, William and M. Wallace Sinaiko—An Investigation of a Counselor Attitude Questionnaire. (1950) Ed. Psychol. M. 10:128-133.

McNeil, Elton B. and J. Robert Cohler, Jr.—The Effect of Personal Needs on Counselor Perception and Behavior. (1957) Pap. Mich. Acad. Sci. Arts Lett. 42:281-288.

Maeder, Alphonse—A New Concept of the Psychiatrist's Role. (1955) J. Psychother. Rel. Proc. 2:38-46.

Mendelsohn, Gerald A. and Marvin H. Geller—Effects of Counselor-Client Similarity on the Outcome of Counseling. (Spring 1963) J. Counsel Psychol. 10, No. 1:71.

Menninger, Karl A.—The Character of the Therapist. (Nov. 1958) Past, Psych. 9:14-18.

Miller, Leonard A.—A Functional View of Counselor Behavior. (1962) J. Rehabilit. 28:18-19.

Murphy, Gladys C.—Counselor Dominance: The Degree of Dominance Attributed to Counselors by Judges as Compared with the Counselor's Concept of His Role. (Doctoral Dissertation, New York Univ., 1957) (D.A. XVIII, 1358, 1958).

Naegele, Kasper D.—Clergymen, Teachers and Psychiatrists: A Study in Roles and Socialization. (Jan. 1956) Can. J. Econ. Pol. Sci. 11, No. 1:8-13.

National Conference of Social Work—Social Work in the Current Scene. The Role of the Clergyman as a Counselor. (New York, Columbia Univ. Press, 1950) pp. 369-377.

Oates, Wayne E., ed.—The Minister's Own Mental Health. (Great Neck, N. Y., Channel, 1961).

Oates, Wayne, E.—The Pastor as a Marriage Counselor. (1955) Marr. Fam. Liv. 17:62-67.

Odenwald, Robert P.—The Priest as Counselor. (1956) Conference Bulletin, Archdiocese of New York, Vol. 33, No. 2, 42-53, 70-76.

O'Gorman, Hubert, J., Jr.—Lawyers and Matrimonial Cases: A Study of Informal Pressures in Private Professional Practice. (Doctoral Dissertation, Columbia Univ.) (D.A. XXII, 1739, 1961).

Orlingsky, Nancy—Patients' and Therapists' Conceptions of the Therapists's Role in Relation to Outcome of Therapy. (Doctoral Dissertation, Univ. of Chicago, 1959-60).

Pasamaniek, B. and S. Rettig—Status and Work Satisfaction of Psychiatrists. A Comparative Study of Psychiatrists in State Employ and Private Practice. (1959) A.M.A. Arch. Neurol. Pschiat. 81, No. 3:399-402.

Perkins, Worcester V.—What Contribution Should the Clergyman Make to Marriage Counseling? (May 1952) Marr. Fam. Liv. 14:124-7.

Peterson, Arnold O. D.—A Factor Analysis of Therapists: An Exploratory Investigation of Therapeutic Biases. (Doctoral Dissertation, Penn. State, 1957) (D.A. XVII, 1121, 1957).

Poole, Aileen—Counselor Judgment and Counseling Evaluation. (1957) J. Counsel. Psychol. 4:37-40.

Ramsey, Glenn V.—Sex Questions Asked by Clergy. In Beigel, Hugo, ed.—Advances in Sex Research. (New York, Harper & Row, 1963) 261 pp.

Randall, John D.—Role of the Lawyer in Society. (Dec. 26, 1959) Okla. B.A. J. 30:2019.

Reaves, Gayle C. and Leonard Reeves—The Counselor and Preventive Psychiatry. (1965) Personnel Guid. J. 43:661-664.

Redmount, Robert S.—Attorney Personalities and Some Psychological Aspects of Legal Consultation. (May 1961) U. Pa. L. Rev. 109:972.

Rettig, S., F. Jacobsen, B. Posamanick—The Status of the Professional as Perceived by Himself, by Other Professionals, and by Lay Persons. (1958) Mid-West Soc. 20:84-89.

Rettig, S., et al.—The Motivational Pattern of the Mental Health Professional. In Social Aspects of Psychiatry. (1958) Psychiat. Res. Rep. No. 10:1-18.

Rice, Laura—Therapists' Style of Participation and Case Outcome. (1965). J. Consult. Psychol. 29:155-160.

Riewald, Arthur G.—The Relationship of Counselor's Tolerance Ambiguity to Counselor Behavior in the Counseling Interview: A Pilot Study. D.A. XXV, 6768-6769, 1965.

Rogers, Carl R.—The Attitude and Orientation of the Counselor. (April 1949) J. Consult. Psychol. 13:82-94.

Rogers, Carl R.—The Characteristics of a Helping Relationship. (1958) Personnel Guid. J. 37:6-16.

Rubin, Stanley I.—A Study on the Self-Concept of Function Within the Profession of Counseling Psychology. (Doctoral Dissertation, Ohio State Univ., 1956) D.A. XVII, 1587, 1957.

Russell, Peter D. and William U. Snyder—Counselor Anxiety in Relation to Amount of Clinical Experience and Quality of Affect Demonstrated by Clients. (1963) J. Consult. Psychol. 27:358-363.

Rutledge, Aaron and Dorothy E. Barrier—Should the Marriage Counselor Ever Recommend Divorce? (1963) Marr. Fam. Liv., 25:319-325.

Schnitzer, Jeshais—Rabbis and Counseling. Report on a Project. (July 1958) Jewish Soc. Stud. 20, No. 3:131-152.

Scott, Winfield H.—A Factor Analytic Study of Therapist Bias. (Doctoral Dissertation, Penn. State Univ., 1958) D.A. XIX, 1447, 1959.

Seeman, William—Clinical Opinion on the Role of Therapist Adjustment in Psychotherapy. (Feb. 1950) J. Consult. Psychol. 14:49-52.

Sizer, Leonard M.—Role Conception, Role Discrepancy, and Institutional Contest: A Study of the Protestant Ministry. (Doctoral Dissertation, State University of Iowa, 1954).

Smith, L. Mader—Parish Clergymen's Role Images as Pastoral Counselors. (1960) J. Past. Care 14:21-28.

Sommer, N. Theodore—The Psychologist and Privileged Communication. (1962) J. Offender Ther. 6:59-61.

Soni, B. C.—Sociological Analysis of Legal Profession: A Study of Mechanism in Lawyer-Client Relationship. (1958) J. Soc. Sci. 1, No. 1:63-70.

Southard, Samuel—The Mental Health of Ministers. (May 1958) Past. Psych. 9:43-48.

Southard, Samuel—The Minister's Role as a Counselor. (May 1953). The Pastor.

Spivak, Mark—Factors Influencing the Formation of a Patient-Percept by Psychiatrists Following the Initial Interview. (Doctoral Dissertation, Univ. of Michigan, 1962) D.A. XXIII, 341.

Streitfeld, Julian W.—Expressed Acceptance of Self and Others in Psychotherapists. (Doctoral Dissertation, Columbia Univ., 1958) D.A. XIX, 176, 1959).

Stroup, H.—The College Teacher as Counselor. (1957) Sch. and Soc. 85:120-122.

Strupp, Hans H.—Toward an Analysis of the Therapist's Contribution to the Treatment Process. (1959) Psychiatry 22:349-362.

Sundland, Donald M.—Psychotherapists' Self-perception and Patients' Perception of Their Psychotherapists. (Doctoral Dissertation, Ohio State Univ., 1960).

Sykes, Wilbert—Feelings and Behavior of the Therapist in the Initial Interview. (1965) Past. Coun. 3:20-22.

Szasz, Thomas S. and Mark Hollender—A Contribution to the Philosphy of Medicine: The Basic Models of the Doctor-Patient Relationship. (1956) A.M.A. Arch. Intern. Med. 97:585-592.

Thompson, Clara—The Role of the Analyst's Personality in Therapy. (1956) Am. J. Psychother. 10:347-367.

Thornal, Campbell—Qualities of a Good Lawyer. (Dec. 1959) Fla. B.J. 33:1191.

Thrush, Randolph S.—Work Measurement and Perceptual Studies With a University Counseling Center. (Doctoral Dissertation, Ohio State Univ., 1958) (D.A. XIX, 2389, 1959).

Tingue, Arthur M.—The Minister's Role in Marriage Preparation and Premarital Counseling. (1958) Marr. Fam. Liv. 20:11-17.

Tirnauer, Lawrence—Anxiety and the Behavior of Psychotherapists in an Experimental Setting. (Doctoral Dissertation, Penn. State Univ., 1959) (D.A. XX, 3391, 1960).

Truax, Charles B. and Robert R. Carkhuff—Client and Therapist Transparency in the Psychotherapeutic Encounter. (1965) J. Counsel. Psychol. 12:3-9.

Vogel, John L.—Authoritarianism in the Therapeutic Relationship. (Doctoral Dissertation, Univ. of Chicago, 1959-60) (1961) J. Consult. Psychol. 25:102-108.

Vordenberg, Wesley—The Impact of Personal Philosophies on Counseling. (1953) Personnel Guid. J. 31:439-440.

Wallach, Martin—Certain Relationships Between Psychotherapists' Attitudes and Their Perceptions of Patient Variables. (Doctoral Dissertation, Univ. of No. Carolina, 1959) (D.A. XX, 2911, 1960).

Warman, R. E.—Differential Perceptions of Counseling Role.   (1960)
    J. Counsel. Psychol. 7:269-274.

Wasson, Robert M. and R. Wray Strowig—Professional Isolation and
    Counselor Role.   (1965) Personal Guid. J. 43:443-446.

Weitz, Henry—Counseling as a Function of the Counselor's Personality.
    (1957) Personnel Guid. J. 35:276-280.

Weyrauch, Walter—The Personality of Lawyers.   (New Haven, Yale
    University Press, 1964) 328 pp.

Whitcomb, John C.—Determination of Relation Between Personality
    Characteristics and Nature and Persistence of Problems in the
    Protestant Ministry.   (Doctoral Dissertation, Univ. Michigan)
    (D.A. XIV, 1182, 1954).

Whitley, Oliver R.—Religious Behavior: Where Sociology and Religion
    Meet.   (Englewood Cliffs, N. J., Prentice-Hall, 1964) 177 pp.

Wrenn, C. Gilbert—The Culturally Encapsulated Counselor.   (1962)
    Harv. Ed. Rev. 32:444-449.

Wrenn, C. Gilbert—The Ethics of Counseling.   (1952) Ed. Psychol. M.
    12:161-177. Also, (Oct. 1952) Minn. J. Ed. 33:39.

Wrenn, C. Gilbert—The Self-Concept in Counseling.   (1958) J. Counsel.
    Psychol. 5:104-109.

Wrenn, R. L.—Counselor Orientation: Theoretical or Situational?
    (1960) J. Counsel. Psychol. 7:40-45.

Yoder, H. Walter—The Locus of Responsibility in Counseling.   (1950)
    Past. Psych. 1, No. 6:39-42.

Zacher, Allan N.—The Professional Responsibility of the Lawyer in
    Divorce.   (1962) Mo. L. Rev. 27:466-479.

Chapter 7

Clients—Their Selection, Problems and Satisfaction

"Are chickens the best judges of eggs? is a fair question to ask after practicing professionals analyze their own professions. It early became clear that one of the most important aspects of our study was to get the picture of counseling through the client's eyes.

It will be recalled that we studied the following: (1) *a control* group (statistically described in the footnotes) who might or might not have been to counseling; (2) *a second group* all of whom were known to have been through psychiatric-psychologcal counseling; (3) *a third group* counseled in a large city legal aid clinic; (4) *a fourth smaller group* (Parents Without Partners) was selected as a second "control group" in presenting one type of counseling problem (marital, but unknown as to whether they had used a counselor or not); a *fifth group* (5), the smallest and least representative, since we allowed certain clergy to select their counselees who would receive questionnaires. Overall, we can say that all of our samples represented the younger side

---

1. The control group was 40% age 20-30, 30% age 30-40, 25% over 40; 70% male, 30% female; 50/50 married — single; 50% Protestant, 14% Catholic, 14% no religion, 7% Jewish; 60% urban, 20% metropolitan, 15% rural; with some socio-psycho training 31%.

of the population, that we concentrated on those under 60 and gave greatest emphasis to those 20-40 years of age.

This chapter is laid out on the following plan: a) a few very general statistics to suggest avenues of inquiry (p. 205); b) the statistics of that part of the control group who went to counselors, question-by-question but without cross tabulation to suggest what was learned by simple Q-sorts (p. 207); c) some summaries of the responses of the group known to have gone to psychiatric-psychological counseling, with emphasis on the interrelation and different perspective of counselor and counselee which we could match up (p. 214); d) a survey of the legal aid group, of necessity less detailed because the respondents were interested in their individual problem and left large sections of the questionnaire unanswered (p. 218); e) a statistical summary with a good deal of emphasis on cross tabulation for the Parents Without Partners group, (p. 224)—our consideration is somewhat extended because of the interest in marriage counseling for all professions; f) a rather limited analysis of counselees of clergy statistics (p. 234); g) a general set of observations that derive from all the groups recorded as tentative observations to our "Series O" questions as to clients (p. 236); and h) some general suggestions for counseling as presented by the client samples (p. 250).

The reader who looks for a detailed and definitive report of observations from statistical tables may find this chapter disappointing. We tried, as shown above, to get suggestive material from a considerable variety of sources; we tried to get replies to a large number of questions; we did not know whether these questions were adequate to explore client reaction to counseling; we were pioneering in the field and highly explorative. We have therefore thought that rather than burden this chapter with literally thousands of tables, giving the impression that each proved a point or conclusion, we would set forth only a few tables as examples of the data with which we worked, would utilize statistics in percentage form where they were readily interpretable and meaningful, and we would primarily present our own observations as drawn from all the material. It is our hope that this may encourage further and more definitive studies of some of the major points.

Because of the wide variety of clients, the kind of counselors they sought (or didn't seek), the kind of problems they presented, their ages and like factors, a complete statistical analysis amalgamating all groups does not seem to give a meaningful picture. If we keep in mind the differences, group to group, some statistics do permit of comparison, generalization and hypothesizing, and others pose interesting questions. We may take as an example, religion. In the general control group—counseled and uncounseled: 15% were Protestants, 7% Jewish, 14% Catholic, 14% without religion, 5% other, 9% no answer. But in the second control group (Parents Without Partners), presenting matrimonial problems, 64% were Jewish, 24% Protestant, 3% Catholic, 5% no religion, 3% other or blank. Why should Jews so completely dominate the latter group? Why so few Catholics in both (it might be expected in the second group)? This is one of many problems needing further inquiry.

a) *General Statistics of Client Samples*

In this one section we try to give an overview of all the persons we surveyed. In samples (1)—general control, and (4)—Parents without Partners, we had cross sections of counselee and non-counselee groups, whereas in (2), (3) and (5) we had only known counselees. We considered it worthwhile to show the composition of our total group ((1)-(5)) in terms of age, sex, residence, religion and whether, why and for what they visited a counselor. There follow, therefore, a few statistics on all the groups, general of necessity but sufficient to record the patterns. Where we deal with questions of going or not going to counselors, we give the control groups (1) and (4) separate from all other groups (2), (3), (5) in each of which 100% were known to have gone to a counselor. Where we speak of a counselee our statistics combine groups (2), (3), (5), and the known counselees in (1) and (4).

	Male	Female
Sex counselee	60%	40%
Sex going to clergy	35%	65%
Sex going to psychiatrist-doctor	40%	60%
Sex going to lawyer	70%	30%

Note: Both men and women preferred that the counselor be male.

	Metro.	Urban	Rural
Home town of counselee	20%	60%	20%

Gone to counselor
  (control groups (1)
  & (4)   Yes 45%   No 55%
  (all groups)   Yes 82%   No 18%
  (less than 5 times 51%; more than 5 times 18%; no answer 13%)

Failed to go
  (control groups   Yes 50%   No 40%   No answer 10%
  only)
  (all groups)   Yes 29%   No 60%   No answer 11%

Reason for not going

solved own problem	30%	cost	10%
not necessary	20%	other	15%
no one could trust	10%	no answer	15%

Subject of problem: Personal-sex 25%, work-school, etc. 20%, values, 20%, conflict with others 15%, miscellaneous 20%

To Whom turned—In this order: clergy, teacher-boss, doctor, lawyer, other specific type counselors, psychiatrist, other. (Friends were greatest source of problem discussion and advice but generally not thought of as counseling).

Basis for selection—In this order: technical competence and reputation, nature of problem, through friend, availability, cost, referral.

Was problem solved: Yes 48% No 20% Not clear 12%
Were you satisfied: Yes 49% No 19% Not clear 16%

Counselees were about even on:
    Satisfaction with directive   with non-directive
    Solved problem self   counselor real contribution
    Sought advice   sought new perspectives

Counselees generally saw the satisfying counselor as:
    Stronger; Object of respect; Building rather than destroying confidence; Handling all aspects rather than referring; Interested only in counselee and not others related to problem.

    b)   *General Control Group Counselee Statistics*
On how many occasions have you been to a counselor?
        40% 1 or 2 times
        22% 3-5 times
        16% 6 times or more
At what age were you to a counselor?
        6% from 10-15 yrs.
        28% 16-20
        36% 20-30
        18% 30-35
        16% 35-45
        25% over 45

Have you failed to go to a counselor when you had a problem?
        41% Yes
        44% No
Why didn't you go?
        36% "should stand on own"
        50% "solved own problem"
        34% "not necessary"
        12% "no one could trust"
        12% "cost"
What was the nature of your problems?
        23% "personal, personality"
        18% "school, work"
        17% "values"
        31% "marital, sex"

To whom did you turn?

    20% doctor

    12% psychiatrist

    16% lawyer

    24% teacher

    34% clergy

    28% professional counselor

    14% to "others"

On what basis did you select the counselor?

    40% "through friend"

    48% "technical knowledge"

    14% miscellaneous

    22% referral

    26% advice

How select the specific person?

    46% "through friend"

    32% "because of person's reputation"

    20% "knew person was available"

    20% "referral"

How long did the counselor give you?

    22% 1 session

    26% 2-5 hours

    24% 6 or more prolonged sessions

Did the counselor try to help you find your own solution or give you his?

    24% Directive (counselor's)

    50% Non-directive

    20% "combination"

Did you have respect for the counselor?

    38% high yes

    73% qualified yes

    24% no

Did you consider him a stronger person?

    50% yes

    18% same

    26% less strong

What did he do to destroy your confidence?

       16% "incompetent"

       16% "lacked concern"

       18% other, manner

Were you satisfied?

       29% lifted burden, reassurance

       21% gave direct advice, answers

       20% helped client find solution

       15% helped gain new perspective

How were you dissatisfied?

        8% general dissatisfaction

       16% lack of interest

       17% cold, impersonal

Was the problem solved?

       43% yes

       33% no or qualified

Did you arrive at solution yourself . . .?

       34% solved self

       36% counselor made real contribution

       19% counselor returned problem to patient

Why do you go to a counselor?

       60% for advice

       40% to gain new perspective

       21% for reassurance, support

Did the counselor refer you to anyone else?

       18% yes

       74% no

To whom?

        6% to a psychiatrist

        5% to a lawyer

        4% to clergy

        3% to employer, teacher

Did he ask to see any other people who were involved with your problem?

       16% yes

       74% no

Whom did he ask to see?

      6% husband/wife

     10% other in dual conflict or relation

Have you ever acted as a counselor?

     45% yes

     36% no

For what kind of people?

     25% students

     20% peers, friends

     8% as official counselor

     4% other, various answers

For what kind of problems?

     10% academic, work

     10% personal

     16% marital

How frequently?

     15% sometimes

     23% often

     2% extended

Do you consider yourself adequately trained to counsel?

     29% no

     7% some

     13% yes

Do you consider yourself adequately experienced?

     29% no

     21% yes

Would you be willing to be interviewed?

     47% yes

     33% no

General reaction to questionnaire.

     50% co-operation

     47% neutral

     2% hostility

We ran innumerable *cross tabulations* among the various factors for each client group. In the *Supplement* at the end of this chapter we show tables for 110 of these cross tabulations of the general control group. We may now summarize these (the figure in parenthesis relates to the corresponding table).

AGE is an important factor in counseling. The younger go to a counselor less frequently (1), for fewer visits (4), but when they have a problem they are more likely to seek counsel (2). For all groups the most prominent reasons for not going to a counselor are: they solved or should solve their own problem; they felt it was not necessary; cost was a deterrent (5); there were no observable differences between age groups as to why they didn't go. The most common problems of all age groups are marital, sex, personal or personality problems. Younger people tend to have more problems involved with school and values than older people (3). Most people go to the clergy for counseling; older people tend to go more to doctors and lawyers; younger people tend to go more to teachers (6).

Cross tab (7) shows that counselees of all ages see their counselors as non-directive and this is most true of young people. All ages tended to be satisfied with the counseling they received (8). They were uniformly satisfied with directive or non-directive aid rather than with technical knowledge, advice, support, etc., of the counselor (9) (10), and with the contribution the counselor made, though nearly as many thought they solved the problem themselves (11). The youngest group was not as sure as the older groups that the problem actually was solved.

There was little age difference on how the counselor was chosen or what the client sought; older people tended to look to the nature of the problem and the counselor's standing, the younger ones to availability (12) (17) (22). The counselor was seen as carrying through and not referring by all age groups (27).

SEX is another obvious variable. Without detailing every item, we may show the result of some cross-tabs. About half have been to counselors, women slightly for more problems and for more sessions (13) (18). Yet, women seem to believe they have more problems because they state that

they have failed to go to a counselor more often than men
(14). Both sexes in equal proportions mentioned that they
solved or should solve their own problems as the reason for
not using a counselor (19). The most common problems for
both sexes were personal, sex, school, work, values. Women
mention the first two slightly more often than men and men
the last three (15). Women turned most frequently to the
clergy, next to doctors; men to lawyers and like counselors
(20). Both chose a counselor for his technical knowledge or
the nature of the problem. But females chose more on the
basis of empathy and friendship (16) (21), and preferred
the less directive (23). Women were a little more satisfied
with the counseling they received, with its non-directive
nature (24) (28). Women regarded the problem as solved
more often than men (25); there appeared no sex differences
in reporting that the counselor made a real contribution (30).
Men slightly preferred going to a counselor for advice,
women to get a new perspective (26).

If we consider *RELIGION* and its effect—approximately
one half of each religious group have been to a counselor,
with Catholics and non-affiliates going less times (32) (33).
Consistently, Protestants and non-affiliates predominated in
failing to go when they had a problem (34), while Catholics
are slightly less likely to list themselves as solving their own
problems (35). Catholics see themselves as having more
personality and value problems; those with no religion have
fewer value problems (36). The three religious groups turn
to the clergy. Catholics most so. Those who list no religion
see themselves as having fewer problems altogether, and as
choosing a specialist counselor (37). Most chose the counselor for technical knowledge or nature of the problem;
Catholics for the latter (44). Catholics chose friends more
often, atheists least often. Jews sought empathy (45).
Catholics seemed more satisfied than others, atheists less
satisfied (39). In (41) Jews and Catholics find satisfaction
with directive counseling more often than Protestants or
atheists, but (38) tends to contradict this. Jews and non-

affiliates were more specific in their dissatisfaction (40). Catholics saw counselor as making contribution more often. Jews were more likely to say they solved the problem by themselves (42) (43).

The matter of *RESIDENCE* causes some significantly different counseling patterns: metropolitan persons go more often (46), for more extended sessions (47), have more problems for they also fail to go most often (48), are less able to solve these themselves (49). The metropolitanite predominates in personality and value problems, the urbanite in marital-sex (50). The metropolitan group tended toward "sophisticated" counseling, the rural toward cheaper, friendly or none—*e.g.* metropolitan to the psychiatrist, specialist, selected for technical knowledge and nature of problem, nondirective; rural to the clergy, friend (51) (52) (72) (73) (80). Metropolitan respondents were less satisfied with the counseling (55), criticized directiveness (56), did not think the problem solved (58) (59), and gave reasons (57). There are more referrals in the metropolitan area (73) (81). The gradation on almost all tabulations is from rural, through urban, to metropolitan; rarely do two areas show the same pattern.

Training in *Psychology, Sociology,* or *Teaching* tends to make a person aware of his personality problems, have fewer value problems, go to a counselor more frequently (and report staying away when should go), seek a professional counselor and one expressing empathy, sense the directiveness of the counselor, believe that a competent counselor contributes to problem solution, usually by making the client solve the problem, are more critical but still tend to be satisfied (62) to (94).

Those who have themselves *acted as counselors* tend to see their counselor as a stronger person (99), to be satisfied with the counselor and the contribution he made (96) (97) (98), to arrive at solutions on their own (101), and to be more sophisticated in their choice (95) (102). Similarly, the more counseling type training the counselee has, the more he associates himself with the counselor, respects him, profits from him and works with him in solving the problem (103)-(110). [*NOTE*: This just may explain why lawyers have so much success (they believe—See ch. VI), because men who come to them are often business or other counselors and leaders and find it easy to use counseling].

c) *Psychological-Psychiatric Clinic Counselees*

The previous section had its primary value in permitting analysis of a near cross-section of the public. What percentage go and do not go to counselors, for what, why? What effect do age, religion, residence and like factors have? In short, what makes a counselee and what are his expectations and reactions. The present section relates to a second study which we did for a different purpose. Here we were questionnairing only those who had gone to a specialized type of counseling, and we had the advantage of knowing the counselor's analysis of the case. While we wished to check some of the statistics of the first section (*e.g.* effect of religion, sex, etc.) we were primarily interested in checking the counselee's *present* evaluation and attitude toward the counseling and a comparison of this to his intake record and the original appraisal of the counselor. We therefore set forth three groups of tabulations: 1-33 summarize the present questionnaire responses, 40-45 are from the counselee's original statements at the clinic, and 46-55 are made up from the counselor's report:

1)	*Age*	Largest group in middle 21-35 = 61%
2)	*Sex*	Female slightly greater = 55%
3)	*Single-Married*	S — 60%, M — 25%, Divorced — 8%
4)	*Religion*	Protestant - 27%, Jewish - 12%, Catholic - 6%, None None 29%
5)	*Training in Psychology, Sociology, Religion or Teaching*	Some — 30%, Specialized — 11%, Grad. level — 3%
6)	*How many times to clinic*	1-2 22%, 3-5 20%, 6-10 21%, 11-15 10%, 15-up 16%
7)	Match up of sex of counselor and counselee (in italics is counse*lor*)	*M*-M 60%, *F*-F 38%, *M*-F 60%, *F*-M 36%

8)	Nature of problem	marital-sex 22%, neurotic-psychotic 39%, inter-personal 21%, personality 28%, school-work 23%, values 12%
9)	How counseling terminated	patient quit 49%, counselor ended 23%, end of term, etc. 11%, still continuing 21%
10)	Directive-non directive	dir. 13%, non-dir. 58%
11)	Counselor Stronger	much 2%, little 41%, weak 22%, very weak 9%, blank 25%
12)	What caused you to respect counselor most/least	interest/lack interest 21%/9%; knowledge/lack of knowledge 24%/4%; active/did nothing 19%/18%; sex same/different 1%/2%; directive/non-directive 21%/7%
13)	Satisfied with counseling	yes 46%, no 37%, blank 17%
14)	Why	brought new perspective 33%, listened 23%, interested 7%, supported 5%
15)	Were problems solved	solved self 37%, counselor helped substantially 24%, disappeared 4%, not solved 28%
16)	Have you been to counseling besides clinic	yes 47%, no 37%
17)	How many occasions	1-2 22%, 3-10 13%, over 10 11%
18)	At what ages	under 21 28%, 21-35 29%, other 27%
19)	Failed to go when had problem	yes 54%, no 18%
20)	Why	ought to solve self 24%, not know available 9%, cost 14%, trival 12%
21)	Kind of problem taken	neurotic-psychotic 21%, personality 12%, sex-marital 11%, values-philosophy 10%, interpersonal 8%
22)	Kind of problem *not* taken	same problems in same order, lesser percentages
23)	How select counselor	referral 26%, knowledge-reputation 15%, cost 3%, religion 3%, friend 3%
24)	Counselor directive/non directive	dir. 15%, non-dir. 23%, combined 9%
25)	Did you respect him	much 4%, some 35%, disliked strongly 1%, disliked some 6%
26)	Did you consider him strong	very strong 2%, some 29%, somewhat weak 8% very weak 17%
27)	Did he do anything to destroy your confidence	yes 14%, no 28%
28)	To build it	yes 27%, no 10%

29) What	in this order: was directive, active, supportive, interested, human, (non-directive)
30) Were you satisfied with counseling	yes 28%, no 13%
31) Why	in this order: permissive-non directive, supportive, directive, active
32) Was problem solved	no 34%, solved self 21%, counselor helped substantially 18%, disappeared 2%
33) Why do you go to a counselor	new perspective 19%, advice 11%, lay burden on another — support 14%, listening-empathy 7%, technical knowledge 2%

TABLES 40-45 TAKEN FROM COUNSELEE'S ORIGINAL INTAKE STATEMENTS.

40) Problem	depression, neurotic-psychotic 26%, school-work 28%, interpersonal 23%, personality, inadequacy 21%, marriage-sex 19%, values 12%
41) Number sessions	1-2 28%, 3-5 21%, 6-10 21%, 11-15 10%, over 15 18%
42) Why came	self referral 44%, other referral (suggestion) 43%
43) For what upsetting occurrences	same as questionnaire 22%, greater on school-work by 9%, recent trauma mentioned 10%, greater on sex-marriage 5%

44) Counselee attitudes		
Hostile	considerable 11%	to none 21%
Empathy	considerable 66%	to none 6%
Defensive	considerable 47%	to none 18%
Distrust	considerable 29%	to none 16%
Anxiety	considerable 35%	to none 22%
Stereotype	considerable 4%	to none 23%

45) Counselee satisfaction		
with counseling	yes 54%	no 24%
with counselor	yes 45%	no 27%
with result	yes 31%	no 32% unclear 27%

TABLES 46-55 FROM COUNSELOR REPORTS.

46) Match up sex counselor-counselee	same 72% dif. 24% (compared to counselee figures).
47) Counselor diagnosis	same as counselee 62%, different 18% (more severe 14%, less severe 4%) deferred 10%
48) Psychiatric labels used by counselor	passive-aggressive 20%, obsessive-compulsive 13%, personality disturbance 12%, adolescent carryover 11%, anxiety 9%, depressive 9%, schizoid 7%, stress 4%, paranoia-phobia 3%, deferred-yo yo 22%
49) Treatment	directive 7%, non-directive 21%, combined 29%, listen 21%, support 34%
50) Counselor involvement	little 12%, medium 52%, great 12%

51)	Need for deeper treatment recognized	yes 40%		no 25%		unclear 21%	
52)	Recommended	yes 34%		no 21%		unclear 20%	
53)	Attitude of counselor	Hostile	considerable	3% none 25% unclear 70%			
		Empathy	considerable	61% none 5% unclear 25%			
		Defensive	considerable	2% none 23% unclear 65%			
		Distrust	considerable	1% none 23% unclear 65%			
		Anxiety	considerable	1% none 22% unclear 66%			
		Stereotyped	considerable	1% none 23% unclear 66%			
54)	Termination	end term 9%, treatment completed 12%, joint decision 33%, by counselor 5%, by counselee 41%					
55)	Counselor satisfaction	with counseling	yes 54%	no 24%			
		with counselee	yes 45%	no 27%			
		with result	yes 31%	no 32%	unclear 27%		

We may draw the following conclusions from this group:

The known availability of an open and low cost clinic adds to counseling use. Proportionately more marrieds, females and Jews and those without religion came. Even though psychiatry claims little can be done under 15 sessions, counseling here was mostly short term (1-6 sessions) and terminated by the counselee (the counselor preferring deeper treatment 40% of the time, but usually not carrying through).

The same general pattern resulting from residence and religion which we have already noted, obtained. This sample was sophisticated in psychology, sociology and teaching and this revealed itself as high in awareness, willingness to seek counsel, expectation, criticism of result yet cooperation where good interrelationship was felt. In the questionnaire, because of lack of space, we had to forego the question of the counselee having himself acted as counselor; but in interviews we found much the same pattern as previously reported.

The client went to get new perspectives, advice and support(note they are going to a frankly "psychiatric" clinic) yet the counselor tried to psychoanalize nearly every entrant (note the large number psychiatrically labelled). The client rates his problems as marital-sex and personality, whereas the clinician views it more as neurotic-psychotic or tends to defer diagnosis. Many fail to go, or fail to go many times, mainly because they are ashamed and believe people should be able to solve their problems (the better educated particularly). Because of the nature of the clinic, referral is a major cause of first contact; but in self-referral the already reviewed factors of training, reputation and cost are operative. Both men and women clients prefer men counselors, remain with them and progress better. Both sexes resent women counselors (men more so except where woman plays mother role). Women counselors seem to prefer men and men counselors to prefer women counselees.

The counselee wanted the counselor stronger (but a surprising number saw him as weak), directive, interested and supportive. The counselors tended to be eclectic, supportive and avoiding involvement; they considered themselves stronger. Both counselees and counselors were most satisfied with counseling, less with the counselor (counselee) and least with outcome. Both rated empathy high (60-65%); the counselees revealed high anxiety, hostility-distrust, defensiveness —but, the counselors embodied some of these same patterns. The counselee saw himself as causing termination; the counselor saw it as mutual or, where the counselee terminated, as premature and needful of deeper treatment. Rarely was the problem "solved" according to either, but both felt there had been help.

An attempt was made to determine whether the client really wanted psychonanalysis (short or long) or mere counseling, and whether certain clinicians were more adaptable to this. We believe that something was lost by the clinic being labelled psychological-psychiatric, that a counselee most often early-terminated when he did not get prompt counseling but was treated by classical analysis ("he sat there and smoked his d - - - pipe"), that the most successful counselors were psychologists with wide experience and common sense (and psychiatrists of the same mold).

d) *Legal Aid*

In our study of clients of legal aid, we had questionnaires passed out to clients as they came to a session; we thus caught the one-interview applicant. We attempted to make the form simpler, because all cases would be charity and of less well educated persons. Even then we found a high percentage of meaningless responses on some questions. We also had the aid of a report by the lawyer and the social worker (where one was involved) on every tenth case. In spite of the limitations of the sampled group (and we found no way to get to lawyers' clients otherwise) we found very suggestive statistics appearing.

First, the raw scores are given and then some conclusions from cross tabulations of the data.

LEGAL AID RAW SCORES

1. Age
   - 4%   under 20
   - 22%   21-30
   - 27%   31-40
   - 20%   41-50
   - 25%   51 +

2. Sex
   - 34%   male
   - 66%   female

3. Marital Status
   - 7%   single
   - 61%   married
   - 17%   divorced
   - 8%   widowed

4. Religion
   - 63%   Protestant
   - 27%   Catholic
   - 2%   Jewish
   - 1%   None
   - 2%   Other

5. Size of Family
   - 18%   1
   - 16%   2
   - 16%   3
   - 11%   4
   - 10%   5
   - 7%   6
   - 4%   7
   - 5%   8 +

6. Total Monthly Income
   - 25%   less than $100
   - 5% $100-150
   - 11%   151-200
   - 11%   201-250
   - 8%   251-300
   - 12%   301-400
   - 5%   400 +

7. How Many Times Did You See the Bureau Lawyer
   - 48%   1
   - 18%   2
   - 11%   3
   - 8%   4

8. What Was the Problem You Took to Him
   - 22%   Bu (business)
   - 39%   Ma (marital)
   - 3%   P (suing)
   - 4%   D (being sued)

10% 5 or more
6% NA

2% Criminal
13% Wages
23% Debt
6% Personal
5% Interpersonal

9. Why Do You Feel You Needed a Lawyer
  60% Legal question
  8% Already in law
  16% Needed advice
  10% No place to turn
  8% Other

10. What Did You Like Most About the Lawyer
  2% Satisfying
  23% Technical knowledge
  2% Non-directive
  7% Acceptance
  48% Actions, manner
  11% Directiveness
  13% Interest
  2% Certainty
  11% Took over

11. What Did You Like Least
  5% No satisfaction
  3% Non-directive
  3% Actions, manner
  5% Took over
  83% No answer—

12. Were You Satisfied With His Counseling
  76% Yes
  16% No

13. Why Were You Satisfied
  13% Solved
  20% Technical knowledge
  8% Listened
  17% Took action
  14% Directive
  5% Interest
  2% Certainty
  23% Took over

14. Did the Lawyer Himself Take Over Your Case and Do All the Work on it
  45% Yes
  29% No

15. . . . or Did He Help You Find Your Own Solution
  25% Yes
  27% No

16. Did He Refer You to Anyone Else
  18% Yes
  49% No

17. Who
  4% a social worker
  8% lawyer
  6% other
  83% no answer

18. Did You See a Social Worker in the Bureau
  30% Yes
  54% No

19. How Many Times
  14% 1

20. Did the Social Worker Help You More Than the Lawyer

7%   2
4%   3
5%   4

21. How and in What Way
    1%   Technical knowl-
         edge
    2%   Non-directive
    1%   Action taken
    4%   Directive
    1%   Interested
    2%   Together with
         lawyer

23. How and in What Way
    9%   Caution
    14% Knowledge
    4%   Confidence
    6%   Adjustment
    4%   Support

25. How Many Times
    9%   1
    16% 2
    8%   3
    2%   4
    13% 5 or more

27. From Whom You Have
    Sought Advice
    27% Lawyers
    14% Doctors
    21% Clergy
    5%   Marriage Coun-
         selor
    18% Social Worker
    24% Friend*
    1%   Psychologist
    7%   Other

29. How Did You Select These
    Other Counselors
    4%   Nature of problem

(% of those seeing Social
worker):
    7%   Yes
    43% No
    47% No answer

22. Has the Help You Received
    From the Lawyer or Social
    Worker Aided You in Hand-
    ling Later Problems
    41% Yes
    26% No

24. Have You Sought Advice
    From Others
    50% Yes
    37% No

26. Over What Years
    14% present
    4%   2 prior
    2%   older
    1%   very old
    21% continuous
    57% no answer

28. What Was the Problem You
    Took To These Counselors
    12% Business
    25% Marital
    1%   Suing
    1%   Being Sued
    1%   Criminal
    3%   Wages
    7%   Debt
    9%   Personal
    3%   Interpersonal

30. With What Counseling Were
    You Satisfied
    6%   Legal aid

---

* Most did not consider friend a counselor, higher % talk to friend.

6%   Knowlege
1%   Empathy
5%   Religion
5%   Friend
2%   Reputation
19%   Referral

31. Why Unsatisfied
1%   Not satisfied
3%   Incompetent
2%   Too non directive
2%   No action
3%   Too bossy
3%   Not interested

33. Did You Feel That You Arrived At A Solution By Yourself
17%   Yes
34%   No

35. Did the Counselor Help You
14%   No
19%   Little
5%   More
4%   Average
7%   Considerably

37. Have You Had A Problem Which You Did Not Take to a Counselor
37%   Yes
24%   No

39. Why Did You Not Go
4%   No one available
21%   Solved self
4%   Too personal
3%   No one cares
2%   Cost

12%   All
5%   Lawyer
2%   Doctor
4%   Clergy
1%   Other
68%   No answer

32. Was Your Problem Solved
20%   Yes
32%   No

34. Did the Problem Disappear on its Own
4%   Yes
41%   No

36. Why Do You Think People Go To A Counselor
5%   New perspective
9%   Nature of problem
25%   Advice
37%   Support
1%   Listener
20%   Technical knowledge

38. How Often (not take)
3%   1
2%   2
4%   3
1%   4
27%   5 or more

40. What Were These Problems
2%   Business
12%   Marital
4%   Debt
14%   Personal
3%   Interpersonal
4%   Health

SOME LEGAL AID CROSS TABULATIONS:

	Men Showed This Pattern	*Women Showed This*
Problem:	business, wages, debt	marital, psychological
Go to or liked lawyer for	technical, knowledge,	new perspective, manners

Whom seek	taking over lawyer	interest, clergy, doctor
Satisfied	more lawyer, less other	more social worker, less
Fail to Take		lawyer
problems	less	more (5 times men)
Why	should solve self	did not know available
Frequency of		
seek advice	less	more
Referral	less	more

Religious effect on counseling showed up in many ways. Protestants more frequently than Catholics took marital problems to the lawyer, liked his manners and interest, sought him for technical knowledge, were satisfied. More Catholics than Protestants took business and personal problems, more frequently did not take problems they had or marital problems, had had more frequent other counseling, came through referral and were again referred elsewhere, sought support, went to clergy for advice. Both groups were about equally vague and doubtful as to how much the counselor contributed. Surprisingly few Jews utilized the service, though it was considerably staffed by Jews.

The lower the income bracket, the more marital and debt problems, the more they came through referral, the more they came to this type free service, the less they were satisfied with the result, the more they felt brushed off. The more money one had the more technical knowledge he sought, the more he solved his own problems, the more often he failed to take problems to others, the more he turned to doctors-lawyers and avoided clergy marriage counselors and social workers, and was more often referred elsewhere.

The less one saw the lawyer, the more he felt left to solve the problem himself, respected the counselor's knowledge but not his actions or interest, the less satisfied he was with the results. The more a person saw a lawyer, the more he felt the lawyer was interested and took over, the more likely he was also to have seen a social worker, and stayed with this one rather than be referred, thus the more he was satisfied.

If the client was satisfied with the counseling he felt helped in handling later problems, tended to find his own solutions. Those who sought advice, support or technical knowledge were most likely to be dissatisfied. Those who had many problems and had visited many counselors seemed "satisfied" but didn't think the problem "solved"; their predominant problem was marital and they had failed to go to counselors most often.

The clients generally felt they came to a lawyer because they saw the core of their problem as legal, they did not like being shunted off to a social worker. They liked most the lawyer's action, knowledge, taking over and support; they were not so interested in empathy and manners. Those going for advice were least likely to report problems which they did not take to counselors. The more a person expected and relied on advice, the more he seemed to seek it, and the less easily was he satisfied.

e) *Parents Without Partners*

In one part of this study we were attaching questions concerning counseling to a survey already contemplated by Parents Without Partners (PWP) which was most concerned with reasons for divorce and effect upon children and child rearing; in another part we asked only our questions of PWP members in another city. We tried to get somewhat the same age, religion, place of residence and education as in the general sample; (questions 1a to 21a, 1c to 10c, 65a-66, 35c-36c) and we tried to ask each party the same question for you/him-her (oneself and mate). The major questions on counseling were from 16b to 37b for self and parallel 46c to 31d for spouse; other pairs of important questions were 29a to 61a and 32c on nature of problem, reconciliation and counseling: 4b to 13b and 48b to 60b, (cf 38c to 45c and 42d to 53d) on personal adjustment since marriage dissolution. [All these portions of the questionnaire form appear in the Appendix].

We have confined ourselves to correlations within the "counseling" portion of the survey and certain obvious correlations of the "counseling" portion with other criteria.

Correlation within the counseling portion can be illustrated by the following: All responses were correlated as to self (a) and (b) and as to spouse (c) and (d) question:

19-21b (Reason for seeking aid) vs 22-24b (Types of counseling used).

22-24b (Type of counseling) vs 25-27b (Basis of choice).

19-21b (Reason for seeking) vs 25-27b (Basis of choice).

22-24b (Type of counseling) vs 37b (Evaluation of help received).

22-24b (Type of counseling) vs 38b (Sexual problems).

19-21b (Reason for seeking) vs 37b (Evaluation of help received).

25-27b (Basis of choice)   vs 37b (Evaluation of help received).

22-24b (Type of counseling) vs 52-54c (Type counseling).

18b (Counsel for self during marriage) vs 48c, 59c.

Many other combinations were used. We have tried more to get a general profile of the respondent and his picture of the ex-spouse. Within these definitions, the following can be said well above a significant chi square level:

The respondent rates self well above the ex-spouse in counseling sophistication—before, during and after marriage. This is particularly true among the divorced as compared to the widowed. The respondent views self as primarily trying to hold marriage together as compared to ex-spouse. The respondent views the ex-spouse as thinking that counseling was worthless or harmful. (48c combined with 31d). For both the respondent and ex-spouse there is the smallest degree of counseling pre-marriage, more during, most since (not true for widowed compared to divorced).

While respondent likes to view self as "to save marriage" compared to "personal adjustment" (56-44%), if one puts "save marriage" and "cooperative gesture" in 19b together and does the same for "personal adjustment" and "personal evaluation," the score reverses to (47-53%). It would seem that these two syndromes were about equal. Overall, by far the largest group go to "private counselors;" clinics are second, clergy third, family physician and group therapy fourth, lawyers fifth. The private counselor is seen about equally to save the marriage or for personal adjustment. Group therapy is primarily for personal adjustment. The family physician and clergyman is used to save marriage. The respondent *says* that the lawyer is seen primarily to save the marriage (2 to 1) yet a check of question 31b shows that for 72% respondent and 75% for ex-spouse, divorce has been decided upon before going to the lawyer. It is probable that the 31b response is more accurate and the 22-24b vs 19-21b correlation is more "wishful thinking."

In trying to determine why people select particular counselors it appears that the questions were not as clear or sharp as we might desire. "Referral" is the most important for all counselors (about 2 to 1 to 5 to 1). This is surprising as to the clergy and family physician. The only place where another factor plays a greater role is "cost" in going to a clinic as compared to a private counselor. One would have expected to find "cost" predominating as to the clergy (no cost); but while it is a strong factor it is not predominant. The only three factors with sufficient frequency to be important, and in that order, are: referral, cost, friend (19-21b, 22-24b, 25-27b). The same results seem confirmed by playing 22b against 25b only. "Prominence" or reputation is generally considered by most professional persons as their greatest drawing card, yet the study fails to show this. There is a slightly greater emphasis on "cost," "prominence," "proximity" for the widowed compared to the divorced. This may be accounted for by the counseling being more "normal" than "crisis" in these cases.

. If we play income (6b) against types of counseling used (22-24b) we find that the lower the income the more frequent it is to use "none," to go to clergymen and family physicians. When we get into the "bourgeoise" level of around $5000 popularity of "group therapy" and mental hygiene clinics plays a disproportionate part; the private counselor begins to become the normal pattern. Lawyers begin to come in. The clergyman and family physician fade out. In the upper incomes (over $8000) the emphasis is definitely on the private counselor. Lawyers are still prominent. The other categories have retreated. Few record "none." At the very top of the scale they go to private counselors or not at all; surprisingly "none" re-appears with frequency.

Can one predict the satisfaction which the client will show with the counseling? We already had a very large sampling of client satisfaction in the other studies we made with persons going to private counselors, clinics; paying, free, etc.; for lawyers, doctors including psychiatrists, clergymen; from various parts of the country. We hypothecated that, if we considered "somewhat adequate" as "neutral," we would find about as much dissatisfaction below the line as satisfaction above it, that there would be more satisfaction with lawyers and doctors and clergymen than with other counselors generally, that there would be more dissatisfaction with clinics (including free or reduced fee) than with privately hired counselors. These predictions were verified by Parents without Partners at significant levels, e.g. private counselor satisfaction was 59% above to 41% below; clinics were 55% above to 45% below, etc.; clergymen were 3 times as frequent above as below. One surprise was in the number who rated the experience actually harmful as compared to inadequate; almost half as many thought it harmful as merely inadequate.

It appears that when the respondent or ex-spouse seeks counseling for personal adjustment or to evaluate personality they will be satisfied with counseling from 2 out of 3 times to 4 out of 7 times. If they seek counseling to save the marriage they will be satisfied and dissatisfied about equally or on a 1 to 1 ratio. Or we may look at the basis of choice of counselor and counselor satisfaction. Friend, prominence, cost as a basis of choice will insure about equal satisfaction-dissatisfaction. Mere geographic nearness, phonebook, newspaper or radio seem to produce dissatisfaction. Referral seems to assure satisfaction about 2 to 1.

Some rather strange (or perhaps not so strange) results appear when correlating income and evaluation of or satisfaction with counseling. The lower income group (under $5000) is most frequently satisfied, or at least not dissatisfied (about 2 to 1 or 3 to 2). Those in the $5000 to $8000 group are about even in satisfaction and dissatisfaction. From $8000 to $14,000 there is more dissatisfaction than satisfaction (about 3 to 2). In high incomes (going to private counselors only) the norm is satisfaction.

It may be hypothecated that the number of times married will have a direct bearing on such questions as reasons for seeking aid, types of counseling, satisfaction, etc. We tested these. The fewer the number of marriages the greater will be the emphasis on saving the marriage. The greater the number of marriages the greater will be the emphasis on personal adjustment and personality analysis. Treatment of children will play a larger role in first marriages counseling, court order a greater role in subsequent marriages. Lawyers, family physicians and the clergymen will be visited in single marriages; group therapy and mental health clinics will take over for multiple marriages. Whereas in first marriage counseling the counselor is selected on every conceivable basis: cost, referral, proximity, prominence, friend, advertising, etc.; subsequent marriages rely almost completely on referral. We find no significant variant on counseling before, during, after marriage and at the present time as related to the number of times married. Before marriage about 8% have had counseling for single marriages, about 10% for multiple marriages (to be expected since counseling in or after the first marriage becomes pre-marriage as to later marriages). During marriage about 47% do receive in first marriages, about 50% in multiple. After marriage it is 58% for first marriages, 56% for multiple. Psychiatry at the present time is 25% for first, 26% for multiple.

A somewhat similar picture can be painted as to the question of the number of years married compared to the various items on counseling. First, there are two marked bumps in the curve of divorces or reasons for seeking counseling, one for marriages of 5-9 years duration and another from 15-19 years. This pretty much coincides with other nationally published studies. Saving the marriage is the more frequent reason for counseling in the earlier stage, personality adjustment at the later periods. Just as above we saw that lawyers, doctors, clergymen were more frequently used where the counselee had fewer marriags, so they are turned to in the earlier years of marriage; private counselors of other types, group therapy and mental health clinics become more important later. Cost, friends, geographic proximity are more important factors in choice of counselor in early years of marriage than in later ones. Referral and prominence take on the major importance in later years.

There is little clear correlation between going to a counselor and the years before separation occurs; at 4-6, 7-9, 13-15 years we show 9% had been counseled before marriage. As to those who go to counselors after separation there is something of a bulge at either end—those under 7 years go about 58% of the time; those over 20 about 72% of the time; in the middle at 10-12 years married only 44% seek counseling. There is no substantial variation as to years married for those presently in counseling—the figure runs from 22 to 25% in all categories. There is a fairly significant observation about gross income and length of marriage. Those under $2000 per year tend to divorce quickly (under 10 years); in the $2000-$5000 bracket the spread is over all the scale, but the highest (25%) is in 7-9 years. From $5000 to $8000 the spread is the whole range but the highest (65%) fall in 5-10 years. The higher you go the later seems the break—at $8000, the highest (40%) is 13-15 years and at $11,000, the highest (35%) is 16-19 years.

We also tried the number of years living apart to see its correlation with various factors: *First*: As to gross income. Those under $2000 tended to remarry quickly, all under 5 years, most under 2. For the $2000-$5000 70% remarried within 2-5 years, but there were still 3% unmarried after 10 years. In the $5000-$8000 category 73% married within 5 years but 6% remained unmarried at 10. However, the over $8000 showed Respondent 69 and Spouse 82% remarrying within 3 years and only 3 and 0% unmarried after 10. *Second*: There seemed almost no correlation between reason for seeking counsel and number of years living apart. The figure was substantially the same for personality sought to protect children as prime cause lived over 1/3 longer apart. *Third*: Very little difference appeared on length of time separate and what counselor they went to. Lawyers, clergy and physicians (family) correlated with the adjustment and saving the marriage; however those who quickest remarriage; lawyers the quickest of all. *Fourth*: The basis for selecting counselor had no correlation with length living separate. *Fifth*: Where in the prior marriage there was agreement on the husband's role or on the wife's role, marriage occurred more quickly the second time. In both cases there were few left after 5 years of separation: 11-13% where agree on H and W roles; 25-32% where disagree as to H and W roles respectively. *Sixth*: Though it was predicted that lack of counsel before and obtaining counsel after separation would show a higher correlation on quick remarriage, the hypothesis was not verified. There were no clear trends; the percentage was within 1 point at under 1 year, 3 years and 10 years. Nor did we find any correlation when there had been counseling both before and since separation; about the same percentage obtained for 2, 3, 5 and 10 years. There was some evidence that those who presently were in therapy did not remarry until therapy was finished and that this added a year or two to separation.

Education level of the respondent and of the spouse was also an important factor correlated with counseling. It became clear that the higher the education the more sought counseling by private counselors and specialists and did not turn to clergy and family physicians. High School: 30% saw private counselor, 35% doctor or clergy, 35% none. College years and college graduates used private counselor 40%, others 25%, none 35%. For advanced degrees it was 45% for private, 20% others and 35% none. It also appeared that respondent's own educational level showed even higher correlation: H.S. 40/45/15. College 35/40/25. Advanced degree 60/35/5. The college level seeks counseling most (25% H.S., 62% college, 13% grads). In general, respondent getting counseling tended to be equal to or one stage above the spouse.

A higher tendency toward counseling appears in higher education:

	Counsel before,	during,	since	now	ex spouse now
High School	5%	48%	56%	25%	10%
College	8	44	55	23	11
Grads	13	71	81	33	14

Reasons for seeking aid were to save marriage and child treatment at lower educational levels; personality development at upper levels:

	Personal Adjustment	Save Marriage	Child Treatment
High School	29%	52%	19%
College	41	50	9
Grads	45	47	8

In choice of counselor, referral and prominence (reputation) became more important at higher education levels and cost considerations decreased:

	Cost	Referral	Friend	Prominence
High School	31%	43%	18%	8%
College	23	59	13	7
Grads	16	58	11	11

The higher the education the less they valued the counseling, though they appear to go more often. High School graduates valued favorably 79%, College 72%, Grad 62%. The rated aids to adjustment after separation show different patterns for each education level. The order for each—HS: children, work, friends, dating, therapy, recreation, church. College: work, therapy, children, friends, dating, recreation, church. Grads: work, children, therapy, friends, dating (no votes for church, recreation).

Another dimension related to many factors is whether the respondent has counseling *during* marriage. If respondent has counseling, then 2/3 of the ex-spouses do; if respondent does not, then 3/4 of ex-spouses do not. The annual income shows a correlation with counseling during marriage —42% of the $5000 group; 49% at $8000; 52% at $11,000, 75% at $14,000; 50% over $14,000 have such counseling. Whether the person grew up in a rural, urban or metropolitan area does not have much relation to seeking counsel: 50% for the rural, 52% urban, 57% metropolitan. Having counseling during marriage does seem to have a positive effect after separation, *e.g.* 69% feel a trend toward better health; a larger percentage seek and continue in counseling (36% who had compared to 16% who didn't). They are on better terms with their ex-spouse (55% to 45%) and grieve less the loss of ex-spouse (4% points different). The counseled do not remain single but remarry within a reasonable time (2-5 years): 72%; 54% remain single the first year. There was no correlation between any of the following and going for counseling during marriages: length of time they went together or were engaged; active or joint participation in organizations; agreement as to H-W roles; sex as an expression of love and affection; whether love and affection diminished during marriage; basis for selection of mates; who was viewed as responsible for break-up. The steadier the husband's job habits and the longer the marriage existed, the greater was the tendency to seek counseling during marriage: 11% married 1-3 years sought it; 47% of those 7-9 years; the highest (62%) was in 10-12 years and 13-15 years (60%). Although, as seen above, counseling during marriage made some adjustments after marriage better, it had the effect also of discontent or uncertainty as shown by two correlations: those who sought counseling during marriage felt society accepted them less (67%) than those who had no counseling (81%). Similarly those who sought counseling during marriage were less indifferent to what their ex-spouse did after marriage: 45% were hurt by spouse remarrying, 43% thought it was all right and 12% were indifferent. Among the non-counseled the figures were 25%, 24%, and 51% indifferent.

The dimension of religion, we have noted throughout our study, is a significant factor. Of the respondents 5% had no religion, 3% were Catholic, 24% Protestant, 64% Jewish, 3% other. There is identity in religion of the separating parties: 60% Catholic, 68% Protestant, 87% Jewish; but the successful marriages showed higher identity. For Catholics and Jews breakup is more likely where *neither* is religiously active (60% Catholics, 53% Jews); for Protestants it is about evenly divided—24% neither active, 28% both active, 24% respondent only active. Interestingly, where both are religiously active or *neither* is religiously active the parties agree much more on religious beliefs and practices than disagree (88% both active, 75% both inactive). But where one is active and other not, they agree only 33%. Parties tended to stay with an active affiliation before marriage and continue this religious affiliation into marriage (75% stay, 25% change); by like token no affiliation before continued (80% continued, 20% change). One party active affiliation is a major cause of discord and continues beyond the break. Likewise greater percentage go for counseling during or after marriage where both have active religious affiliation. (As to premarriage counseling the greatest amount occurs where respondent differs from spouse—perhaps because he or she counsels for this specifically):

Before	Resp. 19%	Both 9%	Neither 4%
During	44	56	40
Since	60	72	50

Note: This may not represent the "religious" as much as the "common" factor because participating in organizations yields same results (Resp. 22%, both 55%, neither 24%). There seems to be no correlation between activeness in religion and such items as reason for seeking counsel, type of counselor, basis of choice and ultimate health.

Overall, Parents without Partners provided a number of important conclusions for us. Even when one has a specific type problem (matrimonial) for which there are well known specialists, he rarely picks the specialist. Confidence in counseling is more important than special knowledge. Counselors are often brought in too late to be of much help. Doctors and clergy tend to serve the less educated and lower income groups. Lawyers even at a late stage are expected to do more than get a divorce. Higher education encourages counseling but is also critical of it. The specific problem (save the marriage) may turn out to be secondary when a counselor is actually sought. The percentage of persons who ought to seek counseling but do not is quite astonishing. The role of friends is very great. The quality of counseling is still suspect. Client openness to counseling appears even more important than counseling ability.

f) *Counselees of Clergy*:

As has been pointed out, this was the smallest group of repliers (about 300). They averaged 34 years of age, were predominantly rural and urban, with little training in the social sciences, about 60/40 unmarried and married. Whereas in the general control sample the repliers were 75% male and 24% female, and total in all groups 60% male and 40% female, the percentage was reversed here 32% male and

68% female. The men who went to clergy seemed younger (20-25) and older (60-), with emphasis on deciding life purpose, premarital problems and aging. They were not proud of turning to clergy. Women had more sessions than men (average 8 compared to 3.2). Both men and women prefer the counselor to be male. Females defined most problems as religious-moral: sex and her role therein, motherhood, vocation (service), relations with parents and others (moral duty) and religion itself. She rates relation with a clergy as "personal" but with a psychiatrist or medic or other counselor as "impersonal".

This group, as expected, confirmed the general observation that a clergyman is the first counselor sought. Two factors seem majorly responsible: free service and ever present availability. Many counselees reported that the clergyman suggested counseling in the process of conversations, study groups, house visits, etc.; that they went because "he was my pastor" or "it arose naturally from our relationship"; few came through referrals. They saw the counselor as non-directive (probably accurately), kindly, concerned, loving, tolerant, stronger and an object of respect, (in some cases almost all-knowing) to a much higher degree than for other counselees-counselors. The prime reason for not taking a problem to a minister was still: "one ought to solve his own problems". But here a new reason appears; "half expected him to suggest I come to him", "lack of his initiative". The counselees brought problems in this order of importance: marital-sexual, values, interpersonal. They sought and got reassurance, tolerance, forgiveness, a new perspective. They were aware that many clergy are now psychologically sophisticated.

Counselees of clergy take their problems to the counselor at an earlier stage, consider this the reason for greater success and urge greater availability at an even earlier point. They like the clergyman to tell them stories of others in the same predicament (a form of gossip as well as assurance that he "knows his stuff"), and believe clergy are the best counselors because they relate the problem and solution to the larger environment in which the counselee is otherwise lost.

Though the clergy (see Ch. 6) talked about many problems being psychosomatic, counselees did not so rate their problems (this may be a clerical "lingo", just as "yo-yo" or "personality disorder" is for the psychiatrist). These clients were most cooperative with the questionnaire but wanted to remain anonymous and not to be interviewed. They revealed problems in the realm of law, psychiatry, finance, marriage counseling, and they found the clergyman handling all problems, rarely referring (a few psychiatrists). Contrary to the general sample there was here no indication that one religious group used counseling more frequently than another. A large percentage of these counselees claim to have given counsel as well as received it.

(g) *Examination of Series "O" Questions as to Clients.*

As we have elsewhere pointed out, we early "threw our minds around" as to possible broad observations as to clients which might come from all the data. These were set forth in XII topic subdivisions and 38 questions as series "O". Many of these have been answered, statistically and otherwise, at earlier points in this chapter. Here, we set forth the list of topics and questions in order that they can be quickly related to the earlier data. And we also add a brief comment in caps after each topic; these comments have been composed from the author's overall "feel" for the questionnaire and interview replies rather than by going back over the specific statistics:

SERIES "O"
CLIENT QUESTIONNAIRES.

Note: These deal with the following areas, as well as the clear categories from the questionnaire itself. See accompanying sheets as ways for asking some of the questions.

I. *Client*:

    a) Who is he? Age, sex, religion, class, degree of training, etc.? [SEE PP 142, 144-149]

    b) Real and ideal client? His self-image? Ideal of counselor, etc? [REAL CLIENT IS OFTEN NOT READY FOR COUNSELING. IDEAL CLIENT ONE WITH ENOUGH ANXIETY TO HAVE HIGH MOTIVATION TO BE HELPED, BUT NOT WITH SO MUCH AS TO INACTIVATE HIM. HATES TO SEE SELF AS DEPENDENT. PREFERS TO BE MET ON LEVEL OF FEELING RATHER THAN INTELLECT, BY CONCERNED, TOLERANT, PATIENT BUT DIRECTIVE COUNSELOR].

    c) His personality? Revealed by what? [MOST REVEALING IS TOTAL TONE OF QUESTIONNAIRE OR INTERVIEW, QUESTIONNAIRE INADEQUATE TO SUPPLY IN MOST INSTANCES. PERSONALITY-TO-PERSONALITY SEEMS MOST IMPORTANT FACET OF COUNSELING. MATCHED=SATISFIED; UNMATCHED=DISSATISFIED].

    d) Communication problem (each of above and all other categories could be broken down in great detail—let's do it here). What is communication problem? What is effect of items like:

Tolerance +	Ajustments ±
Safety +	Values ±
Ego-strength +	Emotional climate ±
Past experiences (punitive) ±	Length interview ±
Understanding +	Empathy +
Love +	Distortion —
Semantics ±	Support ±
Verbal ability +	Silence ±
Covert communication ±	Expectancy ±
Anxiety ±	Authority figure ±

[ALL THESE SEEM IMPORTANT. ALL ARE
MARKED PLUS, MINUS OR PLUS-MINUS ±.
SEE PARTICULARLY CHS. 3 AND 9].

   e) Client view of counselor? Of counseling process?
Of success? [CLIENT NOT AS SATISFIED
WITH COUNSELING AS WAS COUNSELOR.
GENERALLY RESPECTED COUNSELOR;
THOUGHT COUNSELING PROCESS TOO
STEREOTYPED; WANTED MORE EMO-
TIONAL INTERRELATION].

II. *Counselor* (as client sees him):
   a) Same questions as for client?
   b) His variables:

Ideation +	Understanding of client
Values	Self understanding
Personality (x)	Conflict areas or traits
Philosophy	Training
Social background	Sex, age, etc.,(x)
Social status	Empathetic ability (x)
Flexibility (x)	Anxiety
Breadth of interest	Defensiveness
Intellectual curiosity	Biases
Intelligence	Directiveness (x)
Communication (x)	Emotional involvement (x)

[PRACTICALLY ALL THESE MENTIONED
BY CLIENTS AS POSITIVELY OR NEG-
ATIVELY IMPORTANT. THOSE MARKED
(x) MOST FREQUENTLY MENTIONED].

III. *Going to Counselor*:
   a) Timing [CLIENT TIMING GENERALLY BAD.
USUALLY LATE. RESULT OF LACK OF
KNOWLEDGE OF AVAILABILITY AND
FEELING OUGHT TO HANDLE OWN PROB-
LEMS].
   b) Availability [FEW KNOW OF AVAILABIL-

ITY; TEND TO USE FRIENDS AS MOST AVAILABLE; CLERGY COME NEXT; CLINICS].

c) Stage of awareness and readiness, motivation [UNREALISTIC. SEE BELOW].

d) Cost [IMPORTANT FACTOR. LACK OF FAVORS CLERGYMAN. GUIDANCE AND SCHOOL COUNSELORS BEING FREE COLORS THIS. PSYCHIATRIST-LAWYER SEEM AS PROHIBITIVE].

e) What matters to be self handled? [UNEXPECTED FINDING THAT ANY "PROBLEM" SEEN AS PERSONAL AND NOT TO BE SHARED. INTERPERSONAL, ADJUSTMENT, FAILURE, SEX, PARTICULARLY].

f) Fears, expectancies, etc.? Different to different professions? [GENERAL FEAR OF LAWYER; MYSTIFIED BY PSYCHIATRIST; YOUNGER INCREASINGLY ALIENATED FROM CLERGY. GO TO PROFESSION ASSUMED SIMILAR TO WAY WILLING TO VIEW PROBLEM].

g) Difference student or non-student? Social class? Intelligence? [STUDENT MORE COOPERATIVE WITH STUDY; NOT, HOWEVER, BETTER CLIENT. NATIVE INTELLIGENCE RATHER THAN TRAINING SEEMS TO AID RESULT. LOWER CLASS MORE APPRECIATIVE].

IV. *Expectancies*:

a) General expectancies of counseling? Specific of client? [GENERAL EXPECTANCY IS COMPETENCE AND LISTENING EAR. SPECIFIC. EXTREMELY VARIED].

b) Related to this profession? Ill, rational, moral,

etc. dimension? [A STEREOTYPE THAT EACH PROFESSION HAS A SPECIALTY. PROBLEMS SEEN BY CLIENT AS NOT FITTING INTO PIGEONHOLE; BUT WILL DEFINE PROBLEM SO IT WILL BE PROPER TO TAKE TO THIS ONE].

c) Of change? Of cure? Of development? [CURE; NOT CHANGE].

d) Someone to talk with? [THE MOST UNIVERSAL COMPONENT].

e) Cost? [EXCEPT WITH CLERGY, FEAR COST AND ESTIMATE HIGHER THAN IS].

f) Authority figure? Sex preference? Relation to problem? [PREFER MAN COUNSELOR; SOME ELEMENT OF AUTHORITY; DEFINED AS COMPETENT ON THIS PROBLEM].

g) Everybody's doing it? Popular? Let's us see what its like? [THOUGH POPULAR LITERATURE EMPHASIZES OR IMPLIES THIS, NO VERIFICATION BY STUDY THAT THIS WAS IMPORTANT PART].

V. *Goals of counseling* (as seen or understood):

a) Limited goals—get rid of headache, win lawsuit, aid study? [ALMOST ALWAYS STATE PROBLEM AND GOALS IN THIS LIMITED WAY. IS METHOD TO ENLIST AID; THEN EXPECT BROADER COUNSELING AS RELATIONSHIP CONTINUES].

b) Self acceptance [ALMOST NEVER AN ORIGINAL GOAL].

c) Personal integration [USUALLY BROUGHT UP BY COUNSELOR; COUNSELEE HATES TO ADMIT NOT INTEGRATED; SECOND STAGE].

    d) Wholesome interpersonal relationships [ABOUT ONE-FOURTH OF TIME AN ORIGINAL COMPONENT].

    e) Meaning for life [BROADLY, ALL ARE SEEKING THIS. RARELY SO PHRASE. EASIER TO FACE AND ANSWER, SPECIFIC BY SPECIFIC].

    f) Hidden or unrecognized goals [USUALLY EXIST. NEVER TOUCHED IN PERHAPS 50% OF COUNSELING].

VI. *Type of Problems*:

    a) Intra-personal (self motives)

    b) *Inter-personal* (self & others)

    c) Environmental (self, culture, society, situation)

    d) Developmental (lack experience)

    e) Educational (lack skills, information)

    f) *Psychological* (self and other understanding)

    g) Actualizing (self actualization)

    h) Specific *(sex, family,* study, *work, marriage,* money, property)

    i) Religious-philosophical (meaning to life, ethics, morals, God, etc.) [*ITALICIZED* ARE MOST FREQUENT. THERE IS LITTLE "PREVENTIVE" COUNSELING, *I.E.* FOR GENERAL PERSONAL ADJUSTMENT BEFORE PROBLEMS ARISE. EVEN WITH CLERGY WHO CAN SUGGEST COUNSELING AT ANY TIME, USUALLY START WITH SOME SPECIFIC PROBLEM. FUNCTION OF SPECIFIC PROBLEM IS TO GET DIALOGUE GOING].

VII. *Causes of Problems*:

    a) Immediate causes or occasions of.

    b) Conflicts related to each type, as above.

c) Anxiety, stress, illness, trauma. [USUALLY
SOME ONE EVENT TIPS SCALE: LOSS OF
PARENT, BOY FRIEND, JOB, MONEY; BAD
MARKS, SLEEPLESSNESS, ANXIETY BEEN
BUILDING; VAGUELY AWARE OF HIDDEN
CAUSES].

d) Other hidden.

VIII. *Counseling set-up*:

a) Clinical or private, church or business office, etc.
[DEPENDS ON CLIENT SEX, CLASS, ETC.
POORER USED TO CLINICS, CHURCH.
WEALTHIER WANT PRIVATE. SELF
CHOICE BY CLIENT].

b) Availability, knowledge of, cost, etc. [GENER-
ALLY POOR KNOWLEDGE OF COST, AVAIL-
ABILITY, ETC. HEAR FROM FRIEND].

c) Time scheduling [CLIENT FEELS RUSHED,
AFRAID PAYING BY HOUR. CLERGY
MOST RELAXED. FAVOR MORE THAN
ONE HOUR].

d) Self-referral, other-referral [MOSTLY SELF].

e) Screening process (open walk in, tests, acceptance
all clients); receptionist role, office location and
decor, etc. [MOST SUCCESSFUL FROM
CLIENT'S VIEW IS WHERE HAD PREVIOUS
RELATION (*E.G.* PASTOR, DOCTOR).
WHERE THIS NOT SO, OPEN OR ACCEPT
ALL CLIENTS PREFERRED; CLIENT NOT
LIKE TO TAKE TESTS BEFORE SEE COUN-
SELOR. COUNSELOR PREFERS SCREEN-
ING].

IX. *Counseling Process or Technique:*

a) Original interview setting stage, orientation
sheets, etc. [SEEM RELATIVELY VALUE-
LESS TO CLIENT].

    b)   Focus on client as person or situation in which he is involved. [PRIME DEMAND].

    c)   Directive or non-directive. [STRANGELY, PREFER DIRECTIVE].

    d)   Empathetic and shared feeling or cognitive and reasoned knowledge. [THE FORMER, RATHER THAN LATTER IS CLIENT DEMAND].

    e)   Stereotyped or eclectic. [ECLECTIC].

    f)   Supportive or non-supportive. [SUPPORTIVE].

    g)   Freudian or what. [CLIENT DISLIKES NEO-FREUDIANISM].

X. *Relationship of counselor and client:*

    a)   Is counseling mainly relationship (importance)? [YES].

    b)   Professional, friendly, involved, etc. [FRIENDLY AND SOMEWHAT INVOLVED].

    c)   Similarities and differences of personalities, goals, values, etc. and effect on counseling. [SEE ABOVE].

    d)   Continuance, growth, change, termination. [REQUIRES 3-6 TIMES FOR MUCH GROWTH; THE 15 TIMES OF PSYCHIATRY NOT REQUIRED].

    e)   Transference, counter-transference and similar dimensions. [OCCURS IN ALL COUNSELING. FULLY AS MUCH AS IN PSYCHOANALYSIS. MORE SUBTLE; LESS UNDERSTOOD].

XI. *Termination:*

    a)   Early? Pre-completion? Why? [LARGE PERCENTAGE DO TERMINATE PRE-COMPLETION. TOO SLOW. NOT WHAT EXPECTED].

    b)   By whom? [BEST TERMINATION BY MUTUAL ACTION. TERMINATION BY

EITHER SHOWS LACK OF SUCCESS OR SATISFACTION].

c) Effect on satisfaction, success? [SEE ABOVE].

XII. *Evaluation of, successfulness?*

a) Is client a good judge? How ? Why? Questionnaire response? [NEITHER COUNSELOR NOR CLIENT A GOOD JUDGE. WIDE DISPARITY IN THEIR SCORES. CLIENT CAN REFLECT "SATISFACTION"].

b) Reliability of counselor case reports. [ALMOST TOTALLY UNRELIABLE, PARTICULARLY IF FOR SUBMISSION TO SUPERIOR OR REVIEWER].

c) Relation of variables to success: expectancies, similarity personalities, religion, etc. [DEFINITELY: SEE ABOVE].

EXAMPLES OF THINGS TO LOOK FOR
IN
CLIENT QUESTIONNAIRES.

1) Effect of counselor's values—counselor's values as counseling tool. [CLIENT SENSES THAT ALL COUNSELING INVOLVES STATED OR UNSTATED VALUES. PREFER COUNSELOR WITH SIMILAR OR FLEXIBLE VALUES, AND THESE TO BE STATED].

2) Client expectancies? Relation to interview behavior? Change during counseling? Awareness of counselor of counselee expectancies?

3) Relation between counselor and client characteristics? How do counselors differ? Do clients differ based on counselor each had? Why? [A CLIENT DOES DIFFER DEPENDENT ON COUESELOR. IF COUNSELOR FREUDIAN, COUNSELEE WILL TALK FREUDIAN; RELIGIOUS=RELIGIOUS; ETC. WARM BEGETS WARMTH;

AUTHORITY FIGURE CALLS FORTH DEPENDENCE.

4) Effect of social class of counselor and client? Effect on authority type counseling? Types problems? Length time given? Expectancies, etc.? [SOCIAL CLASS OF BOTH VERY IMPORTANT. COUNSELOR USUAL HIGHER CLASS— TENDS TO AUTHORITARIANISM, DEMAND RESPECT, SENSE OF "ALL KNOWING". PROBLEMS VARY BY CLASS (COMPARE LEGAL AID - PSYCHIATRIC CLINIC). MORE TIME AND EFFORT GIVEN TO UPPER CLASS—"MORE TO SAVE". COST BARS LOWER CLASS FROM PSYCHIATRY, ETC.].

5) What accounts for progress in counseling? Similarities of counselor-counselee? Acceptance? Techniques? Expectancies? Commitments? What? [NOT A CONSTANT SET OF FACTORS, BUT THESE ARE IDENTIFIABLE: CLIENT READINESS, APPROPRIATE ANXIETY, DESIRE TO CHANGE, WILLINGNESS TO WORK AT IT, COUNSELOR'S PERSONALITY, ACHIEVING COMBINED MOTIVATION].

6) Importance of *relationship* in counseling? What should it be? *Warm?* Overly warm? Cool? *The common mean? Directive?* Non-directive? *Eclectic?* What and Why? [*ITALICIZED* ARE THE ITEMS FAVORED BY CLIENTS].

7) Content of problems discussed? Is it function of counselee or counselor? Taboo and accepted subjects? [COUNSELOR SEEMS TO HAVE MORE CONTROL OF DETAILS DISCUSSED. HE HAS MORE STRINGENT TABOO OR GUIDELINES. CLIENT MERELY FORMULATES ORIGINAL APPROACH].

8) Casual dimension of problems presented? [CLIENT

NOT AS INTERESTED IN CAUSE AS IN SOLUTION].

9) What differences from study being of students? Or non-students? Type problem, willingness to be surveyed, kind of answers, sophistication, attempt to please, criticism, etc.? [STUDENTS GOOD CLIENT SUBJECTS; SENSE WHAT TRYING TO FIND OUT. TEND TO CRITICIZE CONSIDERABLY].

10) What tests have any predictability as to client? TAT, Strong V.I.B., MMPI, Miller Analogies, *Berkeley Questionnaire,* Bill's Index of adjustment & values, *Taylor Manifest Anxiety scale,* etc. [UNDERLINED ONES FOUND TO BE USED].

11) Client and counselor evaluation? Of readiness for help, diagnosis, prognosis, evaluation and success? [DIFFER MARKEDLY. CLIENT RATES HIGH ON READINESS AND PROGNOSIS. COUNSELOR HIGH ON DIAGNOSIS, EVALUATION AND SUCCESS].

12) Purpose of counseling? Motivation? Support? Analysis? Psychiatric adjustment? Shock? Informational? Reflecting mirror? What? [CLIENT FIXES PURPOSE AS SUPPORT, RELATIONSHIP AND INFORMATION. COUNSELOR SEES AS THERAPEUTIC].

13) Relationship of such things as high verbal activity by client and/or counselor as related to favorable outcome? [HIGH VERBAL ACTIVITY OF CLIENT PARTICULARLY PRODUCTIVE, SAME TO LESSER DEGREE COUNSELOR].

14) What influences quality of communication? Training? Personality? Time Length? Pictures, tests, projection tools, etc.? [PERSONALITY AND REAL INTEREST RATE HIGHEST].

15) Use by counselor of similar cases to analyze? Effect

of counselor showing how often he has handled this problem? [A TECHNIQUE OFTEN COMMENTED ON FAVORABLY BY COUNSELEE. HE DOES NOT SEEM TO VIEW THIS AS BREACH OF CONFIDENCE IN OTHER CASE].

16) Finding and laying out many alternative solutions or approaches? [A METHOD FAVORED VERY MUCH BY CLIENTS].

17) Client's awareness of counselor's distortion in area of own conflicts, uncertainties, lack of adjustment? [CLIENT PICKS THIS UP LIKE RADAR AND MAY WELL THROW IT BACK AT COUNSELOR, OR POKE FUN AT IT LATER].

18) Quick judging and labelling by counselor? Effect on client? [CLIENTS, PARTICULARLY OF PSYCHIATRISTS, SEEM TO LIKE LABELS. BUT THEY RESENT A HURRIED ONE].

19) What are important elements: Nature client's problem, degree client motivation, stage of thought of client about his problem, role client expects of counselor? [AT LEAST THESE FOUR INVOLVED IN ALL FULL REPORTED CASES].

20) Importance and nature of empathy? Must one have for success? [HIGH IMPORTANCE; NEEDED. CLIENT TENDS TO SEE IT AS FEELING HE IS MOST IMPORTANT AT THE MOMENT, HIS PROBLEM IS BEING FACED AND UNDERSTOOD, HE IS TREATED AS A PERSON, BOTH CAN AND WILL WORK TOGETHER].

21) Reliability of client Case Report? [HIGH PERSONALIZED; REWRITTEN, SECOND GUESS].

22) Statements as to discontinuance of counseling? By whom? For what reasons? Effect of schedule set up by counselor? [CLIENT HATES TO ADMIT

COUNSELOR TERMINATED. WILL USE AS MUCH TIME AS COUNSELOR SCHEDULES. GREATEST DISCONTINUANCE AFTER ONE EXPLORATIVE SESSION; THESE ARE NOT REAL COUNSELING].

23) Client resistance, defensiveness, unreadiness for counseling, etc.? Are there verbal signs? What are the signs? [UNTIL BROKEN DOWN SEEMS TO EXIST 3/4 OF TIME. "I DON'T KNOW WHETHER I SHOULD BOTHER", "THIS MAY NOT BE VERY IMPORTANT", "I DON'T REALLY FEEL TROUBLED", "I GUESS THESE THINGS ARE NORMAL", ETC.].

24) Expectation of change or help and its relation to actual occurrence of change or help? [HIGHER THE EXPECTATION BY CLIENT (BUT ALSO RATIO AS TO COUNSELOR) THE GREATER SUCCESS].

25) Actual behavior of client (and of counselor)? How important are physical acts and behavior compared to verbalization and structure of interviews? [CLIENT IS SELF PHYSICALLY EMBARRASSED AT FIRST. PAYS MUCH ATTENTION TO PHYSICAL ACTS: "HE SMOKED HIS G-- D--- PIPE", "TOOK MY COAT AND HUNG IT UP", ETC.].

26) Use of the first interview by client? Later interviews? Methods used? Effect of counselor's reaction to client verbalization? Use of "mmm", "oh", rephrasing, restating, duplicating or silence? Taking notes? Stopping taking notes? Etc. [CLIENT USES FIRST INTERVIEW TO TRY VERBALIZING AND TAKE MEASURE OF COUNSELOR; OFTEN MAKES CLEAR LIKES COUNSELOR, THEN GOES HOME AND WONDERS WHY. DOES NOT LIKE

SILENCES; LIKES TO BE LED ALONG.
DOES NOT LIKE NOTE TAKING; FEELS
DEHUMANIZED. COUNSELOR SHIFTS OF
METHOD TEND TO SHIFT CLIENT TOPIC].

27) What effect can be seen in our own study of use of
questionnaire or an interview? Reaction of client
to questionnaire? To interview? [TWO TRENDS:
CLIENTS DO NOT LIKE TO BE QUES-
TIONED, ASK "WHERE DID YOU GET MY
NAME?" IF GET BY THIS CLIENT RELISHES
CHANCE TO TELL HIS STORY. EDUCATED
ARE MORE USED TO QUESTIONS. INTER-
VIEW ADDS LITTLE ON OUR QUESTIONS
BUT MUCH ON CLIENT AND PROBLEMS
GENERALLY].

28) How much can you tell about the person, his problem,
success in previous counseling—from his questionnaire? From actual answers? From overall response or non-response? [QUESTIONNAIRE
PROVES ACCURATE ENOUGH ON SHORT
ANSWERS. CANNOT CONCLUDE ANY-
THING FROM NON-RESPONSE].

29) Value and reliability of "observation" compared to
interview content, for the client? [FOR SOCIAL
WORKER, PERHAPS. AS TO COUNSELING
WE OBSERVED, OUR VALUATION NEAR
TO THAT OF COUNSELOR AND COUN-
SELEE].

30) Role of counselee? Role fulfillment? Role perception? [UNCLEAR. EXTREMELY VARIED.
QUESTIONNAIRE PERHAPS INADEQUATE].

31) How does client determine desire for counseling?
Availability? Overcome blocks to going to coun-
selor? [SEEMS TO "WORK SELF UP" TO
COUNSELING; TRIES IDEA ON FRIENDS,
OFTEN MAKES A REHEARSED RUN; THEN

WAITS FOR A PRECIPITATING EVENT OR INVITATION].

32) Biases of client? [DEFINITELY APPEAR. QUESTIONNAIRE INADEQUATE TO SHOW EFFECT].

33) Emotional involvement? Love or Agapé? Transference and counter-transference? [DEFINITE EMOTIONAL INVOLVEMENT. LOW ORDER OF LOVE. NOT CLASSIC TRANSFERENCE-COUNTER TRANSFERENCE].

34) Influence of sex? Does this differ as to age? Type of problem? How predict? [ONLY IN BROADEST SENSE ARE WE ABLE YET TO PREDICT (*E.G.* NEARLY ALL PREFER MALE COUNSELOR). YET SEEMS TO RELATE TO LENGTH OF COUNSELING, TOPICS, SATISFACTION, RELATIONSHIP].

35) Difference in self-referral? Others referral? Must one think of self as sick? Weak? Immoral? Illegal? Etc. [FIRST STEP IN COUNSELING SEEMS ALMOST INVARIABLY SELF-REFERRAL. MOST CLIENTS FRAME ISSUE SO AS TO BE LEAST ATTACK ON SELVES; DEFINE PROBLEM AS THE OTHER PERSON'S].

h)   Some General Client Supported Theories

If we are to learn how to counsel and how to teach counseling from the insights clients gave us we shall have to remember the observations at the end of each section of this chapter as to each specific client group and particularly to the Capitalized Statement summaries for Series "O" questions, pp. 237-250. But that will not be enough. We must determine what additional overall theories are supported. This will require us to give more attention to observations such as these:

Clients see nearly all problems as "personal" and hold off seeing a counselor, believing they should solve their own problems. Clergy are seen earliest (more available and in constant touch), doctors next (periodic visits), but to see a lawyer, psychiatrist or marriage counselor may seem like great trauma. Consequently, counselors rarely see the "ideal" client or at the "ideal" time. Also the client does not pick the "ideal" counselor. He has already talked with friends, takes friends' advice as to whom to see, does not normally pick a specialist even when he recognizes what his problem is. He has picked *this* one counselor because he has defined his problem as one he wants this person to handle. Confidence in the counselor is more important than special ability; the client does not see his problem as fitting neat pigeon-holes. Counseling must make itself more available and "normal", but it must also learn to take clients as they are. Counsel must recognize that the greatest specialist may be next door but the client has chosen *him,* not the specialist. He must not shirk his duty.

Counseling is seen by the client as different from psychiatry or psychoanalysis (from which clients shy away). It is seen as much more at the conscious level, like what one would do with a friend but here with a more qualified and less involved person, and without the necessity of admitting that one is sick or abnormal. They want it short term. They want advice and new perspective; they want it to be somewhat directive. They seek a counselor whom they respect and consider stronger. They want him to be interested, involved—not to be cold and impersonal. They want him to give them time and then to act, to do something. They believe counselors tend too much to diagnose and defer decision. The most universal demand is a listening and sympathetic ear.

Clients frame their problems in a limited way. Women emphasize marital-sex, personal problems. Men begin in business, work, money terms. But this is the starting point; neither want counseling restricted thereto.

Clients seek empathy, shared feelings and emotions rather than a purely cognitive-intellectual approach. They seem to prefer the golden mean, the eclectic approach rather than neo-Rogerian or neo-Freudian. They are not as interested in cause as in result. They are aware that client's and counselor's "values" are always involved and they seek similar or flexible ones.

Apparently clients have little knowledge and are threatened by time scheduling (rushed), cost (which seems high for no "product"), referral (why shift me off to another). These need more adequate explanations to the public.

Client readiness, willingness to cooperate, openness in giving information—these may be fully as important as the counselor's competence. Counseling must teach the ability to use the client's strength. Nearly everything we have said in Chapters II and III about good interviewing and counseling are underlined by the client study. And the insights gained from the clients have also dictated the emphasis on socio-psycho dynamics in the next chapter VIII.

SUPPLEMENT
CROSS TABULATION CONTROL GROUP CLIENTS
Items (1) to (12), (17), (27) are on Age.

(1) *Been to a Counselor?*

Age	Yes	No
21-25	39%	60%
26-30	49%	48%
31-35	54%	41%
36-40	48%	48%
41-	46%	51%

(2) *Have You Failed to go to a Counselor?*

Age	Yes	No	No Answer
21-25	47%	37%	16%
26-30	41%	46%	12%
31-35	30%	53%	14%
36-40	54%	39%	7%
41-	57%	23%	20%

(3) *Nature of Problem?*

Age:	21-25	26-30	31-35	36-40	41-
Ad	6%	....	....	....	....
De	7%	....	....	....	....
P	6%	7%	....	....	....
Sex	....	8-5%	....	....	....
MA	....	19-12%	....	....	....
PE	23%	22%	14%	29%	20%
SC	21%	18%	20%	....	....
VA	18%	17%	17%	....	....
....	43%	37%	48%	41%	40%

(4) *How Often Been to a Counselor?*

Age:	21-25	26-30	31-35	36-40	41-
1-2	23%	22%	17%	10%	14%
3-5	8%	10%	17%	16%	10%
over 6	2%	5%	1%	7%	3%

(5) *Reasons for Not Using Services?*

Age:	21-25	26-30	31-35	36-40	41-
SOP	35%	33%	27%	29%	34%
TRI		7%	......	......	......
NTR	9%	7%	9%	7%	6%
CO	4%	10%	14%	10%	14%
NN	24%	17%	23%	23%	14%
O	10%	7%	......	......	......
......	32%	37%	45%	19%	37%

(6) *To Whom Turn?*

Age:	21-25	26-30	31-35	36-40	41-
D	8%	8%	17%	4-13%	5-14%
PS	11-5%	11-7%	......	......	......
L	2%	8%	11%	20%	20%
T	12%	14%	......	......	......
PA	14%	20%	17%	13%	17%
C	16%	13%	17%	3%	11%
F	4%	10%	......	......	......
O	7%	10%			

(7) *Was Counselor Directive?*

Age	Dir.	Non-Dir.	Com.	......
21-25	9%	27%	8%	54%
26-30	13%	28%	10%	49%
31-35	10%	24%	14%	47%
36-40	16%	23%	10%	52%
41-	23%	17%	6%	54%

(8) *Were You Satisfied with Counseling?*

Age	Yes	No	......
21-25	35%	10%	54%
26-30	46%	8%	47%
31-35	45%	6%	49%
36-40	45%	7%	48%
41-	40%	9%	51%

(9) *What Particulars Satisfied You?*

Age:	21-25	26-30	31-35	36-40	41-
D	10%	5%	14%	19%	11%
ND	7%	12%	14%	16%	9%
NP	4%	10%	6%	3%	......

(10) *Was Problem Solved?*

Age:	21-25	26-30	31-35	36-40	41-
Y	31%	44%	41%	51%	40%
N	14%	8%	6%	7%	6%

(11) *Did You Arrive at Solution on Own?*

Age:	21-25	26-30	31-35	36-40	41-
S1	17%	17%	17%	10%	20%
C5	15%	21%	20%	29%	20%
C-P	9%	10%	9%	7%	6%

(12) *On What Basis Did You Choose the Type of Counselor?*

Age:	21-25	26-30	31-35	36-40	41-
NA	15%	18%	21%	22%	23%
TK	20%	22%	21%	30%	23%
EM	5%	10%	9%	3%	5%

Items (13) to (31), except (17), (22), (27) are on Sex.

(13) *Sex vs. — Ever Been to a Counselor?*

	Y	N
M	44%	53%
F	47%	52%

(14) *Failed to Go?*

	Y	N
M	43%	42%
F	49%	36%

(15) *Nature of Problem?*

M	14%	PE	14%	SC	13%	VA
F	19%	PE	9%	SC	9%	VA

(16) *How Choose?*

	NA	TK	EM
M	16%	22%	6%
F	23%	20%	10%

(17) *How Select Specific Person?*

Age	F	Rep.	NA	KN	RE
21-25	18%	8%	46%	8%	7%
26-30	19%	14%	32%	7%	7%
31-36	16%	16%	33%	10%	10%
36-40	20%	20%	38%	5%	5%
41-	23%	17%	40%	10%	6%

(18) *On How Many Occasions?*

	1-2	3-5
M	22%	9%
F	17%	17%

(19) Reasons for Not Using a Counselor?

	SOP	NN
M	26%	16%
F	26%	17%

(20) To Whom Turn for Counseling?

	T	AA	C
M	10%	12%	10%
F	7%	15%	15%

(21) How Select Specific Person?

	F	R
M	18%	12%
F	20%	14%

(22) Why Do You Go to a Counselor?

Age				
21-25	27%	20%	12%	50%
26-30	35%	24%	....	41%
31-35	27%	22%	14%	45%
36-40	29%	....	....	45%
41-	34%	17%	....	43%

(23) Directive or Non-Directive?

	D	ND	Com.
M	13%	23%	10%
F	9%	36%	9%

(24) What Satisfied?

	Ad	D	ND
M	....	10%	9%
F	8%	8%	12%

(25) Was Problem Solved?

	Y	N
M	40%	8%
F	34%	17%

(26) Why Do You Go to a Counselor?

	Ad	NP	SU	TK	LI
M	30%	20%	11%	9%	9%
F	29%	29%	11%	8%	14%

(27) Did Counselor Refer You to Anyone?

Age	Y	N
21-25	6%	37%
26-30	8%	41%
31-35	14%	37%
36-40	7%	41%
41-	20%	26%

(28) Were You Satisfied With Counseling You Received?

	Y	N
M	40%	8%
F	42%	11%

(29) Did You Arrive at Solution on Your Own or . . .

	S1	Dis.	C5	C-P
M	16	6%	17%	8%
F	17%	5%	21%	11%

(30) Did He Refer You to Others?

	Y	N
M	8%	37%
F	11%	40%

Items (31) to (43) are as to Religion.

Religion: Protestant (P)   Jewish (J)   Catholic (C)   None (N)   Other (C)

(31) Have You Been to a Counselor?

	P	J	C	N	O
Y	44%	46%	49%	44%	45%
N	54%	54%	49%	55%	48%

(32) How Many Occasions?

	P	J	C	N	O
1-2	18%	19%	25%	28%	23%
3-5	12%	11%	11%	9%	10%
6-10	4%	3%	3%	1%	6%
over 15	5%	5%	3%	3%	....

(33) Have You Failed to Go?

	P	J	C	N	O
Y	46%	41%	42%	50%	29%
N	40%	41%	39%	43%	60%

(34) Reasons for Not Going?

	P	J	C	N	O
SOP	32%	38%	29%	41%	23%
NTR	9%	5%	7%	6%	3%
CO	10%	8%	6%	6%	6%
NN	20%	32%	21%	16%	26%

(35) Nature Problem?

	P	J	C	N
IP	6%	11%	6%	12%
MA	9%	11%	6%	12%
PE	21%	19%	32%	18%
SC	20%	24%	23%	15%
VA	16%	22%	29%	10%

(36) To Whom Turn?

	P	J	C	N
D	11%	8%	9%	10%
PS	7%	5%	3%	9%
L	9%	5%	11%	10%
T	11%	11%	19%	9%
PA	19%	16%	32%	3%
C	7%	8%	3%	1%

(37 Did Counselor Help You Find Your Own Solution?

D	13%	16%	10%	10%
ND	24%	30%	35%	22%
COM	11%	3%	9%	10%

(38) Were You Satisfied?

Y	40%	38%	49%	34%	31%
N	7%	8%	6%	15%	10%

(39) How Satisfied?

D	7%	22%	17%	9%	3%
ND	11%	16%	10%	6%	6%
TK	6%	....	6%	1%	6%
NP	6%	3%	6%	6%	6%
SU	6%	3%	3%	3%	3%

(40) Was Problem Solved?

Y	37%	38%	42%	44%
N	10%	13%	9%	8%

(41) Did Arrive at Solution on Own?

Si	17%	19%	19%	13%
Dis	6%	11%	1%	3%
Cs	19%	13%	23%	19%
C-P	9%	8%	11%	6%

(42) How Select Counselor?

NA	18%	22%	25%	19%	17%
TK	26%	27%	27%	22%	20%
EM	9%	11%	7%	1%	14%

(43) How Select Specific Person?

F	24%	22%	33%	10%	29%
R	16%	5%	22%	21%	6%
KN	9%	8%	11%	7%	10%
RE	8%	13%	9%	16%	3%
EM	6%	11%	1%	5%	10%

(51) Why Go To Counselor?

Rel.	Ad	NP	SU	TK	W
P	31%	20%	12%	8%	11%
J	22%	22%	5%	22%	8%
C	35%	22%	16%	10%	10%
N	28%	12%	9%	6%	6%

(52) Did He Refer You to Any Other?

Rel.	Y	N	....
P	11%	35%	54%
J	8%	41%	51%
C	10%	43%	46%
N	5%	40%	55%

Items (44) to (56) and (77), (78), (69), (70) are as to Residence.
(Metropolitan, Urban, Rural)

(44) *Have You Ever Been?*

	Y	N
M	49%	49%
U	45%	54%
R	37%	62%

(45) *How Many Times?*

	1-2	3-5	6-10	over 15-
M	22%	14%	5%	3%
U	20%	10%	4%	4%
R	20%	10%	....	1%

(46) *Failed To Go?*

	Y	N
M	46%	33%
U	46%	41%
R	36%	48%

(47) *Why Didn't You?*

	SOP	NTR	CO	NN
M	28%	6%	7%	23%
U	34%	9%	10%	21%
R	35%	6%	4%	19%

(48) *Nature Problem?*

	Ad	De	IP	MA	PE	SC	VA
M	9%	6%	9%	5%	26%	21%	22%
U	3%	3%	9%	11%	21%	18%	14%
R	7%	6%	1%	3%	14%	20%	23%

(49 *To Whom Turn?*

	D	T	PA	C
M	6%	14%	20%	27%
U	10%	11%	16%	11%
R	11%	10%	11%	11%

(50) *Directive or Non-Directive?*

	D	ND	Com
M	8%	36%	12%
U	14%	23%	9%
R	11%	26%	9%

(53) *Were You Satisfied?*

	Y	N
M	39%	16%
U	41%	7%
R	36%	6%

(54) *How Satisfied?*

	D	ND	NP
M	6%	13%	10%
U	10%	10%	5%
R	11%	9%	7%

(55) *Was Problem Solved?*

	Y	N
M	34%	19%
U	41%	7%
R	33%	11%

(56) *Did You Arrive at Own Solution or . . . ?*

	SC	C4	C5	O
M	20%	16%	14%	46%
U	16%	20%	7%	52%
R	16%	14%	10%	62%

(69) *Residence—On What Basis Did You Choose?*

	NA	TK	EM
M	24%	26%	12%
U	18%	24%	8%
R	20%	19%	3%

(70) *Res.—Specific Person . . . ?*

	F	R	KN	RE	EM
M	21%	13%	14%	14%	7%
U	24%	15%	8%	10%	7%
R	19%	16%	13%	....	6%

(77) *Res.—Why Go to a Counselor?*

	Ad	NP	SU	TK	LI
M	23%	26%	14%	10%	10%
U	30%	20%	11%	8%	11%
R	26%	16%	8%	8%	6%

(78) *Res.—Did He Refer You?*

	Y	N	....
M	12%	43%	45%
U	9%	35%	55%
R	6%	36%	61%

Items (57) to (90) are as to training in Psychology-Sociology
rated from 1 (little) to 5 (much)

(57) *Psych. Training-cf-On What Basis Did You Choose the Type of Counselor?*

	NA	TK	EM	....
1	20%	25%	10%	49%
2	30%	34%	2%	32%
3	32%	25%	14%	42%
4	14%	50%	9%	27%
5	26%	37%	14%	34%

(58) *Psych.—How Select Specific Person?*

	F	R	KN	RE	EM
1	31%	13%	8%	5%	6%
2	26%	16%	14%	16%	4%
3	25%	21%	14%	14%	10%
4	23%	41%	14%	9%	5%
5	26%	31%	23%	20%	10%

(59) *Sociology Training-cf-Have You Been To . . .?*

	Y	N
1	39%	61%
2	55%	45%
3	77%	23%
4	60%	40%
5	61%	35%

(60) *Soc.—How Many Occasions?*

	1-2	3-5	....
1	20%	11%	65%
2	21%	21%	45%
3	15%	15%	46%
4	20%	20%	50%
5	12%	12%	54%

(61) *Soc.—Failed To Go?*

	Y	N	....
1	40%	41%	18%
2	59%	31%	10%
3	70%	15%	15%
4	40%	40%	20%
5	46%	50%	7%

(62) *Soc.—Why Didn't Go?*

	SOP	CO	NN
1	35%	8%	25%
2	38%	21%	21%
3	46%	15%	....
4	25%	5%	40%
5	42%	7%	19%

(63) *Soc.—Nature of Problem?*

	MA	PE	SC	VA
1	11%	18%	19%	15%
2	17%	21%	21%	21%
3	7%	23%	23%	15%
4	5%	10%	30%	20%
5	8%	31%	15%	7%

(64) *Soc.—To Whom Did You Turn?*

	D	L	T	PA	C
1	7%	8%	10%	15%	12%
2	17%	17%	7%	24%	24%
3	23%	7%	23%	23%	31%
4	....	10%	15%	5%	25%
5	12%	19%	12%	15%	15%

(65) *Soc.—Why Go?*

	AD	NP	SU	TK
1	27%	19%	14%	6%
2	31%	21%	14%	27%
3	31%	38%	15%	7%
4	30%	15%	10%	10%
5	23%	19%	7%	12%

(66)	Soc.—Did He Refer You?		
	Y	N	
1	11%	32%	
2	7%	59%	
3	7%	54%	
4	10%	40%	
5	12%	46%	

(67)	Soc.—On What Basis Choose?		
	NA	TK	EM
1	18%	23%	8%
2	34%	34%	3%
3	31%	38%	7%
4	10%	40%	5%
5	27%	27%	12%

(68)	Soc.—How Select?		
	F	R	RE
1	28%	11%	8%
2	24%	24%	10%
3	31%	31%	7%
4	20%	30%	10%
5	19%	23%	23%

(71)	Psych.—Have You Been?	
	Y	N
1	41%	58%
2	66%	34%
3	61%	35%
4	77%	23%
5	63%	37%

(72)	Psych.—How Many Times?	
	1-2	3-5
1	20%	10%
2	26%	20%
3	18%	14%
4	32%	27%
5	23%	14%

(73)	Psych.—Failed To Go . . . ?	
	Y	N
1	45%	88%
2	56%	40%
3	53%	32%
4	50%	27%
5	66%	31%

(74)	Psych.—Why Didn't Go?		
	SOP	CO	NN
1	37%	7%	23%
2	40%	16%	22%
3	42%	3%	14%
4	32%	14%	14%
5	46%	11%	23%

(75)	Psych.—Nature Problem?				
	IP	MA	PE	SC	VA
1	10%	11%	24%	15%	18%
2	8%	16%	28%	28%	20%
3	14%	7%	18%	14%	10%
4	18%	9%	18%	41%	32%
5	3%	10%	26%	23%	20%

(76)	Psych.—To Whom Turn?		
	T	PA	C
1	13%	22%	8%
2	10%	18%	28%
3	10%	14%	21%
4	18%	9%	27%
5	11%	14%	31%

(79)	Psych.—Was Counselor . . . ?		
	D	ND	Com
1	8%	32%	9%
2	16%	36%	8%
3	18%	18%	18%
4	23%	32%	14%
5	20%	17%	23%

(80)	Psych.—Were You Satisfied?	
	Y	N
1	38%	10%
2	57%	10%
3	35%	14%
4	59%	9%
5	54%	10%

(81)	Psych.—How Satisfied?	
	D	ND
1	9%	10%
2	24%	15%
3	3%	7%
4	18%	14%
5	11%	14%

(82) Psych.—Was Problem Solved?

	Y	N
1	37%	11%
2	56%	15%
3	32%	14%
4	50%	14%
5	57%	11%

(83) Psych.—Did You Arrive at Solution?

	S1	C5	C-P
1	20%	18%	6%
2	18%	24%	20%
3	14%	14%	18%
4	27%	23%	14%
5	26%	40%	11%

(84) Psych.—Why Go?

	Ad	NP	SU	TK	LI
1	29%	18%	13%	7%	13%
2	43%	34%	16%	12%	12%
3	21%	21%	10%	14%	25%
4	41%	32%	9%	23%	9%
5	34%	20%	6%	20%	6%

(85) Psych.—Did He Refer You?

	Y	N
1	13%	32%
2	12%	57%
3	3%	46%
4	9%	59%
5	14%	46%

(86) Sociology—Was Counselor Directive or Non-Directive?

	D	ND	Com
1	7%	31%	4%
2	38%	14%	14%
3	15%	38%	23%
4	30%	20%	5%
5	8%	23%	19%

(87) Soc.—Were You Satisfied?

	Y	N
1	37%	7%
2	49%	14%
3	62%	7%
4	35%	10%
5	46%	15%

(88) Soc.—How Satisfied?

	Ad	D	ND	NP	SU
1	4%	9%	9%	5%	8%
2	3%	17%	17%	10%	7%
3	15%	7%	15%	15%	23%
4	5%	10%	5%	....	....
5	8%	7%	12%	15%	....

(89) Soc.—Was Problem Solved?

	Y	N	....
1	37%	11%	51%
2	55%	10%	34%
3	54%	7%	38%
4	35%	15%	45%
5	42%	8%	42%

(90) Soc.—Did You Arrive at Solution?

	S1	C1-2	C5	C-P
1	18%	8%	13%	10%
2	21%	....	21%	17%
3	15%	....	38%	15%
4	20%	5%	10%	5%
5	23%	7%	23%	23%

(91) Have You Acted as Counselor-cf-Was Counselor Directive or Non-Directive?

	D	ND	Com
Y	19%	35%	15%
N	10%	27%	5%

Items 91-105 correlate acting as counselor or counseling training with other items.

(92) Have You Acted as Counselor—Did You Have Respect?

	Y+	Y	Y—	N
Y	7%	59%	3%	4%
N	6%	39%	2%	2%

(93) Have You Acted as Counselor—In What Part Satisfied?

	D	ND	NP	SU
Y	15%	13%	9%	9%
N	8%	12%	6%	2%

(94)   *Have You Acted as Counselor—*
       Problem Solved?

	Y	N
Y	52%	14%
N	39%	11%

(95)   *Have You Acted as Counselor—Do*
       You Considerd Him a Strong Person?

	Y	N
Y	38%	19%
N	22%	15%

(96)   *Have You Acted as Counselor—*
       Were You Satisfied?

	Y	N
Y	59%	11%
N	39%	10%

(97)   *Have You Acted as Counselor—Did*
       You Arrive at Solution on Your Own?

	S1	Dis	Cl-2	C3	C5	C-P
Y	25%	9%	7%	7%	26%	13%
N	12%	4%	7%	2%	17%	8%

(98)   *Have You Acted as Counselor—*
       Why Do You Go?

	Ad	NP	SU	TK	LI
Y	33%	29%	16%	13%	15%
N	38%	20%	10%	8%	6%

(99)   *Are You Trained-cf-Is He Stronger*
       Person?

	Y	N
N	36%	18%
Some	32%	16%
Y	40%	22%

(100) *Are You Trained—Were You Sat-*
       isfied?

	Y	N
N	51%	13%
Some	51%	13%
Y	72%	8%

(101) *Are You Trained—Was He Directive*
       or Non-Directive?

	D	ND	Com
N	15%	33%	11%
Some	5%	41%	24%
Y	29%	32%	14%

(102) *Are You Trained—Did You Have*
       Respect?

	Y	N
N	57%	7%
Some	57%	10%
Y	79%	37%

(103) *Are You Trained—How Satisfied?*

	D	ND	NP	SU
N	10%	11%	7%	8%
Some	5%	16%	16%	13%
Y	27%	14%	6%	3%

(104) *Are You Trained—Problem Solved?*

	Y	N
N	51%	15%
Some	37%	13%
Y	60%	16%

(105) *Are You Trained—Did You Arrive*
       at Solution on Your Own?

	S1	Dis	Cl-2	C3	C5	C-P
N	24%	8%	8%	7%	26%	9%
Some	35%	5%	3%	5%	5%	22%
Y	19%	13%	9%	6%	40%	11%

(106) *Are You Trained—Why Go?*

	Ad	NP	SU	TK	LI
N	37%	27%	12%	11%	13%
Some	32%	41%	37%	3%	22%
Y	40%	21%	9%	19%	9%

Bibliography Chapter 7

See Freeman, Counseling — A Bibliography with Annotations
Codes E, F and J

Aarons, Z. Alexander—Indications for Analysis and Problems of Analyzability. (1962) Psychoanal. Q. No. 4, 514-631.

Adams, Walter D.—An Investigation of Differential Client Behavior Occuring to Specific Therapist Activities. (Master's Thesis, Univ. of Denver, 1951).

Allen, Richard B.—The Unhappy Client. (June 1962) Wisc. Bar Bull. 35:51-58.

Apfelbaum, Bernard—Dimensions of Transference in Psychotherapy. (Berkeley, Univ. of California Press, 1958) 90 pp.

Appel, Victor H.—Client Expectancies About Counseling in a University Counseling Center. (Doctoral Dissertation, Ohio State, 1959) (D.A. XX, 3824, 1960).

Arbuckle, Dugald S.—Client Perception of Counselor Personality. (1956) J. Counsel. Psychol. 3:93-96.

Auerbach, J. G.—Value Changes in Therapy. (1950) J. Pers. 1:63-67.

Axelrod, Joseph—An Evaluation of the Effect on Progress in Therapy of Similarities and Difference Between the Personalities of Patients and Their Therapists (Doctoral Dissertation, New York Univ., 1952) (D.A. XII, 329, 1952).

Baker, Elliot—The Differential Effect of Two Psychotherapeutic Approaches on Client Perception. (Doctoral Dissertation, Penn. State Univ., 1957) (D.A. XVII, 1805, 1957) Also (1960) J. Counsel. Psychol. 7:46-50.

Baller, W. R.—Characteristics of College Students Who Demonstrate Interest in Counseling Services. (1944) J. Ed. Psychol. 35:302-308.

Barrington, Byron L.—Prediction from Counselor Behavior of Client Perception and of Case Outcome. (1961) J. Counsel. Psychol. 8:37-42.

Barron, F. and T. Leary—Changes in Psychoneurotic Patients With and Without Psychotherapy. (1955) J. Consult. Psychol. 19:239-245.

Beatty, Billie C.—Counselee-Counselor Identifications. D.A. XXV, 4255 (1965).

Bergman, Daniel V.—Counseling Method and Client Responses. (1951) J. Consult. Psychol. 30:216-224.

Berkowitz, L.—The Expression and Reduction of Hostility. (1958) Psychol. Bull. 55:257-283.

Berkowitz, L.—Repeated Frustrations and Expectations in Hostility Arousal. (1960) J. Abnorm. Soc. Psychol. 60:422-429.

Blaine, Graham B. and Charles McArthur—What Happened in Therapy as Seen by the Patient and His Psychiatrist. (1958) J. Nerv. Ment. Dis. 127:344-350.

Blair, Mildred L.—Criteria for Screening Applications to a Mental Hygiene Clinic. (1950) (Smith Coll. St. Soc. Wk.).

Blum, L. P. and B. A. Sullivan—What Do College Students Think of Counseling? (1953) J. Higher Ed. 24:262-264.

Bordin, Edward S.—The Implications of Client Expectations for the Counseling Process. (1955) J. Counsel. Psychol. 2:17-21.

Butler, John M. and Gerald V. Haigh—Changes in the Relation Between Self-Concepts and Ideal Concepts Consequent Upon Client-centered Counseling. In Carl Rogers and R. F. Dymond, eds.—Psychotherapy and Personality Change. (1954).

Butler, John M.—The Interaction of Client and Therapist. (1952) J. Abnorm. Soc. Psychol. 47:366-378.

Campbell, David P.—The Result of Counseling: Twenty-five Years Later. (Philadelphia, Saunders, 1965) 205 pp.

Cartwright, Rosalind D.—The Effects of Psychotherapy on Self-Consistency: A Replication and Extension. (1961) J. Consult. Psychol. No. 5, 25:376-382.

Chance, Erika—Mutual Expectations of Patients and Therapists in Individual Treatment. (1957) Hum. Rel. 10:167-178.

Chance, June E. and W. Meaders—Needs and Interpersonal Perception. (1960) J. Pers. 28:200-209.

Cleland, Robert S.—Emotional vs. Ideational Emphasis During Group Counseling. (1965) J. Consul. Psychol. 12:282.

Collier, B. N. and Frank A. Nugent—Characteristics of Self-referred, Staff-referred and Non-counseled College Students. (1965) J. Coun. Psychol. 12:208-12.

Coulson, William R.—Client-centered Therapy and the Nature of Man. D.A. XXV, 11, 1964.

Cummer, John P.—A Study of Counselee Satisfaction in Relation to the Interest Level of Faculty Advisers in Counseling Activities. (Doctoral Dissertation, Florida State Univ.) (D.A. XXII, 1083, 1961).

Davis, Stanley E.—An Investigation of Client Character Shows in Interview Behavior. (Doctoral Dissertation, Ohio State, 1953) (D.A. LVIII 18, 1855-1858).

Deskins, A., C. C. Herbert, F. Gorman, T. Margaret, and G. H. Crook—Patterns of Expectation in the Doctor-Patient Relationship. (Paper read at Western Psychological Association, San Jose, California, April 1960).

Devlin, John P.—A Study of Verbalized Self-Attitudes and Reactions to Social Frustration as Methods of Predicting Success in Brief Psychotherapy. (Doctoral Dissertation, Penn. State Univ., 1953).

Duke, Robert D.—Counselee Perceptions of the Counseling Process in California Junior Colleges. (Doctoral Dissertation, Standard Univ. 1960) (D.A. XX, 4309, 1960).

Eaton, Joseph—On the Validity of Treatment Evaluation by Client Associations. (1957) Gr. Psychother. 10:198-211.

Elton, Charles F.—A Study of Client Responsibility: Counselor Technique and Interview Outcome. (1950) Ed. Psychol. M. 10:728-737.

Erickson, K. T.—Patient Role and Social Uncertainty. (Aug. 1957) Psychiatry 3:263-274.

Ewing, T. N.—Changes in Attitude During Counseling. (1954) J. Counsel. Psychol. 1:232-239; (1964) J. Counsel. Psychol. 11:146.

Farm, Arnold L.—Student Attitudes Toward Counselors and the Counseling Center at Michigan State College. (Doctoral Dissertation, Michigan State College, 1952) (D.A. XII, 720).

Ferguson, Robert E.—An Investigation of Client Behavior as a Function of Specific Therapist Formulations. (Master's Thesis, Univ. of Denver, 1951).

Fey, William F.—Aceptance of Self and Others, and Its Relation to Therapy-Readiness. (1954) J. Clin. Psychol. 10:269-271.

Findley, William J.—A Study of the Developmental Pattern of Client Response in the Counseling Process. (Doctoral Dissertation, Colorado State College of Education, 1956-57) (C.S. XVIII, 49).

Frank, Jerome D.—The Dynamics of Psychotherapeutic Relationship. (1959) Psychiatry 22:17-39.

Frank, Jerome D.—Patient's Expectancies and Relearning as Factors Determining Improvement in Psychotherapy. (1959) Am. J. Psychiat. 115:961-68.

Gallagher, James J.—An Investigation Into Factors Differentiating College Students Who Discontinue Non-directive Counseling From College Students Who Continue Counseling. (Doctoral Dissertation, Penn. State, 1951) (P.S. XIV, 445).

Garfield, S. L., et al.—Expectations Regarding Psychotherapy. (1963) J. Ner. Ment. Dis. 137:329-335.

Gibson, R. L., W. V. Snyder, and W. S. Ray—A Factor Analysis of Measures of Change Following Client-Centered Therapy. (1955) J. Counsel. Psychol. 2:83-90.

Goldstein, Arnold P.—Patient's Expectancies and Non-specific Therapy as a Basis for (Un)Spontaneous Remission. (1960) J. Clin. Psychol. No. 4, 16:399-403.

Goldstein, Arnold P.—Patient's Expectancies Regarding Psychological Testing and Test Performance. (Unpublished manuscript, Nov. 1960).

Goldstein, Arnold P. and K. Heller—Role Expectations, Participant Personality Characteristics, and the Client-Counselor Relationship. (Unpublished manuscript, August 1960).

Goldstein, Arnold P.—Therapist and Client Expectation of Personality Change in Psychotherapy. (1960) J. Counsel. Psychol. 7-180-184.

Goldstein, Arnold P.—Therapist-Patient Expectancies in Psychotherapy. (New York, Macmillan, 1962).

Grant, C. W.—Harvard Students Perceive the Counselor's Role. (March 1954) Personnel Guid. J. 32:386-388.

Grant, Charles—A Study of Personality Characteristics of Clients Self-referred and Other-referred to a Student Counseling Center. D.A. XXIII, 2204, 1962.

Greenberg, Harvey R.—The Manipulator and the Mental Hygiene Consultation Service. (1965) A. J. Psychiat. 122:313.

Greenfield, Norman S.—Factors Influencing Utilization of Psychotherapeutic Services in Male College Students. (1965) J. Clin. Psychol. 12:276-279.

Grigg, Austin E.—Client Response to Counselors at Different Levels of Experience. (1961) J. Counsel. Psychol. 8:217-233.

Harvin, Anna F.—Social Factors in Student Counseling Needs: A Comparative Study of Student Counseling Clients and Non-Clients Among College Freshmen. (Doctoral Dissertation, State College of Washington, 1956). (D.A. XVII, 422, 1957).

Hassinger, Edward W. and Robert L. McNamara—Relationships of the Public to Physicians in a Rural Setting. (Missouri Agr. Exp. Sta. Res. Bull. 653, Jan. 1958) 36 pp.

Heilbrun, Alfred B., Jr.—Male and Female Personality Correlates of Early Termination in Counseling. (1961) J. Counsel. Psychol. 8:31-36.

Heilbrun, Alfred B., Jr. and D. J. Sullivan—The Prediction of Counseling Readiness. (1962) Personnel Guid. J. 41:112-117.

Heine, R. W. and H. Trosman—Initial Expectations of the Doctor-Patient Interaction as a Factor in Continuance in Psychotherapy. (1960) Psychiatry 23, No. 3:275-278.

Heller, Kenneth and A. P. Goldstein—Client Dependency and Therapist Expectancy as Relationship Maintaining Variables in Psychotherapy. (1961) J. Consult. Psychol. 25:371-375.

Hiler, Edward W.—Initial Complaints as Predictors of Continuation in Psychotherapy. (1959) J. Clin. Psychol. 15:344-345.

Holzman, Mathilda S.—The Significance of the Value Systems of Patient and Therapist for the Outcome of Psychotherapy. (Doctoral Dissertation, Univ. of Wash., 1961) (D.A. XXII, 4073).

Hulme, William E.—The Counselee Who Exploits the Counselor. (June 1962) Past. Psych. 13:29-36.

Jammes, J. M.—What People Expect From Priests. (1958) Lumen Vitae 13:312-321.

Kadushin, Alfred—Opposition to Referral for Psychiatric Treatment. (1957) Soc. Work 2:78-84.

Kadushin, Charles—Individual Decisions to Undertake Psychotherapy. (1958) Admin. Sci. Q. 3, No. 3:379-411.

Kadushin, Charles—Why People Undergo Psychotherapy-A Research Outline. Bureau of Applied Social Research, Columbia Univ., New York, 1958.

Kaiser, Bydus F.—Parishioners' Perceptions of Ministerial Roles in Pastoral Calling. (Doctoral Dissertation, Boston Univ. School of Theology, 1961).

Kamm, Robert C., and Gilbert Wrenn—Client Acceptance of Self-Information in Counseling. (1950) Ed. Psychol. M. 10:32-42.

Kapit, Hanna E.—Relationships Between Attitudes Toward Therapist and Attitudes Toward Parents. (Doctoral Dissertation, Columbia Univ.) D.A. XVI, 1284, 1956.

Katz, Bernard—Predictive and Behavioral Empathy and Client Change in Short-term Counseling. D.A. XXIII, 2206, 1962.

Keister, Wilbur D.—Counselee Modification of Interview Data as Determined by Post-interview Evaluation. (Doctoral Dissertation, Univ. of Arizona, 1959). D.A. XX, 2176, 1960.

Kessel, N.—Who Ought to See a Psychiatrist. (1963) Lancet 1:1092-1095.

Kirtner, William L.—Client Personality and Problem-solving Approach as Related to Success and Failure in Client-centered Therapy. (Doctoral Dissertation, Univ. of Chicago, 1959-60).

Kirtner, William L. and Desmond Cartwright—Success and Failure in Client-centered Therapy as a Function of Initial In-therapy Behavior. (1958) J. Consult. Psychol. 22:329-333.

Korner, I. N., et al.—The Patient as a Constant in Psychotherapy. (1964) J. Clin. Psychol. 20:403-406.

Kounin, J. S., et al.—Experimetal Studies of Clients' Reactions to Initial Interviews. (1956) Hum. Rel. 9:237.

Kruger, Albert H.—Counselor Holding Power: Clinical vs. Client-centered. (1965) J. Counsel. Psychol. 12:159-166.

Kutash, S. and E. Dengrove—Why Patients Discontinue Treatment in a Mental Hygiene Clinic. (1950) Am. J. Psychother. 4:457-462.

Leik, Robert K. and L. K. Northwood—The Classification of Family Interaction Problems for Treatment Purposes. (1964) J. Marr. Fam. 26:288-294.

Lesser, William M.—The Relationship Between Counseling Progress and Empathic Understanding. (Doctoral Dissertation, Michigan State Univ., 1958). D.A. XIX, 3367, 1959; (1961) J. Counsel. Psychol. 8:330-336.

Levy, Charles S.—Social Worker and Client as Obstacles to Client Self-Determination. (1963) J. Jewish Comm. Serv. 39:416-419.

Lewis, Edwin C.—Counselors and Girls. (1965) J. Counsel. Psychol. 12:159-166.

Lipkin, Stanley—Clients' Feelings and Attitudes in Relation to the Outcome of Client-centered Therapy. (Washington, Am. Psychoanal. Assn., 1954) Psychoanal. Mono. 68, No. 372. 30 pp.

Littman, R. A. et al.—Where Parents Go for Help. (1957) The Coordinator. 6, No. 1:3-9.

Lorr, Maurice—Client Perceptions of Therapists: A Study of the Therapeutic Relation. (1965) J. Consult. Psychol. 29:146-149.

McGowan, John F.—Client Anticipations and Expectancies As Related to Initial Interview Performance and Perceptions. (Doctoral Dissertation, Univ. of Missouri, 1954) D.A. XV, 228, 1955.

MacLean, M. S.—Idealized Image Concept as a Factor in Counseling. (Sept. 1950) Education 70:495-497.

Mangus, A. R.—Role Theory and Marriage Counseling. (1957) Soc. Forces. 35:200-209.

Mechanic, David—Role Expectations and Communication in the Therapist-Patient Relationship. (1961) J. Health Hum. Beh. No. 3, 2:190-198.

Mendelsohn, Gerald A. and Marvin H. Geller—Effects of Counselor-Client Similarity on the Outcome of Counseling. (Spring 1963) J. Counsel. Psychol. 10, No. 1:71; (1965) J. Counsel. Psychol. 29:63.

Most, Elizabeth—Measuring Change in Marital Satisfaction. (1964) J. Soc. Work 9:64.

Nachman, B.—Client Problems and Duration of Counseling. (1960) Personnel Guid. J. 38:486-488.

Nelson, A. G.—Vocational Maturity and Client Satisfaction. (1956) J. Counsel. Psychol. 3:254-256.

Overall, B. and H. Aronson—Exceptations of Psychotherapy in Patients of Lower Socio-economic Class. (1963) Am. J. Orthopsychiat. 33:421-430.

Patients Want Sympathy More than Cures. (Feb. 18, 1956) Sci. N.L. 69:108.

Patterson, C. H.—Client Expectations and Social Conditioning. (1958) Personnel Guid. J. 37:136-138.

Perlman, Helen Harris—The Client's Treatability. (1956) Soc. Work 1:32-40.

Pohlman, Edward and F. P. Robinson—Client Reaction to Some Aspects of the Counseling Situation. (1960) Personnel Guid. J. 38:546-551.

Pohlman, Edward—Changes in Client Preferences During Counseling. (1961) Personnel Guid. J. 40, No. 4:340.

Pohlman, Edward W.—A Study Involving Client Preferences for Counselor Behaviors in Counseling. (Doctoral Dissertation, Ohio State) (D.A. XXI, 3167, 1961).

Porter, E. H., Jr.—Client's Evaluation of Services at the Univ. of Chicago Counseling Center. (1957) J. Counsel. Psychol. 4:274-282.

Prim, Wayne L.—Clients are People (Feb. 1957) Stud. Law J. 2:3.

Reiter, Paul J.—Differential Reactions of Men and Women Patients to Group Psychotherapy. (April 1952) Inter. Group Psychother. 2:103-110.

Ripple, Lillian and Ernestina Alexander—Motivation, Capacity and Opportunity as Related to the Use of Casework Service: Theoretical Base and Plan of Study. (1955) Soc. Ser. Rev. 29, No. 2:172-193.

Rogers, Carl R.—Through the Eyes of a Client. (1951) Past. Psych. 2, No. 16:32-40; No. 17:45-50; No. 18:26-32.

Rogers, Sister Mary Elaine—The Attitude of College Sophomores and Seniors Toward Counseling Procedure with Reference to Certain Personality Factors and Personal Problem Frequency. (Doctoral Dissertation, St. Louis Univ., 1957) (D. A. XVIII, 503, 1958).

Roth, Irwin—The Effect on Outcome of Client's Initial Approach to Life Problems in Psychotherapy. (Doctoral Dissertation, Univ. of Chicago, 1959-60).

Rottschafer, Ronald H.—Client Dependency in Relation to Counselor Style and Induced Client Set. (Doctoral Dissertation, Southern Ill. Univ.) (D.A. XXII, 645, 1961).

Rubinstein, Eli A. and Maurice Lorr—A Comparison of Terminators and Remainers in Outpatient Psychotherapy. (1956) J. Clin. Psychol. 12, No. 4:345-349.

Rudikoff, Esselyn C.—The Self-Concept and Client-centered Counseling. (Doctoral Dissertation, Univ. of Chicago, 1956-57).

Rudikoff, Esselyn C. and Barbara A. Kirk—Goals of Counseling: Mobilizing the Counselee. (1961) J. Counsel. Psychol. 8:243-249.

Samler, J.—Change in Values: A Goal in Counseling. (1960) J. Counsel. Psychol. 7:32-39.

Samler, J.—An Examination of Client Strength and Counselor Responsibility. (1962) J. Counsel. Psychol. 9:5-11.

Schroeder, Pearl—Client Acceptance of Responsibility and Difficulty of Therapy. (1960) J. Consult. Psychol. 24:267-471.

Sechrest, Lee B.—Patients' Interpretations of Their Psychotherapists. (Doctoral Dissertation, Ohio State University, 1956) (D.A. XVII, 1129, 1957).

Shapiro, Stewart B.—Patient Wisdom: An Anthology of Creative Insights in Psychotherapy. (1962) J. Psychol. No. 2, 54:285-291.

Sheerer, Elizabeth—An Analysis of the Relationship Between Acceptance of and Respect for Self and Acceptance of and Respect for Others in Ten Counseling Cases. (1949) J. Consult. Psychol. 13-169-175. Reprint, (March 1957) Past. Psych. 8:35-42.

Singer, S. L. and B. Stefflre—Analysis of the Self-Estimate in the Evaluation of Counseling. (1954) J. Cousel. Psychol. 1:252-255.

Skinner, Kathryn I. K.—Personality and Attitude Characteristics Associated with "Therapy Readiness." (Doctoral Dissertation, Univ. of Texas, 1959) (D.A. XX, 1681, 1960).

Snelbacker, Glen E.—Factors Influencing College Students' Person-Perceptions of Psychotherapists in a Laboratory Analog. (Doctoral Dissertation, Cornell Univ., 1961).

Stein, Aaron—The Nature of Transference in Combined Therapy. (1964) Inter. J. Gr. Ther. 14:413-23.

Strickland, Bonnie R. and Douglas P. Crowne—Need for Approval and the Premature Termination of Psychotherapy. (1963) J. Consult. Psychol. No. 2, 27:95-101.

Strong, Donald J. and Daniel D. Feder—Measurement of the Self Concept: A Critique of the Literature. (1961) J. Counsel. Psychol. 8, No. 2:170.

Taulbee, Earl—Relationship Between Certain Personality Variables and Continuation in Psychotherapy. (1958) J. Consult. Psychol. 22: 83-89.

Terwilliger, Gaines and Fred Fiedler—An Investigation of Determinants Inducing Individuals to Seek Personal Counseling. (1958) J. Consult. Psychol. 22:288.

Todd, William B. and Thomas N. Ewing—Changes in Self-Reference During Counseling. (1961) J. Counsel. Psychol. 8:112-115.

Tuma, A. H. and J. W. Gustad—The Effects of Client and Counselor Personality Characteristics on Client Learning in Counseling. (1957) J. Counsel. Psychol. 4:136-141.

Turner, F. Bernadette—Common Characteristics Among Persons Seeking Professional Marriage Counseling. (1954) Marr. Fam. Liv. 16:143-144.

Van Kaam, Adrian L.—The Experience of Really Feeling Understood by a Person: A Phenomenological Study of the Necessary and Sufficient Constituents of this Subjective Experience by 365 Subjects. (Doctoral Dissertation, Western Reserve Univ., 1957-58).

Vickey, E.—Implications for Marriage Counseling of Self Perceptions and Spouse Perceptions. (1960) J. Counsel. Psychol. 7:3-9.

Werble, Beatrice and C. Henry—Motivation for Using Casework Services, 1. Current Research on Motivation. (Feb.-March 1958) Soc. Casework 39:124-130.

Wheelis, Allan—The Quest for Identity. (New York, Norton, 1958).

Worby, M.—The Adolescent's Expectations of How the Potentially Helpful Person will Act. (1955) Smith Col. Stud. Soc. Work 26:19-59.

Young, Arthur K.—The Relationship of Client Expectation and Counselor Perceptiveness to Client's Willingness to Use Counseling Service. D.A. XXIV, 2991.

Zelle, J. A.—The Strange Shadow of the Imaged Self. (1959) J. Rehabilit. 25:10-11.

Chapter 8

Using The Total Community Counseling Services

Introduction.

Throughout this report we have seen the interrelationship of professions, the way in which clients view their problems as relating to different services, the desire of counselor trainees and colleges for interdisciplinary materials and the recognized need for knowledge of referral routes and usable agencies. We have also placed counseling in that preventive zone between normal social functioning and an individual lost to society. All this underlines the necessity for the helping professions and agencies being organized as a total community helping and counseling service.

Whenever specialization occurs in any service to the public we find the need recognized, and ultimately fulfilled, to synthesize specialties so that nothing is lost to the client. As far back as the American Revolution the Medical Association opproved specialties, and by 1950 twenty specialties were recognized and regulated. Lawyers too have specialized and under 1954 and 1962 plans the American Bar Association has contemplated certification. In medicine the pattern is primarily for separate specialization and then extensive referral. In law, the tendency is to combine numerous specialists in large firms. We are not so much interested

271

in these amalgams of specialists within a profession as we
are in the use of various counseling or helping functions of
different professions. Even in this regard the "clinic" at
which various specialties are offered may take on more meaning for counseling as it has in medical and diagnostic clinics.

Marriage Counseling — A Case in Point.

Marriage counseling, we have seen, has currently sought
to deal with one of society's most central problems and consequently has asked for recognition as a separate profession.
But we have also determined that this is an extremely large
part of the work of clergymen, doctors and lawyers. In fact,
persons take five times as many marital matters to these
professions as they do to all others combined. The clergyman and medic are generally recognized as the ones engaged
in pre-marital counseling. All treat the same problem, albeit
the medic may emphasize sexual conflict, the lawyer financial
conflict and the minister personality conflict.

A comparison of professions shows that the following
percentages claim to do marital counseling: law 91%,
medicine 93%, clergy 97%—compare social workers 50%
and teachers 30%. When it comes to how they handle marriage cases a pretty clear picture of professional interrelation emerges: 53% of the clergy know a marriage counselor
and 48% have referred cases; the figures for doctors are
15% and 21% and for lawyers 19% and 10%. The clergyman
and lawyer handle most cases themselves (48 and 47%
compare physicians (21%); medics refer 1/3 more cases to
psychiatrists than do lawyers and clergymen. All think they
would make adequate marriage counselors; none wants
another profession to do its work; most (45-65%) believe
referral is the proper interrelationship.

Others studying this field came up with the conclusion
that in marital misadjustment there were four types of
causes—medical, religious, legal and financial. Therefore,
in a number of cities (Oklahoma City, Oklahoma and Portland,
Oregon are examples) 4 member panels of physician, clergyman, lawyer and businessman were made available to hus-

band-wife pairs. These report great success (from 75-90%). These panels take referrals (the most frequent are from friends, attorneys, newspaper publicity and employers) and they make referrals (most frequently to doctors).

Many churches now include marital counseling services, and almost without exception these are jointly staffed by ministers, lawyers, social workers, medics, psychiatrists and psychologists. The Family Service Division of the Federated Churches of Los Angeles (Francis Poynter, MSW) has an excellent program and manual. The Domestic Relations Court of Los Angeles (Judge Pfaff) has a similar reconciliation service attached. Many other courts do also. The Pastoral Institute in Washington, D.C. is a counseling center available to ministers and others, staffed by clergymen, psychologists and psychiatrists. One of the most famous is Rev. Norman Vincent Peale's and Dr. Smiley Blanton's American Foundation of Religion and Psychiatry in New York, which has a dozen psychiatrists and four times that many ministers, handles about 500 cases a week and has been thoroughly studied by Samuel Klausner and Charles Kadushin, Bureau of Applied Social Research, in "An Alliance of Pastors and Psychiatrists" and "Steps on the Way to a Psychiatric Clinic."

Other Specialized Joint Efforts.

Although there must be thousands of helping agencies which combine a variety of counselors—from Alcoholics Anonymous to the Big Brother Movement—I wish to mention some of the less well known and more experimental which we noted in the areas of the country where we conducted our research.

In Chicago Nester Kohut has united law and the new specialty of marriage counseling (Ph.D. in psychology). In New Haven Robert Redmount has made the same and even a broader combination. In Downey, California (Los Angeles) the Trotter-Joseff Institute is "an interprofessional approach (law, psychology, sociology) to family relations and probation counseling.''

The Comprehensive Care Program of Cornell Medical Center in New York (Dr. Reader) combines nurse, social workers and medic and that of Northwestern University in Chicago combines five preceptors: 2 medical, 1 psychiatric, 1 psychological and 1 social service. The Legal Aid Division of the Chicago Community Chest combines lawyers, social workers and other counselors. A somewhat similar inter-disciplinary group is the Suicide Prevention Center in Los Angeles.

The Referral Problem—The Point of Departure

Since it is unlikely that most professions will presently join together in clinics, and since the client will invariably seek the most available counseling or that related to his problem as *he* defines it, if he is going to get the best service some form of referral for all or part of his problem seems likely. Although this was not a central part of our research we did try to trace channeling of clients, particularly the poor. We found that on the average the least seriously affected client (particularly if he had little to pay with) encountered on the average six or more persons or agencies before obtaining satisfaction. Geography, religion, finances seem to be the first determiners of where one goes. Then every community develops its referral routes, practitioner interaction, committees and role definitions. In two areas of our study we were able to compare lawyers' and social workers' views and uses of each other. Strong feelings and hostile stereotypes were the rule; social workers saw law as rigid, conservative, non-evolving, settling disputes, active against those committing anti-social acts, an expert and high paid profession but unscrupulous, and approved only the juvenile and ''socialized'' courts. The lawyers associated social work with charity and religion, saw it as fostering immorality and dependency-welfare-statism, did not see it as professional or confidential, viewed it as an impractical and unrealistic "shelter" without much specialized expertness, a place to send nuisance cases. We cite these factors as emphasizing the undercover difficulties which exist in realistic utilization of community services. Every profession, every service agency has similar stereotype views of other agencies in the community. The attitude may be positive or negative; all we can be sure of is that until further education occurs it will probably be inaccurate.

Every community should have a referral index available to all counseling professionals and agencies. Legal Aid of Chicago and Northwestern University Law School put out a good simplified form, for lawyers. The criticism I would make is that it ought to be much broader, listing churches, marriage counselors, teachers, job guidance, adoption and child protection, Big Brother and Sister movements, college entrance helps, banks and lending services, geriatrics and senior citizens, etc. The Index of the Chicago Referral List will give some suggestion of an approach:

Experiment in Multidisciplinary Counseling—
The College Student Counseling Service.

As a part of our study we examined rather deeply several college counseling services in the geographic areas of our survey. On the college campus today is a society in microcosm, one that both sees itself as a separate society and as part of the larger society, one very knowledgeable about counseling and its use. Often times experiments can be tried on a college campus and then later applied to society as a whole (*e.g.* contract medicine). Colleges, further, being composed of many disciplines, have more available and should be more willing to use, the multidisciplinary approach.

In most colleges and universities there have in fact grown up four or five almost completely separate counseling services: 1) guidance and testing, primarily concerned with testing a student's ability and advising on study programs and careers, 2) the health clinic, usually covering everything from decayed teeth and the common cold to schizophrenia, 3) some form of disciplinary counseling, in the dean of students' office or otherwise, 4) religious counseling (defined very broadly) by the religious chaplains or student pastors, and sometimes 5) a general counseling service (offering friendly and psychological counseling). The health clinic is usually the most voracious of these and over the past decade or so has frequently subsumed disciplinary counseling and in some places asked the ministerial counselor to report to it. Considerable jealousy exists between the units and the client often feels himself caught in the middle. It also appears that when counseling combines disciplinary action almost the total value of counseling is lost—the client simply cannot see counseling and discipline as similar in approach, and the counselor cannot keep the functions separate. The most frequently successful interdisciplinary clinic is the "open door" or "walk in" clinic, (illustrated outside our area of study by University of Minnesota and Yale). Here any student may come in for any problem bothering him: grades, money, lack of sleep, sexual questions, or suicidal tendencies. A filled out entry blank and a quick talk with an admissions person gets him to a psychiatrist, psychologist, social worker, or other counselor. From one to fifty sessions may be scheduled; a quick advice, a mere hearing, or deep therapy may result. Such a clinic often finds need to call on other professions—law, medicine, theology.

Two large universities, chiefly as a result of our study and proposals, are planning to set up an even wider open door counseling clinic. It will not be a part of the hygiene department. It will have clergyman, lawyers, doctors, psychiatrists, psychologists, social workers, guidance, marriage and other types of counselors available and working as a team. [We have strongly urged a "peer group" counselor also]. Any problem a student wishes to bring will be handled; he will not have to label himself as sick to come. The key to such a clinic is obviously the trained ability of the intake personnel—can they help the client spot what counselor or set of counselors will be most helpful. This is an experiment, I believe, which needs more study. It ought to be able to evaluate joint efforts and joint conferences compared to referral. The counseling professions will be watching these plans with much interest.

What is said in this chapter comes from our geographic survey areas. Many excellent experiments in college counseling, interdisciplinary offices, open-door counseling, referral listings and like matters have occurred elsewhere and some have been reported. In the areas we studied we found only limited knowledge and use of such national listings as the Membership of the American Association of Marriage Counselors, Directory of Approved Counseling Agencies (by American Board of Counseling Services, Inc.), Counseling Psycholigists (recognized by the APA), Accredited Social Workers and Social Work Agencies, etc. (nearly every profession or calling has a Directory, often with ratings, of its membership). The average professional tended to look upon such lists as advertising media for a particular group. He was much more interested in a local list of facilities available—he would, himself, do the evaluating.

It seemed to us that our interdisciplinary knowledge and use of knowledge was far inadequate to the problem as the client saw it.

Bibliography Chapter 8

See Freeman, Counseling — A Bibliography with Annotations
Code K-1 to K-6 (K-6 particularly)

Adams, James R.—Collaboration of Psychiatrist and Clergyman: A Case Report-The Pastor's Viewpoint. (1964) Fam. Process 3: 262-272.

Alexander, Paul W.—Legal Science and the Social Sciences: The Family Court. (1958) Marr. Fam. Liv. 20:132-139.

Anderson, George C.—The Partnership of Theologians and Psychiatrists. (1963) J. Rel. Health 3:56-70.

Berdie, R. F., ed.—Concepts and Programs of Counseling. (Minn., Univ. of Minn. Press, 1951).

Bietz, Arthur L.—Pulling Life Together: A Source Book for Physicians, Ministers, Teachers and Laymen. (Mt. View, Calif., Pacific, 1952).

Bloom, Betty B. and Jessie Bingham—The Contribution of the School Social Worker. (1955) Understanding the Child 24:114-118.

Bocsky, D.—Factors Associated With the Psychiatric Referral Techniques of a Group of Physicians. (1960) J. Mich. Med. Soc. 59, No. 9:1356-1360.

Boverman, Maxwell—Collaboration of Psychiatrist and Clergyman: A Case Report-The Psychiatrist's Viewpoint. (1964) Fam. Process 3:251-262.

Bowe, V. P.—Marriage Counseling Practices in Salt Lake City Churches. (Master's Thesis, Univ. Utah, 1951).

Brieland, Donald and Norman J. Booth—Child Guidance as a Community Service. (1964) Ann. Am. Acad. Pol. Sci. 355:105-111.

Burke, Hon. Louis H.—The Role of Conciliation in Divorce Cases. (1961) J. Family L. 1:209-226.

Cantoni, Louis J. and Lucile Cantoni—Making Referrals to Professional Counselors. (1965) Education 85:437-438.

Chase, Theodore—Aid to the Legal Profession: The Family Service Association. (Dec. 1958) Boston B. J. 2:13.

Cockerill, Eleanor—The Interdependence of the Professions in Helping People. (Nov. 1953) Soc. Casework. 34:371-378.

Crenshaw, J.—Blueprint for Marriage: Psychology and the Law Join Forces. (Feb. 1962) A.B.A.J. 48:125.

Duhl, Leonard J., et al.—A Mental Health Program for the Peace Corps. (1965) Hum. Org. 23:131-136.

Elia, Andrew D.—Teamwork in Premarital Counseling. (Dec. 1959) Past. Psych. 10:33-38.

Elkin, Meyer—Short-Contact Counseling in a Conciliation Court. (1962) Soc. Casework 43, No. 4:184-190.

Faibanks, Rollin J.—Cooperation Between Clergy and Psychiatrists. (Sept. 1951) Past. Psych. 2, No. 16:19-23.

Family Service Association of America—The Lawyer and the Social Worker. (New York, Family Service Association of America, 1959) 36 pp.

Garber, R. S.—Building an Effectual Physician-Psychiatrist Team. (1960) J. Kentucky Med. Assn. 58:822-826.

Gardner, Yvelin—The Pastor's Use of Community Resources (in Helping the Family of an Alcoholic) (April 1962) Past. Psych. 13:39-44.

Hallinan, Helen W.—Coordinating Agency Efforts in Behalf of the Hard-to-Reach Family. (Jan. 1959) Soc. Casework 40:9-17.

Harper, Fowler V. and Miriam Harper—Lawyers and Marriage Counseling. (Spring 1961) J. Family L. 1:72-88.

Haselkorn, Florence—Some Dynamic Aspects of Interprofessional Practice in Rehabilitation. (1958) Soc. Casework. 37, No. 7:396-401.

Hathorne, B. C.—A Critical Analysis of Protestant Church Counseling Centers. D.A. XXI, 1644; (1960) Past. Psychol. 11:60.

Hiltner, Seward—Tension and Mutual Support Among the Helping Professions. (Dec. 1957) Soc. Serv. Rev. 31, No. 4:377-389.

Isaac, Sol Morton—Status of Lawyer-Social Worker Cooperation. (1963) J. Family Law 3:53.

Jacob, Margaret—Cooperation Between Social Workers in Hospitals and Family Agencies. (Oct. 1958) Soc. Work 3, No. 4:78-85.

Kassan, Martin——The Counseling Service. D.A. XXVI, 1171, 1965.

Keith-Lucas, Alan—The Partnership Between Lawyer and Social Worker in Services to Individuals and Families. (June 22, 1953) Interpreter Releases, New York 30:180-184.

Kerckhoff, Richard K.—Lawyer and the Marriage Couselor. (1952) Mich. S.B.J. 31:26.

Klausner, Samuel Z.—An Alliance of Pastors and Psychiatrists. (Bureau of Applied Social Research. Columbia Univ., New York, 1961).

Klausner, Samuel Z.—Psychiatry and Religion. (New York, Free Press, 1964) 299 pp.

Klausner, Samuel Z.—Role Adaptation of Ministers and Psychiatrists in a Religio-Psychiatric Clinic. (Bureau of Applied Social Research, Columbia University, New York, 1957).

Klink, Thomas W.—The Referral: Helping People Focus Their Needs. (Dec. 1962) Past. Psych. 13:10-15.

Lagey, Joseph and Beverly Ayres—Community Treatment Programs for Multi-Problem Families. (Vancouver, Canada: Res. Dept. Community Chest and Councils of Greater Vancouver Area, Series 2, 1962) 191 pp.

Langford, William S., et al.—The Professional Person-A Mental-hygiene Resource. (1950) Ment. Hygiene, New York, 34:262-286.

Leslie, Robert C.—Cooperation Between Psychotherapists and Pastoral Counselors in the United States. (Nov. 1961) Past. Psych. 12: 23-28.

Macfarlane, Jean W.—Inter-professional Relations and Collaboration with Medicine and Other Related Fields. (1950) Am. Psychol. 5:112-114.

McCleave—Medicine Seeks the Clergy. (1963) J. Rel. Health 2:230-247.

Manning, Jane and Betty Ann Glasser—The Home Visit in the Treatment of Psychiatric Patients Awaiting Hospitalization: A Pilot Study. (1962) J. Health Hum. Beh. 3:97-104.

Miller, Arthur—The Psychiatric Consultant in Family Counseling. (1956) Marr. Fam. Liv. 18:254-258.

Morris, H. H.—Mental Hygiene and the Psychiatrist's Role in a University. (1954) Ment. Hyg. 38:365.

National Association for Mental Health, Inc.—Directory of Psychiatric Clinics and Other Mental Health Resources in the United States. and Territories, 1952, 1954-55, New York, N.A.M.H.

O'Doherty, Eamonn F.—Multidisciplinary Methods in Retrospect. (1948) Psychiatry 11:355-358.

Oglesby, William B., Jr. and J. Barnard—Minister aud Physician as Working Partners. (Sept. 1959) Past. Psych. 10:37-42.

Pfaff, Roger A.—The Conciliation Court of Los Angeles County. In A.B.A., Section of Family Law, Summary of Proceeding 35. (1960).

Powell, Mack—The Mental Hospital Chaplain and Community Clergymen Work Together Through an Orientation Course. (1959) J. Past. Care 13:178-181.

Rapoport, Lydia, and Kate S. Dorst—Teamwork in a Rehabilitation Setting: A Case Illustration. (June 1960) Soc. Casework 41:291-297.

Review of Community Oriented Church Counseling Programs. Facilitating Cooperative Interaction of Religious Groups and Community Health Centers. (Tennessee Department of Mental Health, 1962).

Richards, L. E.—Integration of a Psychiatric Clinic With a Student Personnel Program. (Oct. 1951) Coll. and Univ. 27:38-49.

Roche, Philip Q.—Marriage Council of Philadelphia—A Community Service. Reprinted from Philadelphia Medicine.

Ruffin, John W.—Selected Techniques in Developing a Counseling Program. (1952) Counseling 10, No. 1:4.

Schatzman, Leonard and Rue Bucher—Negotiating a Division of Labor Among Professionals in the State Mental Hospital. (1964) Psychiatry 27:266-277.

Schiller, Patricia—Marriage Counseling in a Legal-Aid Setting. (1960) Marr. Fam. Liv. 22:213-217.

Schmidl, Fritz—The Dynamic Use of the Psychiatric Social Worker's Services Within the Clinical Team. (1950) Am. J. Orthopsychiat. 20:765-775.

Schwartz, E. K. and T. M. Abel—The Professional Education of the Psychoanalytic Psychotherapist. (1955) Am. J. Psychother. 9:253-261.

Stitt, P. G.—Teaming Together for the Whole Patient. (1952) J. Past. Care 6, No. 3:1-10.

Turner, Gary E. and Clifford J. Bodarky—Inter-Discipline Functioning: A Joint Private Practice of Psychiatry and Psychiatric Casework. (1955) Marr. Fam. Liv. 17:355-358.

Voss, Lawrence—Using Religious Counselor in an Institution. Use of Counselor Tried in Theology and Psychological Counseling. (1958) J. Past. Care 12:94-98.

Weil, Frank L.—Cooperation of Church and Social Work. (Proc. 76th National Conf. on Social Work, 1950, 125-234.

Whitehouse, Frederick A.—Teamwork: An Approach to a Higher Professional Level. (Dec. 1951) Excep. Ch. 18:75-82.

Wiesbauer, Henry H.—Pastoral Help in Serious Mental Illness. (Nat. Assn. for Mental Health, 1956).

Zinberg, Norman and Golda Edinburg—Psychiatric Consultation in an Interdisciplinary Setting. (1964) Smith Coll. St. Soc. Wk. 34:126-139.

Chapter 9

Socio-Psycho Dynamics
Of Counseling

The Concepts and Materials on Which to Base
Counseling Theory

We have shown that counseling is neither psychoanalysis
nor psychiatry, though both operate in the realm of interpersonal relationships and relate to the same psychic forces.
Our survey demonstrated that most counselors recognized
this, were dissatisfied with their training in this regard, were
critical of the "schools" of psychiatry which demanded all-
or-nothing acceptance, and asked for or emphasized the
central concepts of sociology-psychology which could be used
in the counseling process. Few counselors saw the need to
be psychoanalyzed. Most, resenting the psychiatrist's asser-
tion that only psychoanalyzed persons could be objective,
tended to observe that counseling operated in the area of
normal life and that psychiatrists and analyzed persons appeared to them less normal than the average client. They
made suggestions of, and asked for, the most modern material
on socio-psycho dynamics in non-specialist language. This
chapter attempts a brief recording of this. It will be found
to deal with factors not considered important by neo-Freud-
ians but which practicing counselors deem pertinent in the

cases they handle, it will review enough Freudianism to relate the counselor to this whole dimension.

The confluence of sociology, psychology and psychoanalysis into a dynamic theory of human behavior and development is the point at which the counselor works. Sociology interests itself in the totality of human experience, insists that the social factor is always present and that society as well as the individual is fulfilling itself through evolutionary stages. Its major research has been in mapping the contemporary social scene to provide the raw data to be used by all disciplines actively dealing with society and the individual's relation to society. Similarly psychology has not primarily been an applied science but rather the clinical and experimental study or "science of mental life" producing information to be used by all applied disciplines (including counseling). It has studied awareness, perception, recognition, memory, consciousness, communication, determinants, drives, goals, animal-man continuum, maturation, aging, group and social processes, testing. Each of these syndromes of material is used by some or all counselors. Our study shows that the most frequently and helpfully used are theories of learning and motivation, individuality and stages of maturing, drives, psychological determinism and goals. Psychoanalysis and psychiatry have furnished the classical theory of personality structure (Id, Ego, Super-ego) and personality growth (oral, anal, phallic, genital stages—producing parallel optimistic, orderly-hoarding, ambitious-envious, reality-balanced personality type). Counselors, as distinguished from analysts, emphasize their need for the above knowledge but refuse to view man with a problem as "sick" or press determinism to the point of seeking answers to all problems in ages 1-10 sexuality.

We have used "dynamic" because we know no other way to express what the counselors and clients whom we studied, asked for. Modern medicine uses the concept of "homeostasis"—the normal organism in balance, not stable but dynamic, ever changing, force springing into action to meet force, biochemical processes and bodies/anti-bodies seeking balance. Psychology-psychiatry has always emphasized this: pleasure-pain; Id-Ego-Super ego; inferiority-compensation; fight-flight; societal-individual; extroversion-introversion. Counseling seeks no static code however excellent. It helps humans face problems and achieve homeostasis through harnessing the creative, explorative, imaginative powers of youth; the feedback of skill, reality and intelligence of adulthood; the societal correction which only humans can achieve through communication, interpersonal reaction and counsel. This is the dynamism the counselor-counselee seek.

The emphasis that will appear in the remainder of this chapter is determined by the demand of both counselors and clients whom we studied that it would be helpful to briefly summarize the major insights of sociology-psychology that must be used for effective counseling, that while socio-psycho dynamics for counselors be grounded in the insights of classical analysis, it embody modern attitudes critical of neo-Freudianism and data that fills out the outline particularly as it relates to people in normal society. Although the social pressures and socialization of modern life, the peculiar problems of the 20th century and the difficulties of understanding choice and decision and motivation were referred to by our counselors as at the very core of their counseling problems, we shall only incidentally refer to these because our respondents considered themselves (and we tend to agree) more experienced and competent in these areas than most of the academic "experts" or writers. Therefore, we shall first treat of the "conscious", "unconscious" and "preconscious", of psychologial determinism, of the Id, Ego and Super-Ego and of personality theory (these are essentially Freud's great contributions). But we shall add to Freudian concepts in each of these, and we shall go on to discuss personality development and problem genesis as pre-school, pre-adolescence, adolescence, adult and societal (a distinct change of Freudian emphasis). And we shall give

some attention to man's peculiar societal dilemmas in this
century.

*Conscious, Preconscious, Unconscious—Levels of Aware-
ness.* The four great insights of Freud and modern
psychiatry probably are: infant sexuality, determinism, the
unconscious and analysis by free association. In place of
a single rational human mind this substitutes the concept of
three levels of awareness (or lack of awareness): the
conscious, preconscious and unconscious. These are viewed
as paralleled by three aspects of personality: the Ego,
Super-ego and Id. The conscious is the everyday mind we
know, the rationality level adapting the individual to his
world. The preconscious is transitional, or as Freud put it—
the antechamber between the inner office (unconscious) and
outside waiting room (conscious); memory is a good example
of preconscious awareness, half-conscious and half-uncon-
scious. The unconscious level is the hardest to reach. In
fact, psychiatry insists that it can only be reached by
hypnosis, dreaming or a free association on the analytic
couch. Yet Freud reached it by semi-trained self analysis,
and Horney and others recognize this potential generally.

The classical Freudian theory of the unconscious is that
a painful emotional experience is "forgotten" into the
unconscious, from which it later appears as unconscious behavior. The maturity of the individual determines what
items can be dealt with consciously and what have to be
regressed into the unconscious. Associated with the theory
of unconscious is that of dreams. Dreams protect sleep, by
putting aside the day's unsolved problems. The dream
records how rationality (Ego) is trying to reconcile the
interior unconscious (Id) and the censorship or conscience
(Super-Ego); it attempts also to relate the day's problems
or residue to the individual's past (largely unconscious)
and thus achieve a fresh combination (conscious, unconscious
or both) of the old and the new. All men dream. A "successful" dream is not remembered, since the above process
has made the adjustment at the unconscious level. The

analyst is able to reach the unconscious and the problems of adjustment through dream interpretation, hysteria, hypnosis and like methods.

The counselor by comparison is not primarily interested in the unconscious in dreams, psychoses, neuroses, psychosomatic disorders and hysteria. He is concerned with the interplay of conscious, preconscious and unconscious in everyday life.

Without trying to fully describe the unconscious, we can give enough characteristics to help us spot when the unconscious is in control. The unconscious maintains the phantasy that it is omnipotent (able to do anything, manipulate anyone). It operates to achieve pleasure. It is uncontrolled by any of the normal rules of the game (the same symbol or word can mean several things or be shifted to an unrelated connection; space and time can be juggled freely; opposites are potentially the same; laws of logic are abandoned). Jung added to Freud that the unconscious is not to be feared, that it is not mainly sexual, that a man embodies an individual and a collective (societal) unconscious, and that herein lies much of the creativity of art, literature, religion, etc. Maslow and others show that from this arises leadership, self-actualization, drive. The matter of conscious and preconscious will be left to the discussion of Ego and Super-ego compared to Id.

The important question raised by most counselors was, "What is the relation of man's intelligence to all this", "how can we integrate and use intelligence?" The current and broader studies of man reinforce the view that the most human characteristic is not an unconscious approximating animal instinct, but intelligence. Man is a purposive machine (like Univac) with a goal or program which sorts all input, suggests a tentative output, tests this against the goal, feeds this back and brings out a corrected output. In man an old brain structure (base of the brain) controlling the instinct system was revamped to connect with the newly formed neocortex of intelligence. It is being strongly suggested that even the unconscious is an intelligent unconscious. Instinct directed *animals* are now seen not merely as automatons, but as driven hither and yon by dissociated subdrives, each grabbing the stage in turn. Intelligence, through sustained integration, keeps man functioning as a whole and in an overall pattern which we call personality. Personality develops self esteem and security through finding that intelligence works. But since instinct mechanisms survive alongside intelligence, frustration or danger will continue to evoke rage and fear. If self esteem is high, rage and fear will not take control and intelligence will function adequately. Contra, if esteem is low.

Psychological determinism primarily means that no human behavior is accidental. All behavior is caused. This continuity moves through forgotten episodes, the unconscious, personality development, conscience, ideals and goals. Many persons have feared a secondary meaning—that all action is determined by the libido and unconscious so that man is not a free agent. The most up-to-date theory (and counseling recognizes this) is that while *Id* and environment control much activity through the unconscious, man has some autonomy as the *Ego* and intelligence through "attention control" make ultimate choices; but, when certain drives are so strong as to completely control attention, autonomy may disappear or be curtailed.

Id, Ego, Super-ego. In all discussions of psychic theory, dynamics, personality, determinism and the unconscious it is necessary to use these three Freudian terms. *Id* is the unconscious libido force, instinctive; originally conceived as eros, life or sex drive but later dualized to include the death or destructive drive. (Recent studies suggest the *Id* is learned and not wholly instinctive, and that what Freud saw as "sex" in the very young was only "pseudo-sex" or the projection of the parents' sex). *Ego* is the hypothecated integrative force governed by the reality principle, the battlefield between Id and Super-ego, the seat of anxiety, repressions, dreams but also of sanity, reason, consciousness. The *Super-ego* is the censor; it begins as parental attitudes, adds societal standards, and matures as conscience. *Id* may be thought of as Amoral man, *Ego* as Reasonable man and *Super-ego* as Moral man. These functions are being located anatomically—*Id* in the mid-brain, *Ego* in the sensory cortex and *Super-ego* in the K-spindles. This trichotomy remains in precarious balance. It gives us tools for recognizing the role of sex, the place of the unconscious, the ego and its defenses, the eternal presence of parents in every man and the like presence of his childhood in each adult.

A few words more need to be said about the *Ego,* for our counselors recognized that it is mainly at this point where counseling works. The *Ego* was first thought to be merely a reaction to *Id*, to have no drive of its own. Now Id is seen as libidinal drives and a pleasure principle and Ego as Ego-drives, Ego-defenses and a reality principle. The Ego functions by dynamic syntheses and viable compromise to maintain the total organism *vis-a-vis* the demands of the "three harsh masters"—external reality, the Id and the Super-ego. Its functions are usually listed as follows (similar to the processes of learning and intelligence): perception, memory, thinking or intellect, deciding or judgment, action or executing, testing, defense.

Ego-defenses are an aspect of the Ego, difficult to list or systematically study. Freudians list ten to twenty of these: repression, sublimation, dreams, projection, introjection, reaction formation, isolation, undoing or nullifying, displacement, denial, compromise, regression, rationalization, fixation, introversion, conversion, character, identification, symbolization, dramatization, transference. It is not to be assumed that psychic balance comes from the Ego or conscious and unbalance from the Id or unconscious, or that Ego defenses are always negative. The Id and unconscious are an important part of man and must have their appropriate place. Ego defenses can be a fearful turning of one's back on reality, but they can also be the very tool for maintaining oneself and mediating external and internal forces.

The generally accepted story of how the *Super-ego* is formed is that some time in the phallic or Oedipal period the child internally takes over the remonstrances (code) of the parents, later adds what he perceives as the larger-than-family societal code and matures this into the still small voice of conscience. Morals, customs, religious ideals, ethics and law enter the Super-ego through the social conscience. How do we move from original Super-ego content to new content? That portion of the Super-ego called the "Ego-ideal", or the goal of what one would like to be, determines what will be further learned. Hopefully, the Super-ego matures. Fromm has forcefully shown that a mature person (and a mature society) is one "who is not subject to irrational (outside) authority, and accepts willingly the rational authority of conscience and reason" (*The Sane Society*, 275).

Personality Theory is another aspect of socio-psycho dynamics that the able counselor utilized. Although almost every psychological, sociological and philosophical school has attempted a theory of personality, no definition is entirely satisfactory. "Character" represents society's appraisal of personality; "personality" is the internal organization of each person adjusting him to everything and everyone with whom he comes in contact. It is best to employ a "stages of development" and a "comparison of theories" approach. The more sophisticated of our examined counselors seemed to agree (as do theorists) on what concepts are generally acceptable and usable:

> The genetic view (particularly in early stages)
> Man as *purposive*
> *Unconscious motivation* and the operation of a *pleasure-reward* formula
> *Continuity of development*
> *Wholistic or the total individual* view
> Importance of *self* and *psychological environment.*

We can sense how great the development of personality concepts has become if we briefly compare Freud and a modern "field" or "vector" theory. Freud posited a theory of personality structure (Id, Ego, Super-ego) wherein the Id or instinctual was dominant; a theory of sexual-infantile personality growth (oral, anal, phallic, genital); with personality types paralleling this growth cycle (optimistic, orderly-hoarding, ambitious-envious, reality-balanced). His thought was pioneering and his broad view of a full-bodied man living both in reality and make-believe, driven by the unconscious but capable of rational thought and action, now frustrated and now satisfied, hopeful and despairing—a complex personality, is the foundation of personality theories. A field theory does not emphasize early experience but rather the contemporaneous; it studies the specific person in a concrete situation, the "normal" person rather than the neurotic. It leaves the explanation of early experience to Freud or others; since early experience is only important as it is one of the existing "factors" or part of the existing "field" from which behavior comes. The "field" is the totality of coexisting, interdependent facts. A need releases energy, increases tension, imparts value and creates force. The emphasis is not on a time sequence, but rather on the increased ability of the adult through development in such matters as variety of thought and action, complexity, extensity, organization, integration, realism, differentiation, boundary definition. Development is a continuous process in which it is hard to see distinct stages.

Finally, to further set the stage for using personality theories, concentrating on the normal functioning adult, we may borrow two listings. Most of the theories refer to *"needs"*. Murray has catalogued needs as: Abasement, achievement, affiliation, aggression, autonomy, counteraction, defendance, deference, dominance, exhibition, harm-avoidance, infavoidance (avoid humiliation), nurturance, order, play, rejection, sentience, sex, succorance, understanding. In defining a truly adult or mature person, most writers refer to some concept of "self-actualizing" or "conscience directed". Maslow has studied mature or self-actualizing persons and lists the following characteristics they possess: a) *realistically* oriented, b) *accept selves* and natural world for what they are, c) *spontaneity*, d) *problem-centered* rather than self-centered, e) air of detachment and need for *privacy*, f) autonomous and *independent*, g) some mystical or *spiritual* experience, h) *identity with mankind*, i) *intimacy with few* but deep love with these, j) values and attitudes which are *democratic*, k) *creativeness*, l) absence of confusion of *means and ends*, m) sens of *humor*, philosophical rather than hostile and n) *resistance to conformity*.

A Modern Integrated Socio-Psycho Dynamics for Counseling.

Again we should note that counselors, as compared to pediatric analysts or classical analysts, see themselves as involved with normal *adults* with only more or less psychological content to their problems. This means that it must be the function of *counseling dynamics* to emphasize more the adult personality than infant sexuality. We therefore take a genetic-wholistic-dynamic pattern overall, with Freudian emphasis for infancy, modified by Erickson and learning theory for the school age, by the self-field insight for adolescence, and the societal-maturity formulation for adulthood. Therefore, the periods we shall examine are:

Pre-School: Personality, Sexuality and Family

School: Personality, Acculturation, Teachers

Adolescence: Toward Maturity, Self, Sex, Education-work

Adulthood: Socialization, Achievement, Responsibility, Aging

The Sane (mature) or Insane (immature) Society.

We shall not repeat the foundation material outlined in the paragraphs above, but shall show applications at appropriate points.

Pre-School. Nearly everything we have heretofore observed—about socio-psycho dynamics, determinism, the unconscious, and the Id, Ego and Super-ego, is set in a human time sequence. The first stage of this development is within the confines of the family and involves ages 1 to 6 years. It is the period to which psychoanalysis originally gave virtually all its attention. It is classically divided into three time periods named after the location of the sensory zone associated with the gaining of pleasure in that period, as follows:

> Oral—to 2 years (self-centered, narcissistic)
> Anal—2-4 years (development of control)
> Phallic, Urethal, Oedipal—4-6 years (outward interest, curiosity)

In the *oral* period the child is one large mouth: moving to the mother's breast, sucking, crying, happily gurgling. He is said to be self centered or narcissistic, in control of mother and environment, unable to be alone, lacking in ego qualities. Something is carried over from this period (in balance or out of balance): pleasure in eating, drinking, kissing or compulsive eating, homosexual perversion, narcissism. Bowel movement and urination are the center of the *anal* period, whether because they give pleasure or are the focus of learning control. The child is supposed to learn the hygiene of defecation, not to handle himself. He is made to conform to family values (clean-dirty, proper-improper, grown up, etc.) by the family's tools of discipline (disgust, ridicule, schedule, spanking, etc.). Bio-neurology shows this is the time the myelin sheath is deposited over the nerve fibers, allowing the striated voluntary muscles to take control over the smooth involuntary muscles. If control is required too rapidly or in ways it cannot be accepted, the child develops neurotic reactions to control (masochism, sadism, obsession-compulsion, projection, manipulation). The period gives rise to a series of comparisons important in later life: holding-letting go, giving-receiving, self-thing, I-thou, autonomy-authority, internal-external perception, reality-imaginary. And classic analytic thought says that these leave personality traits: saving-spending, withholding-giving, precision-sloppiness, cleanness-dirtiness.

The *phallic* period is the Oedipal complex, the most central and criticized Freudian concept. The theory is that the child (4-6 years), begins wide exploration, finds gratification in his sex organs, and turns an experimentation in love outside himself (non-narcissistic) toward the only available other-sexed person, the parent of the opposite sex. From this family triangle is said to be learned the plan for all social relationships. Classical Freudianism says that, since Oedipal love is impossible (the strongest taboo is against incest), sexuality is repressed until adolescence when it can be fulfilled. This converts extra-personal love within the family and toward acquaintances and friends into tenderness and affection, and leaves sexual love to operate toward one love object later, as approved by society. This cycle is believed necessary for adult loving and being loved. To achieve this "good" or "mature" pattern mother and father must feel true object love and affection for the child and true sexual love and affection for each other. Recently it is being suggested (with considerable proof) that what the child does in this period is experience *pseudo*-sex at a time when he cannot use true sex, but that the pseudo qualities will hold over with him to spoil his use of true sex in adolescence; the pseudo-sex is projected by the parents into the experience rather than derived from the child's instinctual drive. Pseudo-sex is that complex of all unconscious drives and conflicts displaced into sex so that sex may carry the scars of anxiety, fear, hate, etc. The new approach would point to how within a few days of birth parents begin to remark how the child looks like one parent, how girlish or manly, with sexual interest, a little animal, etc. We can properly ask whether and how far a given person extends the pseudo-sex period into dirty jokes, masturbation, puritanism, nymphomania, voyeurism, exhibitionism, prostitution, or tendencies in these and like directions. The phallic period is the threshold in societal life. Here begin three-fold (child, 2 parents) and more complex (siblings, parents, grandparents, family friends, neighbors and neighbors' children) relationships. Here begins society's (family's) demand to internalize values (Super-ego) and control (Ego). Freudianism was probably too sexual, too masculine oriented, too Vienna 1890 (cf. new role of male and female, new time schedule in kindergarten and nursery, new influence of toys, T.V., etc.). The emphasis in later paragraphs attempts to reflect some counseling material used to correct this.

Pre-Adolscence: Freud called the period from 6 to 13 "sex latency"; it is better viewed as schooling or accultura-tion. Studies of the National Institute of Mental Health and of the ineffective (disturbed, delinquent) soldiers in World War II show that school is *the* primary affector of person-ality and that low educational achievement was the one con-sistent factor in the disturbed groups. The first drives and conflicts have been weathered, ability to live in the restricted family environment has been achieved (well or poorly), a first set of values has been accepted, the desire to emulate mother or father has been aroused. Now the child must move into the outer world, take on new teachers, experience new influences and life patterns, learn wider values and standards, and begin in earnest the learning-intellectualizing process. The Ego becomes supreme. To be successful, each person must develop and maintain his own self identity and at the same time identify with the larger society. One of the dangers is that the child has unlimited desire to explore but limited ability to integrate. He learns best in the security of ex-ternally fixed rules but with encouragement to experiment as far as his strength permits. Both the family and society are trying to teach the child; the two may not speak for the same values. And the child, grounded in both, is trying to produce a unique character and fit with his peer group. Learning and personality theories are more important to this period than sex. Recent research has shown ability to chart the rules for development here of the self concept.

Adolescence: Adolescence is the change from child to adult. Physically there is the most evident change; menstruation and ejaculation; the power of reproduction; the secondary sex characteristics of breasts, hair, voice change, shoulder-hip structure. The Ego has worked hard to produce a pre-puberty self image; now it must re-form the self image to include the new body. The self image must be adequate. But the more complex the society, the more difficult to answer, "adequate for what?" To catch a man, bear children, establish a good home, explore new thought realms, develop a philosophy of life, become a leader? By now the intellect is formed and society makes it clear that it expects some energy poured into productive work and preparation for work. Education becomes job oriented.

Adolescence has its own unique anxiety—the anxiety of testing for adequacy. The youth is tested for intelligence, personality, adjustment, leadership, eyesight, for college and in athletics. Few are chosen or make the Olympics. And it must be added: it is not merely the inadequate who suffer psychologically, the person who knows he has an IQ of 150 is a real and special problem.

Two dimensions of this testing are particularly significant. Society requires part of the testing to be extremely public—almost like a gladiatorial contest wherein society gloats on one's loss as fully as on another's gain. In a second area, that pertaining to sex and male-female relationships, society demands that experimentation be completely covert. Experimentation does occur, but it is without societal approval. Therefore, added to testing for adequacy are the anxieties of fear, conflict, guilt and uncertainty. The ways of meeting the anxiety are likely to be any of the Ego-defenses which we earlier listed. Some would say that here we come to the most crucial question of adolescence. As sex re-appears will it be true sex or pseudo-sex? Most pre-adolescent sex, as we have seen, is in a sense pseudo; parents, afraid of their own reaction to sex in their adolescent children, tend to evidence pseudo-sex; movies and books are apt to purvey all forms of pseudo-sex, often rationalized, advertised, sentimentalized and moralized. Then society, not permitting free experimentation, pushes sex toward masturbation, fantasies and like pseudo-sexual patterns. When menstruation or ejaculation first occurs, one soils clothes or bedding, and must "face mother" in the same way as in bowel and urinary accidents. It is sometimes a wonder that youth develops any true sex.

This is also the age marked by emotional extremes, tempestuous swings and trying on hundreds of "identities" (ballplayer, movie star, President). It is a time of meeting the widest variety of people, problems and experiences; when the tacit becomes explicit and the known is understood; when the past invites retreat to dependency and the future beckons to maturity; it is marked by the poles of idealism and cynicism; when one's family and peer group both call; when adolescents are expected to behave like adults and are treated like children. Maturity is to create a unique self out of all this (not a half-self or arrested development).

Adulthood: Socialization (Achieving, Responsibility, Aging). We counselors are perhaps most interested in the adult stage, and for these reasons: (1) The age span (20-80) covers 3/4 of a normal life. (2) We are ourselves in this age group. (3) So are nearly all our clients. (4) The problems we handle are adult problems. In a sense, psychiatrists have blocked out as their province, and people visit them to center on, childhood problems. Counselors and their clients approach problems from the opposite end—here is an adult and an adult problem; childhood will be considered only if apparently directly involved. In spite of this connection, we shall not outline adulthood's patterns as detailedly as we have previous stages because they are more conscious than unconscious; to the extent that they are conscious counselors believe they are aware of and deal with them in their own daily experience and observation; and to the extent these are unconscious they delve back into the pre-adult material reviewed in prior sections.

The philosophy and culture of India separates life into four almost airtight compartments: studency, mating-home building, leadership-citizenry, and meditating-aging. In America divisions are far from airtight. Grandma tries to look like the debutante and the latter tries to appear as sophisticated as the matron. Our counselor assumes that because he is adult he knows adulthood. Our study shows that he gradually does achieve this by experience. He would profit by knowledge of available studies on the decision process, the social pressures and problems of modern life and similar factors.

We suggest several adult syndromes of which he should take cognizance: Adulthood is the acting out of earlier training; it seeks to be creative, self actualizing, self correcting, productive, achieving. It is societal; it limits individuality and seeks socialization; its anxiety is socially produced. It is complex in societal pressures and advertising-propaganda, in motivation, experience and Ego-Super ego balance. It is youth and age, parenthood and responsibility, family and society, movement toward unity and maturity.

Young adulthood is marked by education, mate selection, marriage, unabashed sexual love, birth of children, job, productive work, "taking home the bacon", one's own home, one's own friends—these are the period's "firsts." And these years are marked accordingly by their own problems: inability to enjoy sex where *pseudo*-sex or repression remains from prior experience, spring "romance" dying without its being replaced by mature love, the loneliness in a crowd that Riesman insists inflicts our civilization, the difficulty of maintaining individuality in a gray flannel suit or on a production line, keeping up with the Joneses and problems of finance, the alienating rather than productive nature of so many jobs, the inability to be adequate parents as children arrive, the fear of responsibility, the realized lack of philosophy of life, and unachieved maturity. Our counselors listed these young adult problems which walked into their offices every day.

The middle years, 35-55, are when counsel is most often sought (see Ch. 7 as to average client age). This is the period of achievement (and nonachievement), maturity (and lack of maturity). Here are the pressures of society, job, family—the changes that occur in the marriage relationship, the added responsibilities of finances, the loss of drive, the fear of age, the increasing physical ailments, the demands and challenge of one's children and other youth, societal and job mobility. Counseling, rather than depth analysis, is most appropriate to these problems.

In old age we face a new problem. Drugs have alleviated physical ailments and made the period longer; but jobs end earlier and psychological problems loom larger as others take over leadership or challenge authority and as loneliness or idleness move in. Age turns to counselors to plan finances, find philosophy of life and death—the whole new field of gerontology.

The Sane or Insane Society. Flowing out of the middle and later years is the kind of society we have (sane or insane), how we can shape it and how it will in turn shape us. Psychologists and sociologists fairly well agree that society presently is struggling for but lacks maturity. It has lost the goals that originally made man human—reason, justice, love, unity of mankind. It has mastered nature, science, machines and production but failed to eliminate poverty and war. It is paranoic (strong yet fearful), masochistic-sadistic (in war and criminality), schizophrenic, and regressive (preferring childish security to exploration). It produces "class psychoses" so that the upper classes move toward external "success" but internal neurosis; the lower classes are pushed into suspicion, withdrawal, anti-society attitudes that make them unable to play the success game. Some writers have mentioned five perversions that contribute to our individual-societal maladjustment: *intelligence perverted into rationalization, sex perverted into pseudo-sex, communication perverted into deception* (the "fine" art of propaganda, politics and marital chit-chat); *cooperation perverted into exploitation* (one person *using* another to the first's advantage rather than cooperating for a common end or competing to move toward a common goal); *evolution perverted into revolution* (need for societal change apparent but using destructive-neurotic revolution rather than intell-gent-integrative evolution). Social scientists may argue whether man can change before society changes, or whether man must change first in order to change society. The counselor has not time for this argument. He approaches this man-society complex at the crucial point in a problem where man and society meet and each may influence the other. The good counselor is interested in both sides of the question and in himself working with them maturely. He may be advising an Agency or a Judge as well as a client.

The competent, experienced and wise counselor will know what aspect of socio-psycho dynamics will best meet his client's problem. Is it centered in infancy, sex, personality, failure, what? His approach is pragmatic and eclectic. He is dealing with individuals, interrelationships and society. He has a wider spectrum of potential methods than depth analysis on a psychiatrist's couch. And if he is wise, he will use them.

Bibliography Chapter 9

See Freeman, Counseling — A Bibliography with Annotations
Codes J-3, 4; L-I, 2, 4 and particularly Code N

Abrahasen, David—The Road to Emotional Maturity. (New York: Prentice-Hall, 1958).

Ackerman, Nathan W.—Psychodynamics of Family Life. (New York: Basic Books, 1958).

Adler, Alfred—Understanding Human Nature. Trans. by Walter Beran Wolfe. (Garden City, N. Y., Greenberg, 1927).

Adler, Alfred (Alan Porter, ed.)—What Life Should Mean to You. (New York, Capri, 1958).

Albert, Gerald—A Handbook to Increase Awareness Among Non-Professionals, D.A. XXVI, 1165, 1965.

Alexander, F.—Current Views on Psychotherapy. (1953) Psychiatry 16:113-122.

Allport, Gordon W.—Becoming: Basic Considerations for a Psychology of Personality. (New Haven: Yale Univ. Press, 1955).

Allport, Gordon W.—Pattern and Growth in Personality. (New York: Holt, 1961).

Argyle, Michael—Eysenck's Theory of Conscience: A Reply, (1965) 56 Br. J. Psychol. 309.

Arnold, Magda B.—Emotion and Personality. Vols. 1 and 2. (Washington, Columbia, 1960).

Arthur, Julietta K.—You and Yours: How to Help Older People. (Philadelphia, Lippincott, 1960) 315 pp.

Balatao, J. C.—Conscience and Superego. (March 1957) Am. Cath. Psychol. Assoc. Newsltr. Supp. No. 26:1-2.

Balint, Michael and Alice Balint—On Transference and Counter-transwerence. (1939) Inter. J. Psychoanal. 20:223-230. Also in Michael Balint—Primary Love and Psychoanalytic Technique. (New York, Liveright, 1952) 288 pp.

Baller, W. R. and D. C. Charles—Psychology of Human Growth and Development. (New York, Holt, 1961).

Barry, M. J., Jr.—Depression, Shame, Loneliness, and the Psychiatrist's Position. (1960) Am. J. Psychother. 16:580-590.

Barta, Frank R.—The Moral Theory of Behavior: A New Answer to the Enigma of Mental Illness. (Springfield, Ill. Thomas, 1952) 35 pp.

Bateman, Mildred M. and Joseph S. Jenson—The Effect of Religious Background on Modes of Handling Anger. (Feb. 1958) J. Soc. Psychol. 47:133-141.

Bentz, Willard K.—Social Class and Perception of Mental Illness. (1963) Fla. St. U. Res. Rept. Soc. Sci. 6:31-49.

Bergler, Edmund—The Revolt of the Middle-aged Man. (New York, A.A. Wyn, 1954) 308 pp.

Berthoid, Fred—The Fear of God. The Role of Anxiety in Contemporary Thought. (New Yoork, Harper, 1959) 158 pp.

Blake, John A.—The Fourth Category of Personality Needs; A Critical Analysis of a Psycho-Theological Problem. (1953) Ment. Hygiene 37:377-383.

Blanton, Smiley and N. V. Peale—The Art of Real Happiness. (Englewood Cliffs, Prentice-Hall, 1950) 247 pp.

Blanton, Smiley—Love or Perish. (New Yoork, Simon and Schuster, 1957).

Blos, Peter—On Adolscence: A Psychoanalytic Interpretation. (Glencoe, Free Press, 1962) 269 pp.

Boisen, Anton T.—Religious Experience and Psychological Conflict. (1959) J. Past. Care 13:160-163. Also (1958) Am. Psychol. 13:568-570.

Bordin, Edward S.—A Counseling Psychologist Views Personality Development. (1957) J. Counsel. Psychol. 4:3-8.

Braceland, Francis J.—Faith, Reason, and Modern Psychiatry; Sources for a Synthesis. (New York, Kenedy, 1955) 310 pp.

Brookes, Crittenden E.—Personality Theories Underlying Two Views of Counseling. (Doctoral Dissertation, Stanford Univ., 1056) (D.A. XVII, 91, 1957).

Caprio, Frank S.—Helping Yourself with Psychiatry. (New York, Prentice-Hall, 1959).

Carrier, Blanche—Free to Grow. (New York, Harper, 1951).

Carrington, W. L.—Psychology, Religion and Human Need (Great Neck, N. Y., Channel, 1957).

Chase, Stuart—Changes in Public Opinion and Attitudes Between Generations: American Values. (1965) Pub. Op. Q. 29:357.

Coleman, Marie L. and Joost A. M. Meerloo—The Transference Function: A Study of Normal and Pathological Transference. (1951) Psychoanal. Rev. 38:205-221.

Cattell, Raymond B.—Personality: A Systematic, Theoretical, and Factual Study. (New York, McGraw, 1950).

Clark, Walter H.—A Study of Some of the Factors Leading to Achievement and Creativity, with Special Reference to Religious Skepticism and Belief. (1955) J. Soc. Psychol. 41:57-69.

Clinebell, Howard J., Jr.—Ego Psychology and Pastoral Counseling. (Feb. 1963) Past. Psych. 14:26-36.

Cohen, John—Behaviour in Uncertainty and Its Social Implications. (New York, Basic Books, 1964).

Cohen, Yehudi A..—Social Structure and Personality. (New York, Holt-Rinehart, 1961).

Curran, Charles A.—Some Ethical and Scientific Values in the Counseling Psychotherapeutic Process. (1960) Personnel Guid. J. 39:15-20.

Davidson, H. A.—The Reversible Supergo. (1963) Am. J. Psychiat. 120:190-191.

Dempsey, P. J. R.—Values and Therapy. (1958) Bull. Guid. Cath. Psychiatrists 6:13-14.

Deutsch, Morton and H. B. Gerard—A Study of Normative and Informational Social Influences Upon Individual Judgment. (1955) J. Abnorm. Soc. Psychol. 51:629-637.

Doniger, Simon, ed.—Becoming the Complete Adult. (New York, Association, 1962).

Doniger, Simon, ed.— The Nature of Man in Theological and Psychological Perspective. (New York, Harper, 1962).

Dreger, Ralph M.—Fundamentals of Personality. (Philadelphia, Lippincott, 1962).

Dubbe, Marvin C.—What Parents Are Not Told May Hurt. (1965) Fam. Life. Coord. 14:51.

Dunham, W. Warren—Sociological Theory and Mental Disorder. (Wayne State Univ. Press, 1960).

Eames, Thomas H. et al.—Attitudes and Opinions of Adolescents, (1965) J. Ed. 147:1.

Eavey, Charles B.—Principles of Personality Building for Christian Parents. (Grand Rapids, Zondervan, 1952) 321 pp.

Eissler, Ruth S.—The Psychoanalytic Study of the Child. (New York, Intern. Univ. Press, 1965) 566 pp.

English, Oliver S. and S. M. Finch—Introduction to Psychiatry. (New York: Norton, 1954).

Erickson, E. H.—Childhood and Society. (New York: Norton, 1950).

Erickson, E. H.—The Problem of Ego Identity. (1956) Am. J. Psych. Ass'n 4:56.

Eysenck, H. J.—Sense and Nonsense in Psychology. (Baltimore: Penguin Books, 1957).

Eysenck, H. J.—A Note on Some Criticism of the Mowrer-Eysenck Conditioning Theory of Conscience. (1965) 56 Br. J. Psychol. 305.

Eysenck, H. J.—The Structure of Human Personality. (New York: Wiley, 1953).

Falcone, John Cesare—A Study of the Theological and Psychiatric Aspects of Guilt. (Jan. 1961) Past. Psych. 11:59-60.

Federn, Paul—Ego Psychology and the Psychoses. (New York, Basic Books, 1953).

Ferenczi, Sandor—Further Contributions to the Theory and Technique of Psychoanalysis. (New York: Basic Books, 1952).

Ferenczi, Sandor—Stages in the Development of the Sense of Reality, in His—Sex in Psychoanalysis. (New York: Basic Books, 1950).

Field, K.—Field Theory in Social Science; Selected Theoretical Papers (New York: Harper, 1951).

Fisher, Robert M., ed.—The Metropolis in Modern Life. (New York, Doubleday, 1955) 401 pp.

Fishman, J. A.—How Safe is Psychoanalysis? (1952) Jew. Ed. 23 No. 1:45-8.

Freides, D.—Toward the Elimination of the Concept of Normality. (1960) J. Consult. Psychol. 24:128-133.

Freud, Anna—The Ego and the Mechanisms of Defense. (New York: International Univ. Press, 1946).

Freud, Sigmund—Standard Edition of (his) complete Psychological Works. (New York: Macmillan, 1953).

Freud, Sigmund—An Outline of Psychoanalysis. (New York: Norton, 1949).

Friedman, Maurice S.—Healing Through Meeting: Martin Buber and Psychotherapy. (Autumn 1955) Cross Currents 5:297-310.

Friedmann, Eugene A. and Robert J. Havighurst—The Meaning of Work and Retirement. (Chicago, Univ. of Chicago Press, 1954).

Fromm, Erich—The Art of Loving. (New York: Harper, 1956); The Heart of Man (N. Y., Harper, 1964).

Fromm, Erich—The Sane Society. (New York: Rinehart, 1955).

Fromm, Erich—The Philosophy Basic to Freud's Psychoanalysis. (Feb. 1962) Past. Psych. 13:26-32.

Fromm-Reichmann, Frieda—Psychoanalysis and Psychotherapy. (Chicago; Bullard, 1959).

Garrison, Karl C.—Psychology of Adolescence (Engl. Cliffs, P-H, 1965) 487 pp.

Gerard, Margaret—Dynamic Psychiatry. (Chicago: Univ. of Chicago Press, 1952).

Guntrip, H.—Ego-Weakness and the Hard Core of the Problem of Psychotherapy. (1960) Brit. J. Med. Psychol. 33:163-184.

Hall, Calvin and G. Lindzey—Theories of Personality. (New York: Wiley, 1957).

Harrower, Molly—Personality Change and Development. (New York, Grune and Stratton, 1958) 392 pp.

Hartmann, Heinz—Ego Psychology and the Problem of Adaptation. (New York: International Univ. Press, 1958).

Hilgard, Ernest R.—Theories of Learning. (New York, Appleton, 1956).

Hillman, James—Emotion: A Comprehensive Phenomenology of Theories and Their Meaning for Therapy. (Evanston, Ill., Northwestern Univ. Press, 1961) 318 pp.

Hiltner, Seward—Freud for the Pastor. (Jan. 1955) Past. Psych. 5:50.

Hiltner, Seward—Self-Understanding. (Nashville, Abingdon, 1962).

Holt, John—How Children Fail. (New York, Delta, 1965) 181 pp.

Horney, Karen—Neurosis and Human Growth. (New York, Norton, 1950).

Horney, Karen—The Neurotic Personality of Our Time. (New York, Norton, 1957).

Hughes, Margaret M., ed.—The People in Your Life, Psychiatry and Personal Relations by Ten Leading Authorities. (New York, Knopf, 1951) 278 pp.

Johnson, Paul E.—Personality and Religion. (Nashville, Abingdon, 1957) 284 pp.

Johnson, A. M., S. A. Saurek—The Genesis of Antisocial Acting Out in Children and Adults. (1952) Psychoanal. Q. 21:323.

Jung, C. G.—Collected Works. (New York, Pantheon, 1953).

Kahn, Eugene—The Past Is Not Past. (Springfield, Ill., Thomas, 1962) 66 pp.

Kelly, G. A.—The Psychology of Personal Constructs. (New York, Norton, 1955).

Kelman, Harold, Frederick Weiss, Paul Tillich and Karen Horney—Human Nature Can Change. (Oct. 1960) Past. Psych. 11:35-43; (1952) Am. J. Psychoanal. 12.

Kubie, Lawrence S.—The Dilemma of the Analyst in a Troubled World. (1950) Bull. Am. Psychoanal. 6:1-4.

Kunkel, Fritz—In Search of Maturity. (New York, Scribners, 1943).

Leary, Timothy—Interpersonal Diagnosis of Personality. (New York, Ronald, 1957).

Leighton, Alexander—Explorations in Social Psychiatry. (New York: Basic Books, 1957).

LeShan, Lawrence L.—Changing Trends in Psychoanalytically Oriented Psychotherapy. (1962) Ment. Hygiene No. 3, 46:454-463.

Levin, Tom—The Function of the Idealized Self-Image in Transference Formation: A Study of Eight Psychoanalytic Patients to Determine the Function of the Projected Idealized Self-Image in the Evaluation of the Analyst Using Q-methodology. (Doctoral Dissertation, New York Univ.) (D.A. XXIII, 533, 1961).

Lewy, E.—Responsibility, Free Will and Ego Psychology. (1961) Inter. J. Psychoanal. 42:260.

Liebman, Joshua L.—Peace of Mind. (New York, Simon and Schuster, 1946).

Lindemann, Erich, M.D.—The Medical Psychological Dynamics of the Gamut of Normal Experiences of the Normal Individual. In Iago Galdston, Ed.—Ministry and Medicine in Human Relations. (New York, International Universities Press, 1955) pp. 16-32.

Lindgren, Henry C. and Donn Byrne—Psychology: An Introduction to the Study of Human Behavior. (New York, Wiley, 1961).

Lindzey, G., ed.—Handbook of Social Psychology. (Cambridge, Addison-Wesley, 1954).

Loewald, H. W.—The Superego and the Ego-Ideal, Superego and Time. (1962) Inter. J. Psychoanal. 43:264-268.

Lowenstein, Rudolph M., ed.—Drives, Affects, Behavior. (New York, International Universities Press, 1953).

McKinney, Fred—Understanding Personaltiy: Cases in Counseling. (Boston, Houghton-Mifflin, 1965).

Maslow, A. H.—Motivation and Personality. (New York: Harper, 1954).

Maslow, A. H.—Toward a Psychology of Being. (New York: Van-Nostrand, 1962).

Masserman, J. H. and Leon Salzman, eds.—Modern Concepts of Psychoanalysis. (New York: Phil. Lib., 1962).

Masserman, J. H., ed.—Science and Psychoanalysis. (New York: Grueh, 1958-1962, 5 vols.).

May, Rollo—Religion, Psychotherapy, and the Achievement of Selfhood. (1951) Past. Psych. 2, No. 17:29-33. Also (1952) 2:26-33.

May, Rollo—The Springs of Creative Living. (New York, Abingdon-Cokesbury, 1940).

Menninger, Karl A.—The Human Mind, 3rd ed. (New York, Knopf, 1957).

Menninger, Karl A.—Theory of Psychoanalytic Technique. (New York, Basic Books, 1958) 206 pp. (Also 1961).

Merton, Robert K.—Social Theory and Social Structure. (Glencoe, Free Press, 1957).

Merton, Robert K., Leonard Broom and Leonard S. Cottrell—Sociology Today. (New York, Basic Books, 1959).

Milgram, Stanley—Some Conditions of Obedience and Disobedience to Authority. (1965) Hum. Rel. 18:57-76.

Minkowich, Abram—Empirical Contribution to a Theory of Ambivalence. (1965) J. Abnorm. Psychol. 71:30.

Moberg, D. O.—Religious Activities and Personal Activities in Old Age. (1956) J. Soc. Psychol. 43:261-67.

Morgan, C. T.—Introduction to Psychology. (New York, McGraw-Hill, 1961).

Mowrer, O. Hobart—Psychotherapy, Theory and Research. (New York, Ronald, 1953).

Mowrer, O. Hobart—Learning Theory and Behavior. (New York, Wiley, 1960).

Mullan, Hugh and Max Rosenbaum—Group Psychotherapy: Theory and Practice. (Glencoe, Free Press, 1962). 360 pp.

Munroe, Ruth—Schools of Psychoanalytic Thought. (New York, Dryden, 1955).

Murray, H. A.—Explorations in Personality. (New York, Oxford, 1938).

Newcomb, Theodore M.—The Persistence and Regression of Changed Attitudes. (1963) J. Soc. Issues 19:3-14.

Oates, Wayne E.—The Religious Dimensions of Personality. (New York, Association, 1957) 320 pp.

Peale, Norman Vincent and Blanton Smiley—The Art of Real Happiness. (New York, Prentice-Hall, 1956).

Peck, Robert F. and Robert J. Havighurst—The Psychology of Character Development. (New York, Wiley, 1960).

Polatin, Phillip and Ellen Philtine—The Well-Adjusted Personality: Preventive Psychiatry for Everyday Use. (Philadelphia, Lippincott, 1952).

Pruyser, P. W.—Toward a Doctrine of Man in Psychiatry and Theology. (March 1958) Past. Psych. 9:9-13.

Rachman, S.—Learning Theory and Child Psychology: Therapeutic Possibilities. (1962) J. Child. Psychol. Psychiat. No. 3, 3:149-163.

Reik, Theodore—Dogma and Compulsion; Psychoanalytic Studies of Religion and Myth. (New York, International Universities Press, 1951).

Riesman, David—The Lonely Crowd. (New York, Doubleday, 1955).

Rogers, Carl R.—Learning to be Free. Part I (Nov. 1962) Past Psych. 13:47-54. Part II (Dec. 1962) Past Psych. 13:43-51.

Rogers, Carl R.—The Nature of Man. (May 1960) Past. Psych. 11:23-26.

Rose, Arnold M.—Factors Associated With the Life Satisfaction of Middle-Class, Middle-Aged Persons. (1955) Marr. Fam. Liv. 17:15-19.

Rosenfield, H.—The Super Ego and the Ego-Ideal. (1962) Inter. J. Psychoanal. 43:297-305.

Russell, Claire and W. M. S.—Human Behavior. (Boston, Little Brown, 1961).

Salzman, Leon—Developments in Psychoanalysis. (New York, Grune and Stratton, 1962) 301 pp.

Sarason, Irwin G.—Contemporary Research in Personality. (New York, Van Nostrand, 1962).

Saul, Leon—Emotional Maturity: The Development and Dynamics of Personality. 2nd ed. (Philadelphia, Lippincott, 1960).

Sheeley, W. F.—A Brief History of Psychiatric Education for the Non-Psychiatrist. II. The Age of Reason—and Beyond. (1962) Psychosomatics 3:379-389.

Sheen, Fulton J.—Peace of Soul. (Garden City, N. Y., Garden City Books, 1951) 292 pp.

Sherwood, J. N., M. J. Stolaroff and M. M. Harman—The Psychedelic Experience: A New Concept in Psychotherapy. (1962) J. Neuropsychiat. 4:69-80.

Shulman, Bernard H.—A. Comparison of Allport's and the Adlerian Concepts of Life Style. (1965) Ind. Psycho. 3:14.

Siegman, A. W.—Authoritarian Attitudes in Children: The Effect of Age, IQ. Anxiety, Parental Religious Attitudes. (1957) J. Clin. Psychol. 13:338.

Srole, Leo, et al.—Mental Health in the Metropolis: The Midtown Manhattan Study. (New York, McGraw-Hill, 1962).

Sullivan, H. S.—The Interpersonal Theory of Psychiatry. (New York, Norton, 1953).

Szasz, T. S.—The Myth of Mental Illness: Foundations of a Theory of Personal Conduct. (New York, Hoeber, 1961) 350 pp.

Taylor, Janet A.—Drive Theory and Manifest Anxiety. (1956) Psychol. Bull. 53:303-320.

Tillich, Paul—Existentialism, Psychotherapy, and the Nature of Man. (June 1960) Past. Psych. 11:10-18.

Ungersma, A. J.—The Search for Meaning (Philadelphia, Westminister, 1961) 188 pp.

Weigert, Edith—The Superego and the Ego-Ideal. (1962) Inter. J. Psychoanal. 43:269-271.

Weiss, Edwardo—The Structure and Dynamics of the Human Mind. (New York, Grune and Stratton, 1960) 496 pp.

Wickes, Francis G.—The Inner World of Choice. (New York, Harper, 1963).

Wilder, J.—The Impact of Psychotherapy on Society. (1962) Am. J. Psychother. 16:1-4.

Chapter 10

In Conclusion

In a very real sense there is no way to "conclude" a study such as this. The author was aware that certain groups had attempted to preempt the word "counseling", did not favor the use of the term by lawyers, medics and clergymen, and would look with a jaundiced eye on a study of "counseling in the United States" that emphasized counseling by these professions. He was also apprised of the very limited study that had been made of these professions and of the absence of study of their counseling dimension. He was not originally prepared for some of the conclusions which came from even our tentative and explorative study:

The predominate place of counseling in each of the professions.

The fact that clients did more often seek these professionals than turn to so-called counseling specialists.

The clear distinction between counseling and psychoanalysis and the insistance on this by clients.

The hesitancy of the old professions to emphasize their counseling and openly charge for it.

The lack of selection of student trainees who would make good counselors and the inadequate training in counseling fundamentals in the professions.

The deficit in good teaching material.

The common elements in good interviewing and counseling, apparently sensed by both counselors and clients. The ability to state these elements and the socio-psycho dynamics to be applied.

The specific place in counseling and the specific client group of each profession.

The poor catalogue of interdisciplinary community services and appropriate referral routes.

This book has attempted some explorative ways of responding to these observations. If it contributed toward these professions and their clients understanding better the nature and place of counseling; if it persuaded them not to yield the field to those claiming counseling as a psychological specialty; if it roused in them a commitment to improve their counseling training and to fit without rancor, jealousy or cabal into the total societal attempt to aid persons in trouble before they are lost to society; then the book and the time spent in research is justified.

In quite another sense there can be no "conclusion." In our files are hundreds of statistics not yet adequately explored, hypotheses not adequately tested, insights not yet shared. Though the author's *Counseling: A Bibliography with Annotations* and *Legal Interviewing and Counseling Cases* have been greeted as pioneering works, there is much more to do to create interdisciplinary studies and teaching tools and to make us aware of the lessons and literature in fields other than our own. It is hoped that others will make use of our data and conduct further independent research. Such efforts as the newly launched *Law and Society* project and *Journal* at Wisconsin-Northwestern Universities are the kind needed. The program of the *Continuing Education of the Bar,* California, is another example.

Finally, this report cannot be a conclusion, but hopefully only a beginning in another dimension—interdisciplinary learning. Theology's development of an admission test (TSI) frankly geared to selecting potential counselors is a lesson which needs to be learned in all the professions. Each profession has its own particular tools, and these must be used professionally by each group: manipulation of power by the lawyer, placebos and miracle drugs by the medic, confession, faith, absolution by the minister. But each discipline has discovered some things applicable to common elements of counseling which should be shared with the other professions. Thus, religion has unquestionably most clearly recognized that counseling must be taught and has developed the best tests and technique for selecting candidates on the basis of their likelihood of becoming good counselors. On the other hand, religion has probably gone too far down a blind alley—the clinical pattern of ministers working in mental hospitals and with the mentally ill as an assumed proper method of training counselors who usually work with "normal" individual (religion is just beginning to sense its error). And medicine has developed the clinical training and observance of experienced medical personnel to a degree that religion and law have not approximated. It has been able to persuade its "clients" to thus expose themselves as subjects of training. Many other cross currents could be similarly noted.

May I, in the final paragraph shift to the first person? I have enjoyed this project and the opportunity of working with the Walter E. Meyer Research Institute of Law, and the savoring of what I think is one of the most dynamic movements in teaching, in counseling, in the professions. I urge others to further study and write in these fields.

INDEX

315